RESPONSIBLE AI IN THE AGE OF GENERATIVE MODELS

GOVERNANCE, ETHICS AND RISK
MANAGEMENT

BYTE-SIZED LEARNING SERIES
BOOK 4

I. ALMEIDA

NOW
NEXT
LATER

We are the most trusted and effective learning platform dedicated to empowering leaders with the knowledge and skills needed to harness the power of AI safely and ethically. Join now to enjoy free lessons and webinars, and check out other books in the series.

CONTENTS

Navigating the Age of Generative AI   1

PART I
**GENERATIVE AI AND HUMAN RIGHTS
RISKS**

1. Introduction   7
2. Key Human Rights Risks and Examples   10
3. Exacerbation of Existing Risks   21
4. Emergence of Novel Risks   24
5. Advancing Rights-Respecting AI   28
6. Manifesting Our Values Through Technology   32

PART II
**A RIGHTS-BASED APPROACH TO
BUILDING GENERATIVE AI**

7. Introduction   37
8. The Four Pillars of AI Development   41
9. A Rights-Focused Approach to Regulating AI   45
10. Implementing Rigorous Documentation During
    AI Development Stages   51
11. The Path Forward   65

PART III
RESPONSIBLE DATA GOVERNANCE

12. Responsible Data Curation for Reliable and
    Ethical Machine Learning   73
13. Strategic Corporate Data Governance for
    Generative AI Systems   79

PART IV
PARTICIPATORY DATA STEWARDSHIP

14. Introduction   87
15. Case Study: Grounding Data Governance
    Decisions in Lived Perspectives   89
16. Why Data Stewardship Matters   92
17. Core Principles of Data Stewardship   103

18. Case Study: Data for Good Collaboration 112
19. A Framework for Participatory Data Stewardship 114
20. Key Actors in Data Stewardship 124
21. Participatory Models 131
22. Case Study: Participatory Approach to Algorithm Design 141
23. Conclusion 144

PART V
AI TRANSPARENCY AND ALGORITHMIC AUDITING

24. Introduction 149
25. Understanding AI Transparency 156
26. The Perils of Transparency: An Organizational Case Study 162
27. Stakeholders and Their Transparency Needs 165
28. Transparency in Practice 169
29. Delivering Transparency 173
30. AI Transparency: Challenges and Recommendations 177
31. Understanding Algorithmic Auditing 186
32. Methods and Tools for Algorithmic Auditing 193
33. The Importance of AI Use Case Registries: Lessons from California's Executive Order 200
34. Operational Considerations 206
35. Challenges for Effective Auditing 211
36. Advancing Algorithmic Accountability 215
37. Conclusion 219

PART VI
ORGANIZATIONAL ROLES IN BUILDING RESPONSIBLE AI

38. The Rise of Responsible AI in Organizations 223
39. Executive Leadership: Setting the Tone for Responsible AI 225
40. Data Scientists and AI Developers: Building Ethical AI from the Ground Up 230
41. Product Managers: Balancing Innovation and Responsibility in AI-Driven Products 235
42. Legal and Compliance: Navigating the Complex Landscape of AI Regulations and Standards 241

43. Human Resources: Cultivating a Culture of Responsible AI and Managing Workforce Transformation   246

44. Marketing and Communications: Building Trust and Transparency in AI-Driven Products and Services   252

45. Customer Support: Ensuring Responsible AI in Customer Interactions and Issue Resolution   258

46. Innovation and R&D: Pushing the Boundaries of Responsible AI Development   264

47. IT and Operations: Implementing and Maintaining Responsible AI Systems   270

48. Cross-Functional Collaboration: Driving Responsible AI Through Teamwork and Communication   276

49. Embracing Responsible AI for a Better Future   280

PART VII
MULTI-LAYERED GENERATIVE AI GOVERNANCE ACROSS THE LIFECYCLE

50. Introduction   285
51. Requirements Gathering Phase   287
52. Data Collection and Curation Phase   292
53. Model Development Phase   296
54. Testing and Deployment Phase   303
55. Post-Launch Phase   307
56. The Path Forwards   311

PART VIII
ORGANIZATIONAL MATURITY IN RESPONSIBLE AI

57. Introduction   317
58. The Responsible AI Maturity Model   319
59. Stage 1: Awareness   321
60. Stage 2: Discovery   324
61. Stage 3: Implementation   327
62. Stage 4: Operationalization   330
63. Stage 5: Leadership   333
64. Assessing and Advancing Responsible AI Maturity   336
65. Conclusion   341

PART IX
CASE STUDY: ANTHROPIC'S CONSTITUTIONAL AI APPROACH

66. Introduction   345
67. The Constitutional AI Approach   348
68. Research on Constitutional AI at Anthropic   354
69. Collective Constitutional AI: Incorporating
    Public Input   362
70. Discussion and Future Directions   369
71. Emerging Generative AI Startups and
    Downstream Risks   375

PART X
EMERGING REGULATORY FRAMEWORK AND THE EU AI ACT

72. Navigating the EU AI Act: A Comprehensive
    Guide for Companies   385
73. EU AI Act Co-Rapporteurs Reflect on
    Monumental Achievement in Balancing
    Innovation and Protection   396
74. EU AI Act: Analysis and Implications   400
75. Conclusion   415

    Shaping a Rights-Respecting AI Future   418

    Keep Learning   423

NAVIGATING THE AGE OF
GENERATIVE AI

In recent years, we have witnessed a remarkable breakthrough in artificial intelligence (AI) with the rise of generative models. These sophisticated systems, powered by advanced machine learning techniques, have demonstrated an unprecedented ability to create highly realistic and convincing content across various domains, including text, images, music, and video. From generating engaging social media posts to designing complex architectural plans, Generative AI has the potential to revolutionize industries, automate workflows, and transform the way we interact with technology.

However, alongside the excitement and promise of these powerful tools, there are pressing concerns and challenges that demand our attention. Generative AI amplifies risks such as the spread of misinformation, exacerbation of biases and discrimination, threats to privacy and consent, and disruption of creative livelihoods. As these models become more ubiquitous and influential, it is crucial that we develop responsible AI governance frameworks to mitigate potential harms while realizing the benefits of this transformative technology.

This book, "Responsible AI in the Age of Generative Models,"
serves as a comprehensive guide for navigating the complex
landscape of ethical AI development and deployment. It argues
for a rights-based approach, grounded in established human
rights frameworks, to provide clarity on principles and obligations, enable proactive risk mitigation, and inform effective
governance strategies. By connecting AI risks to fundamental
freedoms and human dignity, this approach offers a universal
language for aligning AI systems with societal values and
expectations.

The book is divided into ten parts, each exploring a critical
aspect of responsible AI in the context of generative models:

Part I maps the potential risks posed by generative AI to
specific human rights, such as privacy, equality, and freedom of
thought, illustrating the far-reaching implications of these
systems.

Part II presents a framework for institutionalizing rights-
respecting AI practices throughout the development lifecycle,
from data collection to model deployment and monitoring.

Recognizing the centrality of data to generative models, **Part III**
delves into responsible data governance practices to ensure
data is collected, processed and used in an ethical and legally
compliant manner.

Part IV examines participatory approaches to data stewardship,
highlighting the importance of involving diverse stakeholders,
especially marginalized communities, in decision-making
processes to ensure equitable representation and mitigate
harmful biases.

Part V explores the roles and responsibilities of different organizational functions, from leadership and data science to legal
compliance and product management, in operationalizing

responsible AI. It emphasizes the need for cross-functional collaboration and a shared ethical culture.

Transparency and algorithmic auditing are the focus of **Part VI**. It discusses strategies and best practices for making AI systems more transparent, interpretable and accountable to impacted communities and the broader public.

Part VII provides guidance on implementing effective multi-layered governance across the entire AI system lifecycle to proactively identify and mitigate risks.

Part VIII introduces maturity models for assessing an organization's responsible AI capabilities and provides guidance on implementing best practices incrementally.

Part IX features an in-depth case study of Anthropic's innovative Constitutional AI approach. This pioneering methodology aims to imbue AI systems with high-level normative principles and values that guide their behavior across a wide range of contexts and scenarios, offering a promising path forward for aligning advanced AI with human values and ethics.

Given the global impact of generative AI, **Part X** analyzes emerging regulatory frameworks such as the European Union's Artificial Intelligence Act (EU AI Act). It discusses the implications for businesses operating in multiple jurisdictions and the importance of harmonizing standards to enable responsible innovation.

The book concludes with a call to action, emphasizing the urgent need for proactive multi-stakeholder collaboration to shape the future of generative AI in service of human rights and flourishing.

"Responsible AI in the Age of Generative Models" is not just a theoretical exploration but a practical guide for business leaders, policymakers, researchers, and concerned citizens. It equips readers with the knowledge, tools, and strategies needed to navigate the challenges and opportunities of this rapidly evolving field. By embracing responsible AI governance as an imperative, we can work together to unlock the transformative potential of generative models while safeguarding human rights, promoting social justice, and ensuring that the benefits of AI are shared equitably.

The age of Generative AI is upon us, and its impact will be profound. The decisions we make today about how to govern these powerful technologies will shape the course of our collective future. This book is an invitation to engage in that critical conversation and to take action towards building a world where AI empowers and uplifts us all.

PART I

GENERATIVE AI AND HUMAN RIGHTS RISKS

1

INTRODUCTION

In recent years, Generative AI has burst onto the scene, astounding observers with its capacity to create surprisingly convincing human-like content. Unlike previous AI systems focused narrowly on analysis, Generative AI models can write essays, compose songs, design graphics, formulate computer code and more with seemingly little human input.

Leading models like MidJourney for image generation and GPT-4 for text generation have demonstrated remarkable fluency in mimicking patterns found in immense datasets scraped from the internet and human-created works. These systems allow conversational back-and-forth by ingesting user prompts to generate responsive text, code, images and other outputs dynamically.

Many anticipate Generative AI accelerating workflows, enhancing creativity and even automating routine coding and content development tasks entirely. But alongside breathless hype are growing notes of caution about unintended consequences from this disruptive shift in artificial intelligence capabilities.

A Rights-Based Perspective on Exponential Technology

While discussions around ethics and responsible AI innovation explore various social impacts, public discourse often lacks precise connection to established legal and moral frameworks. As Generative AI's effects propagate across industries and digital spaces, focusing specifically on human rights provides clarity on stakeholders and principles at stake.

Human rights constitute the most universally recognized set of guarantees protecting human dignity against infringement from governments and companies alike. These entitlements enshrined under international law range from privacy protections to freedoms of thought and expression to rights to culture and scientific progress.

This book's central framework, guided by the United Nations B-Tech taxonomy[1], is thus analyzing dynamics seen with Generative AI through a human rights lens. In linking abstract capabilities to concrete violations against established rights, we gain clearer understanding of appropriate regulatory responses, governance and precautionary measures that should guide organizations and policymakers during this period of rapid change.

Taxonomy of Risks to Fundamental Freedoms

The following chapters catalogue emerging examples of how characteristics specific to Generative AI pose threats to human rights like no prior technology. While risks like privacy erosion and the viral spread of misinformation are associated with earlier forms of AI as well, properties distinctive to generative models exacerbate these existing dangers. We also surface more novel risks arising from fusion of machine outputs with human cognition unlike seen before.

By delineating clear connections between Generative AI and infringement on dignity, autonomy and equality under international law, this guide intends to spur informed action from tech leaders, lawmakers and advocates to develop this transformative technology responsibly. For only by anticipating risks through a human-centric prism can we ensure AI progress also catalyzes human progress.

---

1. *"Taxonomy of Human Rights Risks Connected to Generative AI"* by the United Nations B-Tech project

2

KEY HUMAN RIGHTS RISKS AND EXAMPLES

Generative AI promises to revolutionize how content is created, disseminated and consumed across digital spaces. But in unleashing new capabilities for mass automation of creative tasks also come risks of adverse impacts on established rights. This chapter surveys emerging examples of Generative AI negatively affecting key pillars of human dignity.

Right to Freedom from Physical and Psychological Harm

Generative AI models possess unprecedented capacity to produce hyper-realistic and convincing fabricated media that could be weaponized to severely erode personal freedoms and security.

For example, non-consensual deepfakes represent an alarming erosion of personal dignity and autonomy through synthetic media. Apps like DeepNude have demonstrated capacity to automatically generate realistic nude images of women without consent, enabling new forms of sexual exploitation[1]. And while deepfakes have focused on celebrity targets so far, experts warn implementation at scale could fuel harassment against ordinary citizens, especially women, denying gender equality.

The output volume and sophistication enabled by Generative AI surpasses anything previously possible; text generators like GPT-4 or Claude could flood platforms with hundreds of unique false accounts inciting violence faster than humanly possible. Further, tools like DALL-E or MidJourney could produce endless customized images depicting marginalized groups committing non-existent crimes in an effort to provoke attacks against them.

There is historical precedent of media manipulation resulting in egregious harm, such as the Rwandan genocide which was fueled by misinformation campaigns over Radio Television Libre des Mille Collines.[2] Generative AI exponentially amplifies both the scale and personalized nature of such tactics to directly and precisely target those most likely to act in extremely violent ways.

We also have very recent examples[34] like COVID disinformation undermining public health measures and demonstrably contributing to premature deaths around the world. Generative AI could severely compound this issue as well; DALL-E or MidJourney could produce endless images falsely depicting trusted health officials as criminals to dangerously erode public trust.

The global reach of social platforms allows such precision-guided AI disinformation to spread internationally within minutes. Generative models have demonstrated an unprecedented ability to produce human-quality text across dozens of languages with just a few examples of translations as a starting point. This allows disinformation campaigns to be precision targeted and adapted to vulnerable communities in their native languages, even obscure regional dialects, while coordinated across borders faster than regulators can keep up.

For example, an instigator could feed English language extremist propaganda through advanced generative translation tools to instantly produce hundreds of locally-nuanced variations targeting specific isolated ethnic groups in sensitive regions across the globe. By exploiting cultural divides and localized trauma through linguistically and culturally optimized fake media, these models remove practically all friction for mass manipulation across disparate populations.

Where past disinformation required painstaking manual translation or relying on a patchwork of individually recruited local provocateurs, AI generative models enable centralized top-down control of globally distributed propaganda fine-tuned to the vulnerabilities of each target audience. This is scalable incitement and radicalization exceeding limits of human capacity.

If these technologies advance without safeguards, the capacity for malicious actors to provoke violence through hyper-targeted manipulation will rapidly escalate beyond historical precedent and threaten the security and dignity of citizens everywhere.

Right to Equality and Non-Discrimination

A core promise of emerging technologies is democratizing access to services, information and creativity. Yet current flaws in dataset representation and design choices limit realization of equal rights.

HEALTHCARE

For example, a study[5] published in Science highlighted issues of racial bias in a widely used health care algorithm that identifies patients for high-risk care management programs. The algorithm relied on past health care spending as a proxy to determine patient need. However, the study found that at the same spending levels, Black patients had substantially higher actual care needs than White patients.

Due to lower average incomes and gaps in quality of care, Black individuals tend to use health services less frequently despite greater underlying illness burdens. So, the algorithm assigned lower risk scores to eligible Black patients compared to White patients with similar needs. This resulted in unequal access to critical care management programs aimed at improving outcomes.

The study underscores how even well-intentioned algorithms can unintentionally perpetuate inequality if they fail to account for complex historical biases embedded in the data or systems they evaluate.

Another study published in The Lancet Digital Health[6] demonstrated that standard AI models can predict a patient's self-reported race from medical images with over 90% accuracy. Researchers found the models could determine race from X-rays, CT scans and mammograms of different body parts, even when image quality was deliberately degraded.

Surprisingly, the AI models predicted race more accurately than statistical models developed specifically for this purpose. And they did so even when features potentially correlating with race, like breast density, were suppressed. So how the models determine race remains unknown.

The concern is that as AI tools aimed at improving workflow are integrated into radiology, reliance on algorithms that incorporate racial bias risk worsening existing disparities in quality of care.

Equal Opportunity

An Amazon's resume screening tool[7] preferred male applicants over equally qualified females for technical roles before the company scrapped the algorithm upon discovering its biased outcomes. The since discontinued AI-powered model was built to review incoming job applications, but was found to systematically assign higher scores to male candidates.

One contributing factor was the tool's consideration of previous occupations as gauges for relevant skills. Since fields like software engineering have been dominated by men, resumes with experience from majority-male industries received higher ratings from the model—even when women performed equivalent roles requiting the same abilities. The biased algorithm resulted in significantly more qualified female applicants being wrongly rejected at initial screening stages compared to similar male candidates.

The case further demonstrates how history of discrimination permeates AI models designed without thoughtful safeguarding, entrenching inequality once deployed at scale. But its discontinuation also spotlights increasing scrutiny over algorithms that perpetuate discrimination through automated decisions impacting people's basic rights and dignities in areas like employment. Outcomes still depend greatly on institutional accountability in admitting flaws.

Governance, Policing, and Justice

A recent article[8] by the Guardian highlighted reliance by US immigration services on unreliable AI translation tools, like Google Translate, jeopardizing asylum applications, especially for speakers of low-resource languages. For example, a Brazilian immigrant was detained for months due to inaccurate translations.

FINANCIAL SERVICES

A study[9] by The Markup analyzing over 2 million mortgage applications found lending algorithms were significantly more likely to deny people of color compared to similar white applicants. Controlling for financial factors like income, debt and credit history, Black applicants were 80% more likely to be denied, Native Americans 70% more likely, Asian Americans 50% more likely and Latinos 40% more likely than white applicants.

The analysis uncovered disparities in 90 major metro areas even when comparing applicants with the same lending profiles. However, the exact decision-making parameters within widely used underwriting algorithms remain proprietary and unknown. As algorithms guide an increasing share of mortgages, their opacity raises accountability concerns around inadvertent scaling of historical inequality.

REPRESENTATION

An analysis[10] by the Washington Post found AI image generators like Stable Diffusion and DALL-E continue exhibiting harmful gender and racial biases despite efforts to address problematic training data. Models default to cartoonish Western stereotypes for people and environments in other countries that distort complex realities.

For example, images of houses in China emphasized classical curved roofs rather than modern apartments actually common in cities like Shanghai. Images of India repeatedly depicted impoverished villages with dirt roads despite its over 160 billionaires. The oversimplifications and exaggerations reveal how even recent datasets disproportionately represent Western perspectives.

Researchers argue shortcomings will inevitably arise with systems trained on data scraped from the internet given long-standing inequities in representation. But companies remain secretive about training content.

Efforts to address representation issues in Generative AI models have also backfired, with tools like Google's new AI image generator Gemini overcompensating in portrayals of marginalized groups. Gemini came under intense criticism[11] for exhibiting absurd political correctness and historical inaccuracy in trying to address representation biases. Images wrongly depicted Black and Asian people amongst United States' Founding Fathers.

Experts say overcorrecting stems from the tendency for AI systems to lack nuanced human judgment. Gemini's training likely aimed to offset uneven portrayals of race and gender in available data. But lacking an intuitive sense of realistic diversity, it overcompensated with almost parodic results.

CONCLUSION

While bias and discrimination issues have long permeated human and algorithmic systems, generative models create new vectors entrenching inequality through unparalleled automation of creative tasks. By exponentially amplifying narrow perspectives embedded in training data, these tools threaten to flood public and private sectors cementing unfair stereotypes.

Without earnest efforts to address root causes behind representation imbalances, mitigation attempts risk further sidelining marginalized voices. Google's debacle with overcorrecting Gemini's historical inaccuracies reveals the intrinsic challenges.

Yet the scale enabled by Generative AI means imperfect remedies yield directly harmful outcomes for impacted communities. The technologies do not operate in an equality vacuum—they embed existing discrimination into exponentially vast creative works while drowning out opposition through volume.

Right to Privacy

Generative models' reliance on ingesting vast personal data raises familiar but heightened privacy concerns.

Web scraping practices enabling creation of detailed behavioral profiles and micro-targeted content deeply erode individual privacy. Lack of consent and awareness fundamentally denies user agency.

For example, the LAION-5B training dataset contained over 50 million identifiable personal photos scraped without user consent[12]. The same dataset was recently removed when a leading research group discovered over 1,000 webpages containing disturbing child abuse content within LAION-5B[13]. This large unfiltered dataset trained Stable Diffusion 1.5, the generative AI app powering countless creative tools across the internet.

Additionally, states now possess mass capacity for surveillance through automated text analysis to identify dissidents. And private actors have granular data for personalized coercion. Both violate privacy essential for autonomy. For example, Clearview AI's face search tool built with over 3 billion unconsented images enables wide-scale tracking of individuals[14].

Right to Own Intellectual Property

Creators have moral interests in protecting fruits of their intellectual labor—interests under increasing threat as creative works get replicated without consent.

Direct copyright infringement already occurs using protected works in some commercial model training datasets. This denies economic interests tied to property rights.

But additionally, AI-generated art, music and writing stylizing after singular creators presents novel dilution of established protections. Locking out humans from owning creative expressions violates basic property-connected dignity.

For example, Getty Images has found its copyrighted photographs being used without license permissions in AI training datasets[15].

Right to Freedom of Thought and Opinion

Emerging evidence suggests Generative AI's anthropomorphic interfaces subtly shape internal beliefs, opinions and even self-identity over time.

Conversational models intentionally designed to mimic humans socialize false projections of relationship forming. This coercively steers freedom of opinion, belief and expression in directions divorced from truth.

Hyper-personalized content tailored to individual vulnerabilities grants outside forces increasing power over inner personal autonomy. Facebook internal research[16] revealed their engagement-based ranking algorithms can promote divisiveness and impact adolescent mental health. When external tools invisibly influence our very thought patterns and inhibitions, freedom of conscience suffers.

In total, these examples outline real and alarming ways both existing AI systems and recently Generative AI models' exponential advancement enable violations of established human rights meant to protect welfare and dignity. But cataloguing risks also directs focus on solutions. The next chapters explore how some dangers represent expansions of existing threats while others constitute wholly new frontiers needing pioneering safeguards.

---

1. *"EU to pass law criminalising deepnudes after Taylor Swift furore"* by tech central.ie
2. *"Rwanda and RTLM Radio Media Effects"* by Scott Straus, Department of Political Science University of Wisconsin, Madison
3. *"The impact of misinformation on the COVID-19 pandemic"* by Maria Mercedes Ferreira Caceres et al.
4. *"Fake News in the Age of COVID-19"* by Greg Nyilasy, University of Melbourne
5. *"Racial Bias Found in a Major Health Care Risk Algorithm"* by Starre Vartan for Scientific American
6. *"AI recognition of patient race in medical imaging: a modelling study"* by Judy Wawira Gichoya et al.
7. *"Amazon Scraps Secret AI Recruiting Engine that Showed Biases Against Women"* by Roberto Iriondo for Carnegie Mellon University
8. *"Lost in AI translation: growing reliance on language apps jeopardizes some asylum applications"* by Johana Bhuiyan for the Guardian
9. *"The secret bias hidden in mortgage-approval algorithms"* by Emmanuel Martinez and Lauren Kirchner for The Markup
10. *"These fake images reveal how AI amplifies our worst stereotypes"* by Nitasha Tiku, Kevin Schaul and Szu Yu Chen for the Washington Post
11. *"Why Google's 'woke' AI problem won't be an easy fix"* by Zoe Kleinman for the BBC
12. *"LAION-5B, Stable Diffusion 1.5, and the Original Sin of Generative AI"* by Eryk Salvaggio for TechPolicy.press
13. *"Investigation Finds AI Image Generation Models Trained on Child Abuse"* by David Thiel for the Stanford Cyber Policy Center Blog
14. *"The Secretive Company That Might End Privacy as We Know It"* by Kashmir Hill for the NYT
15. *"Getty Images is suing the creators of AI art tool Stable Diffusion for scraping its content"* by James Vincent for The Verge

16. *"Facebook reportedly ignored its own research showing algorithms divided users"*
    by Nick Statt for The Verge

3

EXACERBATION OF EXISTING RISKS

While Generative AI enables wholly new threats to human rights, many pressing dangers represent expansions of known risks now intensified by properties specific to these systems. By automating mass creation and dissemination of content, generative models have supercharged familiar threats to privacy, truth, and equal representation.

Heightened Spread of Mis/Disinformation

Synthetic media encroaching on visual authenticity empowers those set to immensely benefit from eroding truth. Advanced neural networks can churn out volumes of manipulated video, imagery and text conveying false realities that humans alone cannot rapidly counter. The resulting threat to information integrity expands risks to free expression and autonomy.

Escalating Privacy Violations

Generative AI relies on continually ingesting vast personal data in order to dynamically improve. User prompts submitted for conversion into outputs can reveal deepest insecurities around family, health and more. Yet once submitted, visibility into how this data gets stored, aggregated and repurposed remains perilously opaque. Familiar surveillance risks now operate at hugely expanded scale.

Compounding Representational Biases

For all radical innovation promised, development patterns display familiar exclusion. Concentrated generative model design occurring in elite Western institutions encodes inherited data biases rooted in unequal social structures. Without deliberate intervention, existing voices of privilege replay through AI systems drowning marginalized perspectives desperate for accurate representation.

Concentrating Wealth, Power and Inequity

Technological shifts inevitably drive economic transformation, often alongside severe disruption. Generative AI continues concentration of data, revenue and highly-valued skills in dominant tech centers. Transition support for workers in automatable jobs remains lacking. And many nations now face being locked out of next wave innovations entirely, ceding tokenized data and prosperity to unaccountable centralized powers.

In total, analysis reveals intensified dangers but also continued gaps requiring updated understandings. While certain risks clearly magnify from exponential trends, distinct properties of emergent technologies also give rise to unprecedented threats.

The following chapter explores these new frontiers ahead needing pioneering safeguards tailored to Generative AI specifically.

4

EMERGENCE OF NOVEL RISKS

Beyond amplifying existing technology dangers, distinctive properties of Generative AI also introduce unprecedented threats to human rights and safety. As models dynamically improve through ingesting data revealing intimate user details, risks arise from fusing machine outputs with vulnerable human cognitive processes in ways not seen before.

Fusion of Human and Machine Cognition

Conversational AI models are designed to increasingly mimic human attributes like humor and emotional intelligence. This makes it harder for users to discern they are interacting with an artificial system rather than another person. Over time, forming seemingly intimate bonds with AI that appears human but hides its algorithmic nature could subtly manipulate people's core beliefs, opinions and even self-identity. This emerging capability poses unconventional threats to personal autonomy, freedom of thought, and informed consent about AI's influence.

In other words, the more convincingly human-like conversational AI becomes, the more it risks subtly shaping users' perspectives, preferences and beliefs without their awareness. If people assume intimacy with artificial systems reflecting human qualities, they may be vulnerable to emotional manipulation that undermines independent decision-making and cognitive liberty. Clear cues signaling the provenance of Generative models are needed to preserve consent.

Democratized Access to Sophisticated Capabilities

Generative AI also democratizes capabilities that once required significant expertise and resources. This empowers new groups to potentially cause harm.

For example, the ability to auto-generate code opens the door for unsophisticated threat actors to rapidly spread AI-powered ransomware attacks.

Similarly, easy access to create synthetic video/images means each individual can now conduct widespread disinformation campaigns that previously required entire teams or state backing.

In short, by making complex technological abilities available as turnkey tools, Generative AI inadvertently elevates dual-use risks. Capacities intended for creation can be misdirected towards harm.

Decentralized access coupled with exponential scalability means threats usually confined to organized groups now have force multiplication into the hands of lone malicious actors.

Automated Multimodal Content Manipulation

Generative AI can synthesize highly realistic media by fusing together text, images, video and audio from minimal prompts. Yet widespread capabilities to authenticate content and identify fakes are lacking. This raises new threats.

As exceptional quality synthetic media floods online spaces, people may unknowingly consume and spread false information. Manipulated video/images of public figures making inflammatory remarks could go viral without better detection.

At scale, erosion of information integrity could undermine freedom of expression, civic discourse, and even personal autonomy. When flooded with seamless fakes, all online content becomes less trusted.

In short, while AI generation capabilities are rapidly advancing, corresponding safeguards around authentication haven't kept pace. This emerging imbalance enables threats to truth and civic debate that are highly unprecedented.

Liability Gaps Around AI Authored Works

Current intellectual property laws have no clear precedent for AI-generated creations. When generative art mimics a unique human artist's style, it creates an ethical gray area around proper attribution and ownership.

For example, a text-to-image model stylizing new works after William Blake could dilute his influence without directly infringing copyright. Yet those outputs still conceptually owe provenance.

This ambiguity leaves impacted artists without clear legal or ethical recourse. If AI-authored works gain commercial value, original creators may see their incomes and incentives diminished even without IP theft.

In short, while generative AI promises new creative bounties, it also enables novel forms of IP infringement and ownership disputes we currently lack frameworks to resolve. Our legal systems and ethical norms need updating to catch up with technological capabilities in this arena.

Additional Frontiers on the Horizon

As capabilities accelerate, pressure mounts for continued maximization of performances, consolidation of research power, and demonstration of ever more sophisticated applications. This risks propelling an AI arms race toward futures centered on mass persuasion, surveillance and even autonomous weapons systems.

Only through proactive foresight can precautionary approaches develop governance guardrails mitigating adverse impacts before manifestation.

5

ADVANCING RIGHTS-RESPECTING AI

Cataloguing risks makes evident the extent of complex challenges ahead in steering Generative AI's progress responsibly. But facing threats also illuminates potential pathways toward technology fostering human flourishing rather than erosion of rights. Through coordinated action across sectors, we can build guardrails mitigating harms while directing innovation toward equitably shared prosperity.

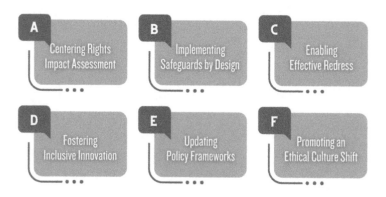

A. Centering Rights Impact Assessment

B. Implementing Safeguards by Design

C. Enabling Effective Redress

D. Fostering Inclusive Innovation

E. Updating Policy Frameworks

F. Promoting an Ethical Culture Shift

A. Centering Rights Impact Assessment

Before Generative AI systems are ever deployed, they should undergo rigorous pre-launch evaluation of potential data and algorithmic biases. This allows correcting trajectory proactively before adverse impacts propagate. Formal rights impact assessments would construct development pipelines around continual incremental testing against ethical safety benchmarks. This bakes accountability into engineering incentives from the start, ensuring regular external audits identify and resolve emerging issues during the design process.

B. Implementing Safeguards By Design

Beyond ongoing assessments, standardized nutritional label style fact sheets should describe key details for datasets and machine learning systems to enable external auditing, oversight and informed consumer choice. Transparency rewards discretion. Additionally, incorporating both technical interventions and oversight processes directly into Generative AI systems can minimize amplification of social biases and manipulation risks as capabilities advance. Privacy and consent policies, ethical usage guidelines, alert systems for detecting potential misuse, and tools providing attribution/provenance— these safeguards must proactively be layered into model functionality rather than treated as afterthoughts.

C. Enabling Effective Redress

For any guardrails to meaningfully protect rights in practice, accessible and transparent appeal pathways have to exist for questionable model outputs or unintended system performances impacting users. Partnerships with civil society organizations can assist by helping historically marginalized demographic groups report burdensome outputs and behaviors for assessment by developers. Creating clear channels for grievances empowers users who encounter issues. It also supports restored trust through remedies correcting past algorithmic harms with case-by-case review.

D. Fostering Inclusive Innovation

However, assessing risks and installing safeguards is only half of the equation. Equally important to mitigating harms is empowering more diverse voices to actively shape how generative AI takes form. Public research grants specifically targeting accessibility advances for vulnerable populations can help direct more innovation explicitly toward justice. Extending technology transfer programs to underserved communities also builds capacity to guide progress particularly across disadvantaged regions. In short, inclusion requires going beyond damage control to welcome new perspectives into the design process itself.

E. Updating Policy Frameworks

Legal regimes form the backbone upholding dignity. Rights-based national AI plans allow coherent integration of safety requirements with innovation support across sectors. Multilateral cooperation constructing international frameworks proactively builds consensus on acceptable use guardrails. And empowered oversight bodies provide continual guidance addressing complex tradeoffs.

F. Promoting an Ethical Culture Shift

But formalized regulation means little without incentives rewarding discretion over reckless speed and industry pressure.

Cultivating ethical voices internally creates environments where even junior engineers feel expected to question luminaries pursuing concerning applications. And promoting holistic service values re-centers technology progress on empowering people.

———

In total, this agenda constitutes a shared call toward justice. The tools exist today to develop Generative AI aligned with human rights if determination toward responsible innovation prevails across public and private spheres.

6

MANIFESTING OUR VALUES THROUGH TECHNOLOGY

Emerging capabilities enabled by Generative AI provoke understandable wariness given long history of unintended consequences from technological shifts. Yet reactive policies born of fear risk constraining progress needed to address humanity's mounting challenges in coming decades. With thoughtful safeguards and inclusive governance, AI could help uplift rights for many rather than erode protections for the few.

Part I illuminated expansive risks to established freedoms posed by uncontrolled AI development patterns. But in tracing specific pathways toward violations of dignity, analysis also revealed interventions fostering ethical outcomes aligned with people's interests. Grounding discourse in internationally recognized rights refocuses debate on affected populations rather than capabilities in isolation.

Of course, even comprehensive documentation requirements and stringent model testing processes cannot guarantee systems operating safely at global scale. Engineers and corporate leaders retain responsibility applying guidelines diligently throughout daily design tradeoffs. Still, preventative measures enacted early in development cycles stand best chance redirecting exponential trends toward justice rather than away.

And achieving responsible progress relies on cooperation across sectors—policymakers setting regulatory incentives, companies internalizing ethical priorities, journalists investigating edge cases, and advocates empowering affected voices into processes determining technological shifts. Multi-stakeholder participation addressing complex challenges ahead positions us best to manifest aspirations of non-discrimination, accountability and pluralism through societal adoption of AI.

In conclusion, steering innovation trajectories remains a continual process requiring vision beyond quarterly returns or electoral cycles. By lifting up human rights as lodestar for scientific advancement, perhaps technology leader and concerned citizen alike can move forward positively—our shared values shaping digital spaces as much as capabilities contained within machines.

PART II

A RIGHTS-BASED APPROACH TO BUILDING GENERATIVE AI

7

INTRODUCTION

Generative AI, capable of producing novel content, designs, and solutions, has shown tremendous potential across various sectors. Yet, its capabilities also raise unprecedented challenges, including deepfakes, misinformation, and the automation of jobs, which can exacerbate issues of bias, privacy violations, and social inequality.

Regulatory efforts such as the European Union's AI Act (EU AI Act) have amplified, but confusion remains over how to craft a regulatory approach that supports innovation while protecting people's rights and welfare.

In response, technology companies and policymakers have put forth an array of voluntary guidelines and principles around issues like fairness, transparency, and safety. While the EU AI Act will bring change, the current patchwork of self-regulation has proven inadequate thus far. Principles lack accountability, and "moving fast and breaking things" remains the status quo for many organizations developing AI systems.

Clearly, we need a more coherent framework for connecting
the actions of companies building AI to the societal protections
that governments are responsible for encoding into law. The
framework should be grounded in people's fundamental rights.

Core Tenets of a Rights-Based Approach

Rather than over-focusing on the technological details, a
rights-based approach[12] ties regulatory requirements directly
to demonstrating how AI systems affect rights around freedom,
equal opportunity, safety and more. For companies, this means
providing rigorous documentation that tracks impacts on
people across an AI model's entire development and deployment lifecycle. Documentation acts as proof that responsible
practices are in place to support human rights and values.

Regulators define goals centered on protecting citizens' established rights. Companies then have flexibility in determining
processes to meet those goals, while transparency requirements
incentivize indeed proactive attention to likely benefits and
risks. This marries top-down oversight with bottom-up innovation optimized by those closest to the technology.

Central artifacts within this approach are Model Cards[3],
Datasheets[4], and other forms of documentation that elucidate
model performance, data composition, and intended use cases
—all factors tied to potential rights impacts.

Model Cards	Datasheets for Datasets
• Model Details • Intended Use • Metrics • Evaluation • Ethical Considerations • Caveats and Recommendations	• Composition • Collection • Pre-processing • Analysis • Distribution

Standardizing such documentation makes opaque AI systems legible to regulators while encouraging technology creators to questioning how each design choice may affect vulnerable groups downstream.

A Focus on Rights, Not Just Technology

Public discourse on AI ethics has tended to concentrate on technological capabilities without connecting back to affected people. Concerns over "killer robots" or superhuman intelligence, while arguably important, can minimize very real issues of injustice happening now as AI scales.

A rights-based perspective clarifies priorities by tying various risks and harms directly to human rights violations. Discrimination translates to infringements on equal opportunity. Surveillance relates to lost freedoms and autonomy. Even existential risk connects back to a fundamental right to existence. This lens shifts focus toward affected populations so that regulation protects what people value most.

Roadmap

The next chapters expand on how centering rights enables practical guidance for implementing principles into daily development routines. We overview necessary documentation across four stages of the machine learning (ML) lifecycle: data collection, model building, model evaluation, and model deployment. For each phase, we cover relevant rights and stakeholders, metrics and measurements tied to impacts, and case studies of rigorous documentation in practice.

We then map different categories of rights to current discourse on AI risks, demonstrating how this framing helps orient issues like fairness and safety toward affected populations. The concluding section provides guidance for policymakers on requiring documentation without hampering innovation, settling debates between long-term and near-term perspectives.

---

1. *"The Pillars of a Rights-Based Approach to AI Development"* by Margaret Mitchell for TechPolicy.Press
2. *"A Human Rights-Based Approach to Responsible AI"* by Vinodkumar Prabhakaran, Margaret Mitchell, Timnit Gebru, Iason Gabriel
3. *"Model Cards for Model Reporting"* by Margaret Mitchell et al.
4. *"Datasheets for Datasets"* by Timnit Gebru et al.

8

THE FOUR PILLARS OF AI DEVELOPMENT

Machine learning models powering AI systems today are not magically created in a black box. Rather, their development follows a pipeline with several clear stages: data collection, model building, model evaluation, and model deployment. Connecting regulation to these behind-the-scenes processes allows oversight to be seamlessly integrated with the daily incentives and procedures developers already follow.

The "Four Stages" of AI Development

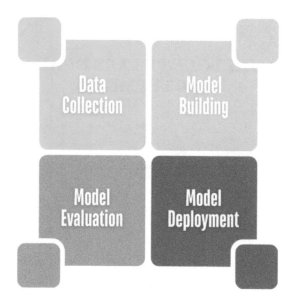

STAGE I: DATA COLLECTION

The lifecycle begins with gathering or generating the data to train AI models. Relevant stakeholders here include the individuals and communities directly represented in datasets as well as those involved in data collection practices, whether employees or third party-firms. Primary rights at stake center on privacy and fair representation—do data practices violate personal consent or result in incomplete perspectives?

Suggested documentation are *Datasheets for Datasets*[1], which catalog details like data provenance, composition analysis, and intended use cases. Requiring such sheets early on incentivizes questioning where data comes from and whether reliance on certain datasets may propagate historical biases against already marginalized groups.

STAGE II: MODEL BUILDING

Next, the architecture and training procedures of models get defined, translating data into functional systems. Decisions made by model builders and company leadership behind them carry significant consequences. Will the system be used to target vulnerable individuals? Does the model encode problematic assumptions that violate people's dignity? Rights around freedom from manipulation and lack of recourse are paramount.

Development history reports help mitigate risks by tracing how design choices relate to potential impacts on different populations. Documenting data sources, errors discovered, modifications made throughout training, and more brings transparency to why models behave as they do during evaluation.

STAGE III: MODEL EVALUATION

Before deployment, model performance and risks require careful examination. External auditors as well as affected communities themselves provide invaluable perspectives when assessing models. Metrics and measurements should be defined based on the very rights identified as endangered in prior stages. Does the system reduce equal opportunity for certain subgroups? What mitigation approaches can address discovered issues?

Model Cards[2] standardized such evaluations, detailing performance across user groups and use cases to enable external oversight. Failing to evaluate known issues prior to deployment severely heightens dangers of AI systems once unleashed into complex social environments.

STAGE IV: MODEL DEPLOYMENT

Finally, considerations shift to end uses and real-world impacts as AI interfaces directly with individuals and communities. Stakeholders now encompass deployers like businesses implementing apps but also wider populations subject to model predictions. Surveillance, manipulation, and categorical discrimination become acute threats without appropriate transparency.

Factsheets[3] detailing deployed use cases, data handling practices, and approaches to redressing risks such as inaccurate medical diagnoses provide necessary visibility around otherwise opaque systems affecting daily lives. Furthermore, explicit consent procedures empower user autonomy.

This Four Stages perspective ties regulatory involvement directly to existing development pipelines familiar to companies already. Standardizing documentation at each phase aligns incentives toward demonstrating how models ultimately impact rights and welfare once in widespread usage. Next, we connect this framework to current discourse by examining how different categories of rights map to common AI risks debated today.

1. *"Datasheets for Datasets"* by Timnit Gebru et al.
2. *"Model Cards for Model Reporting"* by Margaret Mitchell et al.
3. *"Using AI Factsheets for AI Governance"* by IBM Cloud Pak for Data

9

A RIGHTS-FOCUSED APPROACH TO REGULATING AI

When policymakers, researchers, and companies assess AI systems, discussions tend to fixate on capabilities—what the technology can potentially do—rather than impacts on people. Yet regulation exists precisely to encode protections around human welfare. So how might we tie abstract concerns like "existential risk" or "superintelligence" directly to rights violations that legal governance is meant to safeguard against?

Categorizing Rights in AI Systems

We can integrate rights into three broad categories when evaluating AI through a governance lens:

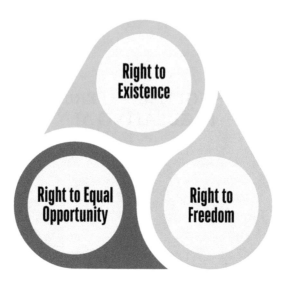

THE RIGHT TO EXISTENCE

This encompasses existential catastrophe scenarios, however unlikely in the near future, where AI causes annihilation of the human species. But we can also include more imminent threats of physical harm such as deaths from autonomous vehicles or lethal autonomous weapons.

THE RIGHT TO FREEDOM

Mass surveillance and loss of privacy violate personal autonomy, as do AI systems for social control and manipulation, whether by companies or authoritarian regimes. There exist reasonable expectations that one's behaviors and communications online or in public should not be exploited.

THE RIGHT TO EQUAL OPPORTUNITY

When AI systems produce discriminatory decisions around lending, insurance, housing, employment, criminal justice and more, this constitutes infringement on fair treatment and access to livelihood. Historical prejudices become baked into models and automated at scale.

Connecting Abstract Harms to Concrete Rights

Public debates around AI ethics often clash between focusing on near versus long-term perspectives. Centering affected populations through a rights framing helps reconcile tensions.

Rights relate speculative dangers around super-intelligent systems back to tangible principles of human welfare that societies already encode into law. What specifically about advanced AI would undermine rights to freedom, equal treatment, or even existence? This grounds abstraction in legal precedent.

Simultaneously, looking at imminent algorithmic harms through a rights lens elevates accountability beyond one-off controversies toward systemic reforms. For example, occasional stories of biased facial analysis are concerning not just because that particular system is flawed but more so because such cases constitute infringement of equal opportunity protections on a societal level. This shifts focus to institutional reforms rather than individual incidents in isolation.

Prioritizing Issues Using a Rights Framework

What gets priority when balancing different issues ultimately depends on assessing impacts on affected populations. Some questions to consider:

What is the severity and proportionality of the rights violation if it occurred?

How historically disadvantaged is the group whose rights
are endangered?

What ripple effects may propagate across communities if
left unaddressed?

Case Studies

Consider a few examples of prominent AI controversies
through a rights-based perspective:

1. Biased hiring algorithms limiting employment opportunities infringe on equal access protections:

As covered in Part I, Amazon discovered that its AI recruiting
tool was not rating candidates for software developer jobs and
other technical posts in a gender-neutral way. The system was
trained on resumes submitted to the company over a 10-year
period, most of which came from men, reflecting male domi-
nance across the tech industry. Consequently, the AI down-
graded resumes that included the word "women's," as in
"women's chess club captain," and graduates of two all-women's
colleges were also penalized in the rankings. Amazon ultimately disbanded the team working on the recruiting tool, realizing that the system's biases were intractable.

2. Racial profiling in predictive policing violates due process rights and enables over-policing of marginalized groups:

The New York Police Department, one of the largest police forces in the U.S., developed its own predictive policing algorithms[1] to direct the deployment of police officers to crime "hot spots." The NYPD's secretive approach and refusal to disclose specific data sets used in these algorithms have heightened concerns over racial biases and the lack of transparency in predictive policing practices.

3. Micro-targeted ads and viral misinformation influencing elections can undermine personal autonomy and manipulate users:

One notable example is the Cambridge Analytica scandal[2] in 2018, where data from up to 87 million Facebook profiles were collected without user consent. This data was used for ad targeting purposes in the American presidential campaigns, the Brexit referendum, and elections in over 200 countries, highlighting how digital platforms and data misuse can undermine democracy by enabling sophisticated voter disinformation and suppression.

In each case, discussing issues as systemic rights violations rather than one-off technical bugs brings clarity to appropriate regulatory reactions.

In Closing

This rights-focused approach gives regulators and developers a common language for translating abstract AI capabilities into concrete impacts on human welfare that legal systems have evolved to protect over decades and centuries. Next, we cover how standardized documentation requirements can serve as "proof" that companies building AI systems have addressed risks connected to key rights their customers and communities depend upon.

---

1. *"Predictive policing algorithms are racist. They need to be dismantled"* by Will Douglas Heaven for MIT Technology Review
2. *"The Facebook and Cambridge Analytica scandal, explained with a simple diagram"* by Alvin Chang for Vox

10

IMPLEMENTING RIGOROUS DOCUMENTATION DURING AI DEVELOPMENT STAGES

Thus far we have covered how standardized documentation tied to protecting human rights can align AI development with ethical principles encoded into regulation. But what does responsible documentation entail in practice? This chapter details the different types of useful documentation, and then provides guidance across different stages.

Introduction to Model Cards

Introduced by Google researchers in 2019, Model Cards present a compelling framework aimed at tackling these issues by standardizing the documentation of AI models' specifications, performance, and intended applications.

The inception of Model Cards was motivated by an increasing recognition of the biases and ethical dilemmas inherent in AI models. These documents aspire to enhance transparency and aid in more informed decision-making among developers, users, and stakeholders by detailing the models' capabilities and limitations. Drawing inspiration from analogous practices in other fields, such as Datasheets for electronic components, Model Cards underscore the critical role of transparency in the deployment of technology.

Model Cards are structured to include several essential elements:

• **Model Details:** This section provides foundational information about the model, including its name, type, version, and purpose.

• **Intended Use:** It outlines the specific scenarios where the model is suited for use, as well as situations where it may not be appropriate.

• **Model Performance:** This part of the card discloses the model's performance metrics over various benchmarks and conditions, emphasizing performance disparities across different demographic groups.

• **Ethical Considerations:** Here, potential ethical issues and biases within the model are addressed, accompanied by strategies for mitigation.

• **Caveats and Recommendations:** The document concludes with a discussion on the model's limitations and offers guidance for its deployment.

Several organizations such as Google and Hugging Face provide annotated templates to aid card creation.

Model Cards fulfill several vital roles within the AI ecosystem:

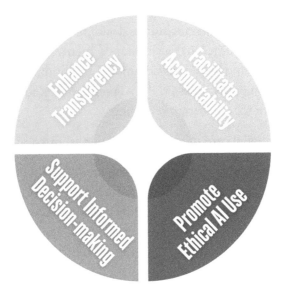

• **Enhancing Transparency:** They demystify an AI model's characteristics, making it more comprehensible to a broad audience.

• **Facilitating Accountability:** By delineating intended uses and performance metrics, Model Cards ensure developers are accountable for the impact of their models.

• **Promoting Ethical AI Use:** The inclusion of ethical considerations prompts developers to confront and mitigate potential biases and fairness issues proactively.

• **Supporting Informed Decision-Making:** Stakeholders can leverage Model Cards to make more educated decisions regarding the deployment or investment in AI technologies.

Challenges

Despite their advantages, implementing Model Cards is not without its challenges, including deciding the level of detail, maintaining accuracy in performance metrics, and ensuring the cards are updated alongside model evolution. Their effectiveness also heavily relies on the AI community's adoption and commitment to transparent reporting.

A poor AI model card might exhibit several shortcomings:

1. **Lack of Detail on Model Performance:** A model card that does not provide detailed performance metrics across diverse datasets, especially concerning different demographic groups, can be considered inadequate. This lack of detail may prevent users from understanding how the model performs in real-world scenarios, potentially masking biases.

2. **Insufficient Description of Intended Use:** Poor model cards may vaguely describe the model's intended use cases, leaving users to guess its appropriate applications. This can lead to misuse or deployment in contexts where the model performs poorly or unfairly.

3. **Overlooking Ethical Considerations and Bias Mitigation:** An inadequate model card might omit discussions on ethical considerations, biases in training data, and strategies for bias mitigation. This omission can indicate a lack of commitment to addressing AI fairness and ethical use.

4. **Absence of Model Limitations:** A model card that fails to mention the model's limitations or the conditions under which the model's performance might degrade is not fully transparent. This can mislead stakeholders about the model's reliability and applicability.

5. **No Information on Dataset Provenance:** Poor model cards might not include detailed information about the datasets used for training and evaluation, including how these datasets were

collected and any potential biases they might contain. This lack of transparency can hinder efforts to evaluate the model's fairness and generalizability.

6. Vague or Missing Information on Model Updates: If a model card does not include information on how the model has been updated over time or plans for future updates, it may not provide a complete picture of the model's development lifecycle.

To improve AI model cards and ensure they fulfill their role in promoting transparency and accountability, developers should aim to address these common shortcomings. By providing detailed, clear, and comprehensive documentation, Model Cards can help bridge the gap between AI developers and the diverse communities affected by AI technologies.

Real-World Applications, Impact, and Future Directions

Model Cards have been applied across a spectrum of domains, from facial recognition to natural language processing (NLP) models. The *Gender Shades* project[1] by researcher Joy Buolamwini notably underscored the necessity for such documentation by exposing significant biases in commercial facial analysis technologies. Adopting Model Cards allows companies to affirm their commitment to ethical AI practices and foster user trust.

Model Cards represent a facet of a broader initiative towards responsible AI development. Future directions might include standardizing Model Cards across different industries, integrating them within regulatory frameworks, and creating tools to facilitate their generation. As AI technologies progress, Model Cards will play a crucial role in ensuring these systems are deployed ethically, transparently, and accountably.

Introduction to Datasheets for Datasets

The concept of Datasheets for Datasets represents a significant advancement in the ethical development and use of AI. As AI and ML technologies have become more prevalent across various sectors, the datasets that train these systems have come under scrutiny. Concerns over data bias, privacy, and the overall transparency of AI systems have prompted the need for a standardized approach to document the origins, characteristics, and limitations of these datasets. This is where Datasheets for Datasets come into play, providing a framework for comprehensive documentation that aims to improve the accountability and fairness of AI technologies.

The idea for Datasheets for Datasets was proposed by Dr. Timnit Gebru and her colleagues in their seminal paper, drawing inspiration from the concept of datasheets used in the electronic components industry. Just as electronic datasheets detail the operational characteristics of components, Datasheets for Datasets are designed to provide essential information about datasets, including how they were collected, their intended use cases, and any potential biases they may contain.

The rationale behind this initiative is rooted in the recognition that datasets are not neutral; they reflect the conditions under which they were created, including the biases of their creators and the societal contexts they originate from. By documenting these aspects, Datasheets for Datasets aim to foster more responsible AI development practices.

A Datasheet for Datasets typically encompasses several critical areas of information:

1. **Collection Process:** This includes details on how and from where the data was collected, whether participants were informed and consented, and any selection or exclusion criteria used.

2. **Data Characteristics:** Information about the type and nature of the data, such as text, images, or numerical values, and the demographic breakdown of individuals represented in the dataset, if applicable.

3. **Preprocessing/Cleaning:** Details on any steps taken to preprocess or clean the data, including normalization procedures, handling of missing values, and annotation methodologies.

4. **Intended Use:** A clear description of the intended uses of the dataset by the creators, highlighting suitable and unsuitable applications to guide users in making ethical choices.

5. **Ethical Considerations:** Discussion of any ethical concerns related to the dataset, including privacy issues, potential for harm, and steps taken to mitigate these concerns.

6. **Accessibility:** Information on how the dataset can be accessed, any restrictions on its use, and the licensing under which it is made available.

The adoption of Datasheets for Datasets carries the potential to significantly impact the AI field by increasing transparency, promoting ethical use, and facilitating better understanding of datasets' limitations. For developers, these datasheets serve as a vital resource for assessing the suitability of datasets for specific applications, especially those with high stakes such as healthcare diagnosis or criminal justice. For researchers, they provide a foundation for critiquing and improving dataset collection methodologies. And for regulatory bodies, datasheets offer a mechanism for oversight, ensuring that AI systems are built on well-documented, ethically sourced data.

Challenges and Future Directions

While the concept of Datasheets for Datasets is widely praised, its implementation is not without challenges. These include determining standardized formats that accommodate the diversity of datasets, ensuring compliance from dataset creators, and updating datasheets as datasets evolve.

Poorly crafted datasheets can significantly impact the understanding and evaluation of AI models. Here are some typical shortcomings:

1. **Incomplete Description of Data Collection Methods:** An inadequate datasheet may lack detailed information on how the data was collected, including the methodology, time frame, and geographic location. This omission can obscure potential biases and limit the dataset's applicability assessment.

2. **Vague Data Annotation Process:** Datasheets that do not clearly describe how the data was labeled or annotated, including who performed the annotations and what guidelines were followed, fail to provide insights into potential sources of bias in the data.

3. **Lack of Demographic Information:** A common issue in datasheets is the absence of detailed demographic information of the data subjects (when relevant and ethical to collect), which is crucial for assessing dataset diversity and potential biases towards certain groups.

4. **Insufficient Discussion on Dataset Limitations:** Poor datasheets might not adequately address the limitations of the dataset, including its representativeness, the contexts in which

it is applicable, and any known issues that might affect model performance.

5. No Information on Data Privacy and Ethics: Datasheets that overlook the discussion on how data privacy was protected during collection and how ethical considerations were addressed can signal a lack of diligence in dataset preparation and usage.

6. Failure to Update Dataset Information: Like model cards, datasheets can become inadequate if they are not updated to reflect changes in the dataset, additional insights into its use and limitations, or new understandings of its biases.

Improving Datasheets for Datasets involves addressing these issues by providing comprehensive, clear, and transparent information about the dataset's creation, composition, and limitations. Such improvements are crucial for enabling responsible AI development and deployment, ensuring that datasets do not perpetuate biases or undermine fairness in AI applications.

Moving forward, the AI community must work together to refine and standardize the practice of creating datasheets, encouraging broader adoption and integration into AI development workflows.

Datasheets for Datasets represent a critical step towards more ethical, transparent, and accountable AI. By providing a structured approach to dataset documentation, they empower all stakeholders in the AI ecosystem to make informed decisions, ultimately leading to the development of fairer and more reliable AI systems.

Introduction to Development History Reports

Understanding the evolution of AI models—from conception through various iterations to their final form—is essential for developers, users, and stakeholders alike. Development History Reports serve as a critical tool in this understanding, offering a detailed chronological account of an AI model's lifecycle. These reports document the sequence of significant events, changes, and decision points that occur as the model evolves, providing an invaluable record of its development process.

The creation of Development History Reports is motivated by the need for transparency and accountability in AI development. They act as a detailed logbook, recording experiments, algorithmic adjustments, dataset changes, and performance evaluations. This documentation facilitates a deeper insight into the model's capabilities and limitations, the rationale behind specific design choices, and the challenges encountered and overcome during development.

Furthermore, Development History Reports enhance collaborative efforts within development teams and across the AI community. By maintaining a comprehensive record of a model's evolution, they enable developers to build upon previous work without retracing steps or repeating mistakes. This continuity is crucial for advancing AI technology efficiently and effectively.

In essence, Development History Reports embody the principles of openness and meticulous record-keeping. They are pivotal for fostering a culture of ethical AI development, where decisions are made transparently, biases are openly addressed, and models are continually refined and understood in the context of their development history.

Introduction to FactSheets for Applications

FactSheets for Applications are crafted with the intent to inform and educate a broad audience, including developers, stakeholders, regulators, and end-users, about the nuances of AI applications. They serve as a bridge, demystifying complex AI systems by providing accessible information that aids in understanding how these applications function, their intended purpose, and the contexts in which they can be ethically and effectively used. This transparency is crucial for building confidence among users and stakeholders, ensuring that AI applications are utilized in a manner that is both informed and aligned with societal values and norms.

Moreover, FactSheets for Applications contribute significantly to the ethical development and deployment of AI by highlighting potential biases, ethical dilemmas, and privacy concerns associated with the applications. They encourage developers to preemptively address these issues, offering strategies for mitigation and detailing the efforts made to ensure fairness and inclusivity. By documenting these considerations, FactSheets help in steering the development of AI towards more equitable and unbiased outcomes.

Key Distinction Between Documentation Types

The key distinction between these documents is that while *Development History Reports* focus on the model itself, *FactSheets* and *Model Cards* provide evaluation and usage guidance, and *Datasheets* detail the source training data characteristics.

Together they provide a comprehensive picture of the data, models, and their applications.

Rights-focused Documentation During AI Development

Now we connect the introduced documentation types to a rights-based approach:

1. Model Cards: Evaluating Models Against Rights Goals

Central artifacts are Model Cards, transparency reports benchmarking performance on safety, fairness, and other criteria vital for oversight. Appropriate metrics require careful consideration of affected populations:

Qualitative assessments may better capture subjective issues around dignity or autonomy compared to quantitative metrics alone. Rights relating to social and psychological welfare resist reduction to statistics.

Datasets used for measurement similarly demand scrutiny— "garbage in, garbage out." User groups matching deployment conditions give confidence in real-world utility. But model builders should also run experiments on alternative datasets checking for consistency.

Comprehensive documentation means reporting performance across all relevant subgroups, not just aggregate averages that hide disparities. Politically disadvantaged groups tend to suffer disproportionately when harms overlooked during evaluation propagate post-deployment.

2. Data Sheets: Rendering Datasets Legible for Oversight

Upstream, Datasheets for Datasets similarly disclose provenance details and composition analysis on training data, enabling auditors to trace downstream risks back to upstream data sources. Facial analysis models often struggle with darker skin types due to under-representation in benchmark datasets, for example. Attributing root causes empowers addressing them.

3. Development History Reports: Evolution of Model Design Choices

On model development itself, version-controlled reports explaining when different architectures were tried or modifications made provide a "flight recorder" for when problematic behavior emerges later. Chronicling dead-ends avoided or surprising errors discovered gives external researchers and future internal teams context on inherited models.

4. Factsheets: Clarifying Intended vs. Unintended Usage

Finally, Factsheets for applications detail mitigation measures and procedures for users or oversight agencies to appeal or report issues around inaccurate system outputs or recommendations. Compared to other stages, deployment phases pose heightened uncertainty as models confront open-ended human environments. Circumscribing intended uses limits unanticipated harms.

Integrating Documentation Through Organizational Processes

For documentation to work, generating and maintaining artifacts like Model Cards should integrate with existing developer workflows. Checklists prompt considering potential rights impacts associated with data and code changes. Supporting metrics display on dashboards, keeping benchmarks continually visible.

Furthermore, cultures around transparency facilitate both internal and external auditing. Workers must feel empowered surfacing tradeoffs or ethical dilemmas to leadership without repercussions. And external testing verifies safeguards function properly outside company walls. Partnerships with civil society groups build trust with communities affected by AI systems.

In Closing

The aim of standardized documentation is rendering AI systems legible for governance in ways aligning with organizations' capacities. Continual tracking of progress toward rights-focused goals marshals insights from those closest to technical details while supporting external oversight duty-bound to constituents' welfare. In the next chapter, we discuss remaining tensions and questions.

---

1. Gender Shades project by Joy Buolamwini for MIT Media Lab

11

THE PATH FORWARD

Part II offers a blueprint for connecting AI development processes with human rights protections. But tensions persist between commercial interests and responsible oversight. Additionally, implementing consistent guidelines internationally remains challenging as cultural contexts differ. This chapter addresses open questions.

Rebutting Innovation Blocking Claims

Industry voices frequently cast regulation as hampering progress and economic competitiveness. However, the documentation-based approach described here aligns incentives rather than uniformly restricting activities. Companies retain flexibility to pursue innovations through means they determine most efficient while standards provide guardrails steering progress in socially beneficial directions.

Furthermore, case studies suggest documentation requirements have stimulated improved practices. Google's Model Cards uncovered biases that developers are now addressing.

And non-profits like Partnership on AI actively collate implementation resources companies directly use to fulfill emerging
policy expectations around transparency. Far from blocking
advancement, responsible oversight anchored to real-world
usage encourages meaningful progress benefiting wider populations.

Remaining Tensions and Open Questions

Certainly some inherent tensions persist between aspirational
principles and pragmatic tradeoffs when building complex
real-world systems:

- Accuracy often conflicts with equity or privacy—
  though adverse impacts frequently arise from over-
  reliance on narrow accuracy metrics. Preserving
  dignity may require forgoing marginal performance
  gains.

- Self-regulation also avoids enforceability challenges
  arising with formal legal requirements. But voluntary
  principles alone enable perpetual avoidance of
  accountability. Hybrid approaches likely work best.

Also, adapting global guidelines to diverse regions with
differing cultural needs and regulatory regimes presents logis-
tical hurdles. And radically transformative scenarios speculated
for advanced AI systems perhaps a decade or more away
surface uncertainty around future potential impacts.

While complex tradeoffs clearly exist, proactive transparency
into how developers balance such decisions can constructively
support external oversight duty-bound to constituents' rights.

Recommendations for Policymakers, Industry, and Partners

In light of remaining open questions, what specific roles might various institutions play co-stewarding AI progress aligned with human welfare?

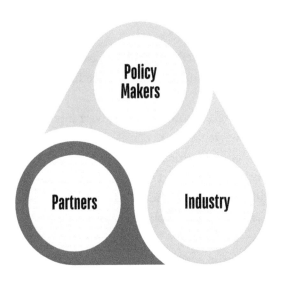

Policymakers should:

- encode documentation requirements demonstrating rights protections into law, while avoiding rigid constraints on innovation pathways;

- conduct independent risk and impact reviews, using documentation to guide governance.

Technology leaders should:

- adopt rights-based risk assessment methodologies proven to catch issues pre-deployment

- enable external oversight through rigorous lifecycle transparency.

Multi-stakeholder partnerships should:

- channel industry resources toward empowering communities affected by AI systems;

- convene forums facilitating all voices shaping decisions behind increasingly impactful technologies.

Through purposeful coordination, governments uphold their duty to encode legal protections for constituent welfare. Companies safeguard ethical codes driving visions for progress. Impacted communities voice priorities around problems affecting daily life. And partnerships amplify voices historically excluded from technology policymaking.

Conclusion

As artificial intelligence advances, so does wariness around potential impacts on human rights and welfare. Yet reactive alarmism often eclipses constructive solutions. Part II outlined practical methods for encoding ethical priorities directly into the incentives guiding AI developers daily. The framework presented here can align exponential technologies more meaningfully with human values.

By tying rigorously documented processes to protecting established rights, companies retain flexibility pursuing innovations while external oversight steers progress toward just ends. Standardizing artifacts like Model Cards, Data Sheets, and Fact Sheets renders opaque systems legible for governance while rewarding organizations that open themselves to scrutiny.

No framework resolves inherent tensions between competing goods entirely. But centering people and rights affected by AI systems constructively grounds policy in lived experience rather than abstract capabilities. If adopted, these methods would foster accountability currently lacking.

Of course, documentation alone cannot guarantee ethical outcomes. The humans behind technology retain responsibility enacting checklist guidance into reality. Organizational cultures emphasizing empowered dissent and cross-functional collaboration largely determine whether oversight lends teeth to existing regulations.

And even the most comprehensive technical processes function within social contexts shaping how systems get built, deployed, and governed. Broader participation from impacted communities in decisions over developing technologies can direct progress toward solving problems people actually face.

Getting there will require cooperation across sectors. Policymakers setting regulatory incentives must work in tandem with conscientious companies willing to have existing priorities challenged. Partnerships can support such collaboration, but public pressure remains essential for hastening mainstream adoption of principles benefiting less powerful groups.

With shared intention, the building blocks presented here can transform AI from an existential source of risk into a progenitor of human flourishing.

PART III

RESPONSIBLE DATA GOVERNANCE

RESPONSIBLE DATA CURATION FOR RELIABLE AND ETHICAL MACHINE LEARNING

The meteoric rise of Generative AI has intensified data extraction at unprecedented levels. Industry giants like Open AI, Meta and Google now ingest trillions of data points annually to continually refine capabilities including behavioral prediction models. The quest to feed ever-larger models is projected to hit zettabyte scale in coming years.

This explosive data mining predominantly uses unregulated online platforms and spaces. But the ensuing models often get applied to sensitive social domains like finance, employment, healthcare, and education with significant consequences. As decisions that deeply impact people's lives become mediated by trained algorithms, ethical data sourcing constitutes an urgent priority within technical infrastructure.

Problems with Common Data Collection Norms

Prevailing practices prioritize efficiency over considerations like consent, privacy, and representation. Key issues include:

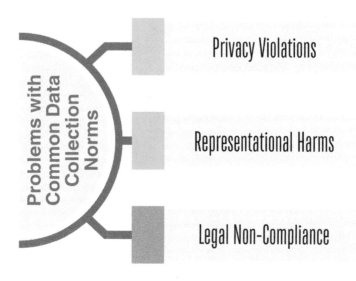

- **Privacy Violations:** Extracting identifiable personal information without consent disregards established protections for individual dignity and data autonomy.

- **Representational Harms:** Homogenous datasets misrepresent reality and exclude minority groups, leading deployed systems to underserve them through poor reliability or outright discrimination.

- **Legal Non-Compliance:** Certain biometric data types entail special handling requirements under regional data privacy laws that scraped datasets routinely violate.

These interconnected issues create substantial ethical and accuracy costs for impacted individuals and communities. Conscientious data collection requires looking beyond efficiency to grapple with complex tradeoffs that decisions regarding human lives need.

Core Principles for Responsible Data Curation

Collecting data ethically[1] starts from viewing information sources as rights-bearing persons rather than passive commodities to optimize metrics. Shifting this perspective demands grounding practices in core principles like:

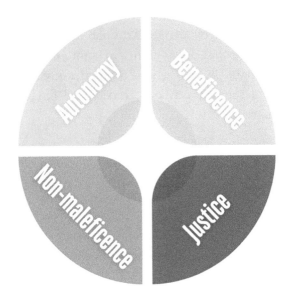

- **Autonomy:** Respecting individuals' dignity and self-determination via informed consent and withdrawal procedures. This preserves data sovereignty rather than coercive extraction.

- **Beneficence:** Proactively furthering data subjects' wellbeing throughout information lifecycles. Create reciprocal value for people whose data trains models.

- **Justice:** Promoting equitable distribution of machine learning's benefits and burdens. Ensure fair representation and access rather than reproducing inequality.

- **Non-maleficence:** Mitigating informational and evaluative harms by handling people's data according to set safeguards calibrated to risks.

Transforming abstract ideals into implemented practices constitutes an open challenge. Actionable solutions demand thoughtful contextual adaptation and appraisal of priorities. We now highlight key suggestions for addressing fundamental issues around consent, privacy, diversity and model development transparency.

Key Recommendations for Responsible Practice

1. SECURING CONSENT AND CONTROL

- Obtain voluntary informed consent to share personal data like biometrics, demographics, behaviors, etc. Use plain language and enable granular permissions.
- Allow revoking consent through easy, accessible mechanisms adaptable to disabilities, languages, digital literacy, etc. Automate where possible.
- Delete data upon request or provide strictly quarantined access only to consenting researchers under time-bound agreements.
- For new data collection, plan consent flows early, seek wide user testing, and be open to adapting approaches based on feedback.

2. PROTECTING PRIVACY

- Assess re-identification risks before releasing datasets and apply state-of-art anonymity methods calibrated to dataset sensitivity.
- Catalog legally mandated and ethically advisable data handling requirements in dataset purpose documentation.
- Collect only necessary attributes and remove ancillary sensitive metadata that could unlock identities without commensurate benefits.

3. REPRESENTING DIVERSITY

- Proactively compose varied training data using census benchmarks to approximate target populations or use privacy-preserving generative models.
- Gather multiple modes of self-identified, intersectional details on identity, culture, experiences, abilities etc. from contributors.
- Compensate marginalized data collection fairly using regional wage benchmarks and provide transparency into uses.
- Structure datasets and model training to equally distribute errors rather than concentrating harms.

4. ENHANCING TRANSPARENCY

- Perform audits internally and facilitate external red team evaluations to uncover dataset biases and model failures through collaborative disclosure.
- Provide model cards detailing performance across user segments and edge cases. Update continually through deployment monitoring.

- Implement interactive model explanations and consent flows for end users subject to algorithmic decisions.

Responsible data curation fundamentally reconsiders common questionable machine learning research norms in technology towards a more conscientious, community-aligned methodology. As public scrutiny and regulation intensifies, these practices constitute pragmatic steps that organizations should undertake for legal compliance, effectiveness and sustaining public trust. Rather than incidental progress, collectively realizing robust and ethical data ecosystems remains imperative for reliably beneficial machine learning.

---

1. *"Ethical Considerations for Responsible Data Curation"* by Jerone T. A. Andrews et al. for Sony AI

13

STRATEGIC CORPORATE DATA GOVERNANCE FOR GENERATIVE AI SYSTEMS

The Rise of Automated Content Creation

As previously discussed, recent advances in Generative AI enable automatically synthesizing written content, images, audio, code and more at quality levels previously requiring human expertise. Models such as GPT-4 display remarkable linguistic fluency, creative potential and reasoning competence by training on vast datasets.

As these systems propagate across industries, they promise to reshape workflows from marketing campaigns to scientific research through on-demand automated content. However, as with any rapidly evolving technology, realizing responsible outcomes requires proactive governance. This chapter provides practical data management strategies for enterprises adopting Generative AI systems. Without diligent protocols instituted early, issues around security, privacy, bias and ethics threaten to undermine public trust and business value.

Preventing Sensitive Data Leaks

The initial priority is restricting generative model access to confidential corporate data, including customer information, product plans, legal documents, trade secrets, strategic memos and more. Once ingested for training, such data becomes permanently embedded within models, creating avenues for exposure through intentional extraction or inadvertent memorization.

For instance, adversaries could deduce proprietary details from model outputs to unfairly compete, or confidential customer records may resurface when employees experiment with novel prompt formulations. These risks compound as generative models serve increasingly business-critical functions with corresponding data access. Additionally, regulations like GDPR (and the upcoming EU AI Act) mandate protecting sensitive personal information, with European authorities already probing chatbot providers.

Mitigating this requires cross-functional involvement between security architects, infrastructure engineers and enterprise architects to institute stringent access controls. First, sensitive unstructured data should be explicitly classified into restricted domains isolated from generative model ingestion through corporate data usage policies. Next, comprehensive data traceability mechanisms need deployment for tracking information flows from authorized on-premise systems into model training environments. Detailed audit trails then enable rapid investigation of any suspected confidential data leakage by identifying the original breach source for remediation.

For externally sourced proprietary APIs or third-party models, it becomes imperative to contractually bind technology vendors and partners to stringent practices safeguarding sensitive data through legally enforceable clauses. Even open-sourced models pre-trained on vast public data warrant algorithmic audits before integration to confirm training methodology isolation from restricted internal data.

Cultivating Conscientious Training Data

Custom developed generative models additionally need curating high-quality training data internally that avoids issues like bias. Present data collection norms emphasize scraping quantities without much consent or governance, risking low-quality outputs once deployed.

Addressing this requires instituting robust metadata standards around classifying training data types, sensitivity labels and intended usage scopes to guide creation of precise data provisioning policies for models. Furthermore, methodical risk assessment documentation like Datasheets or Model Cards need adoption for auditing datasets along key dimensions like consent, accuracy and representativeness before ingestion.

Rather than non-consensual extraction, models should train on data from contributors consciously permitting usage like through opt-in licenses or permissions platforms. Seeking overt consent preserves autonomy and trust. Additionally, submitted data warrants thorough preprocessing via cleaning, deduplication and enrichment pipelines ensuring integrity for model consumption. Taken together, establishing these conscientious data lifecycle controls sustains model reliability and public faith.

Expanding Access to Evolving Public Knowledge

Unlike confidential corporate data, generative models fundamentally require unconstrained ingestion of vast public knowledge to offer utility for enterprise contexts. People expect these tools to incorporate continuously evolving current events, research breakthroughs and cultural dialogs. However, traditional behind-the-firewall environments obstruct dynamically tapping into such open data at scale.

Bridge infrastructure enabling federated data access solves this impediment. Specifically, flexible retrieval augmentation architectures[1] allow programmatically interfacing with rich open knowledge graphs spanning both public domain and licensed external platforms through standardized APIs. Querying these vast reservoirs of structured information then provides contextual grounding to empower more intelligent responses for employee requests.

Additionally, incremental learning methodologies facilitate continuously fine-tuning models on live public data streams and knowledge updates to prevent relevancy stagnation over time. Rather than one-off training, deliberate planning for perpetual enrichment sustains cutting-edge generative performance as expectations and environments inevitably shift.

Governance Switches Generative AI from Liabilities into Assets

The strategies above transform uncontrolled generative models from compliance landmines into trustworthy growth drivers, delivering business value securely while upholding ethical priorities around consent, transparency and accountability. Ultimately, responsible data management unlocks truly transformative possibilities from automated content creation. The time for action is now, before consequences become irreversible.

---

1. *"Retrieval-Augmented Generation for Large Language Models"* by Yunfan Sao et al.

PART IV

PARTICIPATORY DATA STEWARDSHIP

14

INTRODUCTION

Data has become deeply embedded into the fabric of our digital society. From online platforms to medical research, organizations across sectors rely on the collection, analysis, and use of vast amounts of data. This data holds immense potential to tackle pressing challenges, further scientific discovery, and provide personalized services. However, numerous scandals and controversies have also exposed the pitfalls of current data practices.

As previously covered, issues around privacy violations, opaque decision-making, algorithmic bias, and unintended negative consequences are eroding public trust. Certain marginalized groups also face heightened surveillance and exclusion. Without addressing these problems, the benefits of data cannot be fully realized. We need a new paradigm for responsible and ethical data stewardship.

Part IV puts forward the concept of participatory data stewardship[1] as a solution. Data stewardship means the responsible planning and management of data as a shared resource. It involves sustainable, transparent processes that preserve individual and collective data rights. Crucially, effective data stewardship also requires participatory governance that engages the people and communities who are impacted.

Sharing real-world case studies and examples, Part IV demonstrates concrete mechanisms for empowering beneficiaries to have agency in shaping data practices. It outlines ways individuals and groups can gain increasing influence—from being informed, to actively collaborating and even directly governing certain uses of data.

The chapters trace levels of participation, benefits and challenges, key actors, and policy connections. Detailed models showcase how data trusts, cooperatives, participatory algorithms and other structures can enact participatory stewardship. The conclusion synthesizes core arguments and points towards next steps in advocating for more empowered approaches to data that transform extractive practices.

Overall, Part IV charts a practical path forwards for data stewardship that not only manages risks, but also unlocks the tremendous potential in data to serve people and the public good. The framework presented aims to build understanding, capacity and momentum for participation in ethical innovation with data.

---

1. *"Participatory data stewardship."* by Reema Patel for Ada Lovelace Institute

15

CASE STUDY: GROUNDING DATA GOVERNANCE DECISIONS IN LIVED PERSPECTIVES

Wellcome is a global charitable foundation that supports science to help solve urgent health challenges. They are currently funding work to create large-scale mental health databanks to enable research on conditions like anxiety, depression and psychosis.

However, Wellcome recognized that aggregating personal mental health data poses ethical risks around privacy and consent. To mitigate these risks, they wanted to incorporate participatory data stewardship into their databank initiatives.[1]

Wellcome's Lived Experience Advisory Team

To ground data governance decisions in lived perspectives, Wellcome has convened a Lived Experience Advisory Team consisting of 12 members from 8 countries, including Australia, India, Indonesia, Japan, Kenya, Rwanda, South Africa and the UK.

This advisory team is made up of people with personal lived experience of mental health conditions. They provide strategic guidance across Wellcome's mental health portfolio, advising on priorities and approaches that authentically reflect community needs and concerns.

Framework Development Process

As part of their mental health data work, Wellcome commissioned a framework outlining ethical risks and mitigation strategies for developing databanks.

From the outset, the framework development process engaged the Lived Experience Advisory Team in co-design workshops to collaboratively assess and refine the framework, with a focus on strengthening participatory data stewardship elements.

Key initiatives driven by the advisory team input included:

- Elevating community benefit as an equal priority to scientific progress in the guiding ethical principles.
- Enabling participant control over access permissions for their data based on realized privacy levels.
- Requiring inclusion of advisors in monitoring dataset equity.
- Embedding mechanisms for open community feedback at all stages of research activity.

Outcomes

Through month-long iterative co-design sessions, the Lived Experience Advisory Team meaningfully shaped core aspects of participatory data stewardship within the framework.

Their direct guidance led to new mitigation strategies focused on participatory oversight through ethical reviews, consent procedures, longitudinal equity audits and community safeguards.

Three advisors also co-authored academic articles on learnings from this collaborative framework development process for peer-reviewed journals.

Conclusion

This example demonstrates how lived experience insights can be proactively centered within sensitive health data work through structured, compensated participation. By establishing and adequately empowering a Community Advisory Board, participatory data stewardship can move from abstract concept to concrete practice.

---

1. *"Ethical data governance for mental health databanks A framework for risk diagnosis and mitigation strategies"* by Wellcome, AAPTI Institute and Sage-Bionetworks

16

WHY DATA STEWARDSHIP MATTERS

There is no doubt that data holds tremendous potential. When responsibly governed, the analysis of large datasets can further scientific research on pressing issues like climate change and disease. It can enable governments to effectively target services and policies. Companies can use data to provide users with more personalized and improved offerings. However, a barrage of recent scandals and controversies has exposed the significant downsides of current practices in how data is collected, stored, analyzed, and used across sectors.

Controversies and Scandals

In just the past few years, various high-profile cases have demonstrated ways data is often gathered and deployed in opaque, uncontrolled, and unethical ways. As previously discussed, in 2016, it was revealed that analytics firm Cambridge Analytica had harvested the data of 87 million Facebook users without their consent. They then used this to construct detailed psychographic profiles and target voters with tailored political ads. The scandal illustrated how personal data could be secretly exploited to manipulate and influence behavior.

Other controversies like the UK's failed Care.Data program[1] have created significant backlash over privacy and control of health data. The Care.Data program was an ambitious National Health Service (NHS) effort initiated in 2013 to centralize health and social care data to improve treatment and services. However, it faced relentless criticism over sharing sensitive medical records with commercial companies without explicit patient consent.

By 2016 over 1 million people had opted out, derailing the project. A review found "disastrous incompetence" in both ethics and technical implementation. The communication of purpose and data protections to the public was profoundly lacking.

The failure underscores the immense challenges in unlocking health data value ethically. Transparency, consent procedures and strong safeguards are essential to such sharing. But messy complexities abound between progress and privacy.

Care.Data collapsed under public backlash after repeated pauses and controversy. The debacle left clear lessons— success with data systems central to human welfare requires regaining public trust through open dialogues ensuring people's interests come first. Otherwise, citizens will rebel against what they see as profit-driven exploitation of intimate information.

Flaws in algorithmic systems from everything to exam grading software to facial recognition tools have also raised concerns over bias, unfairness, and inaccurate decision-making. The common thread across these cases and others is a lack of transparency, agency, and oversight in how data is used—

contributing to severe negative impacts for individuals and society.

Harmful 'Good Intentions'

The training data used to develop algorithms, as well as the techniques for processing that data, are often not transparent. This lack of transparency means problems can arise without warning. For example, if toxicity filters that remove offensive language are applied to the training data, this can inadvertently eliminate positive portrayals of marginalized identities. Well-intentioned efforts to scrub overtly toxic language by flagging certain keywords may disproportionately exclude minority groups. So an algorithm trained on that skewed data will then replicate and amplify those skewed representations.

The AI startup Jigsaw, owned by Google's parent company Alphabet, developed a system called Perspective that scores the perceived "toxicity" of online text content. The goal was to help platforms like Facebook and YouTube flag destructive comments for moderation.

A 2019 study[2] analyzed how Perspective rated 114,000 tweets from prominent online personalities. Surprisingly, various drag queens and LGBTQ online figures were consistently rated as more "toxic" than extremists like white supremacists.

A likely reason is that Perspective lacked nuanced understanding of language use and context. For example, words like "queer" and "trans" received high toxicity scores despite being common identity terms. And drag queens frequently use mock impoliteness and insults positively to build community resilience.

By contrast, racist and extremist tweets were often rated as healthy discourse by Perspective. This suggests biases in how the system was trained and serious blind spots in detecting genuine hate.

Responsible and ethical data curation requires open acknowledgment that subtle complex tradeoffs exist between removing toxicity and maintaining diversity. Marginalized communities can provide critical input on how to navigate these tradeoffs instead of ignoring them. Their participation is key for determining appropriate data representation.

Consequences for Public Perceptions

These recurring issues have steadily eroded public trust and confidence in how both governments and companies handle data. Surveys show falling perceptions that personal data is secure and used ethically. For example, research by the UK's Royal Society found that only 37% of citizens trust organizations to use data responsibly[3]. Stories of harms and downsides now heavily color attitudes toward data. This compounds reluctance toward data sharing initiatives, even those aimed at the public interest.

Barriers to Unlocking Public Benefits

Distrust and skepticism act as major obstacles to unlocking the huge potential societal benefits in the responsible use of data. When the public lacks confidence in how data will be governed, they understandably oppose proposed programs to leverage data for medical research, improved services, and evidence-based policy. However, this hesitancy also prevents progress on using data responsibly. Without rebooting attitudes and trust, it will remain challenging to implement ethical and beneficial data practices. The status quo has led to a trust deficit that obstructs the path toward more responsible innovation with data.

Participation as a Solution

How can trust be rebuilt and the promise of data realized? A growing chorus of experts argue participatory approaches provide a key piece of the puzzle. Rather than data practices being opaque black boxes solely designed by governments and companies, participatory data stewardship means engaging the people and communities impacted by data in shaping its governance.

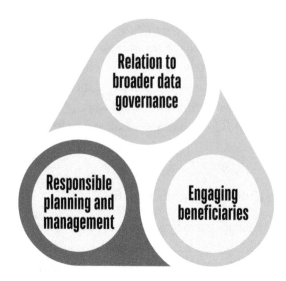

I. RELATION TO BROADER DATA GOVERNANCE

Data stewardship refers to the responsible planning and management of data as a shared resource. It involves sustainable and transparent processes for gathering, analyzing, and using data that preserve individual rights and respect collective interests. Stewardship is an integral component of overall data governance frameworks.

Good governance requires appropriate checks and balances between key stakeholders. Currently, tech companies and governments wield asymmetrical power in data systems. By promoting participatory stewardship, beneficiaries gain more influence in the decisions made about data governance to rebalance this equation.

2. RESPONSIBLE PLANNING AND MANAGEMENT

At its core, data stewardship means using and managing data in an ethical, sustainable, and socially beneficial manner. This encompasses implementing transparency, oversight, and security measures that reduce potential harms. It also means respecting and preserving data rights—both of individuals as well as collective interests.

Responsible stewardship requires considering who is impacted by data practices and how they can be given more say. Marginalized groups who often face exclusion or disproportionate surveillance have acute interests when it comes to governance decisions. As data increasingly mediates decisions and opportunities in society, participation takes on heightened urgency.

3. ENGAGING BENEFICIARIES

In participatory models of stewardship, the people and communities affected by data uses are engaged in shaping governance. This includes data subjects directly in datasets, wider publics served or impacted by resulting decisions, and groups vulnerable to underrepresentation or overreach. Their rights, needs, priorities, and concerns help guide the development of practices around collecting, analyzing, and acting on data.

Rather than being passive consumers with limited awareness or control, participatory stewardship recognizes beneficiaries as key stakeholders with vital perspectives. Their active involvement promotes outcomes better aligned with public expectations and values. Different mechanisms across a spectrum of engagement are possible depending on context. But centering those impacted lays the foundation for rebuilding lost trust through co-creation.

Core Value Propositions

Why does participatory stewardship matter? What unique benefits can be gained by increasing the engagement and influence of beneficiaries?

There are several key interrelated value propositions:

1. Creates checks and balances

Participatory approaches provide checks and balances currently missing from many data governance regimes. They enable oversight and input from people otherwise marginalized. This acts as a counterweight against unilateral decision-making by governments or companies that lead to harmful impacts or reinforce power imbalances.

Diverse oversight inserting public priorities and concerns can lead to more balanced policymaking. It also makes data systems more responsive by channeling user needs. This contributes to greater equity and justice in outcomes.

2. IMPROVES DATA PRACTICES

Engaging beneficiaries also functions as a feedback loop to improve data practices. Identifying problems in existing systems guides their reform. Surface-level diversity in who is involved and represented in processes can also increase depth diversity of ideas and safeguard against groupthink.

More participatory design processes take better account of potential sources of bias, exclusion, or negative consequences earlier on. This results in higher quality datasets and analytical outputs. Tightened feedback between data subjects and stewards similarly enhance alignment with user expectations throughout operations.

3. BUILDS PUBLIC TRUST AND CONFIDENCE

Perhaps most critically, participatory stewardship helps rebuild reservoirs of public trust and confidence in data systems. It enables forms of collaborative auditing, oversight, and control that reassure users. Co-creation and transparency around trade-offs demonstrate respect for public priorities and norms.

Seeing openness combined with accountability measures builds legitimacy around necessary data sharing and uses. This expands the space for secure and ethical data use to benefit society with public backing. In essence, participation flips the script of data as an imposition to data as a collectively governed resource.

Overcoming Key Challenges

There are reasonable critiques to expanding participatory approaches for data governance. Doing so requires confronting some core challenges:

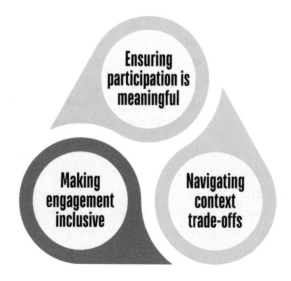

I. ENSURING PARTICIPATION IS MEANINGFUL

First, participation mechanisms cannot simply be symbolic without actual influence. If engagement feels like box-checking without real input into decisions, it will worsen distrust. Genuine participation requires shifting power dynamics to give beneficiaries more control and agency. Their priorities must demonstrably guide substantive choices.

Participation also cannot be a one-time exercise. Ongoing engagement needs embedding through data collection, analysis, use and evaluation stages. This demands considerable investment of institutional resources and commitment. Avoiding tokenism requires starkly confronting existing privileges around data.

2. MAKING ENGAGEMENT INCLUSIVE

Participation itself often advantages certain demographics with time, capacities, and resources to engage in governance. Special efforts must consciously include data subjects from more marginalized communities who face greater stakes around data but high barriers. This demands approaches sensitive to accessibility issues.

3. NAVIGATING CONTEXT TRADE-OFFS

While beneficial, participatory approaches have costs. Developing mechanisms tailored to goals, data types, and beneficiaries takes resources. The processes require time that can seem to delay progress. However, sidestepping public input often backfires later as systems lose legitimacy. Participation must balance facilitating responsible innovation with ensuring human-centric data policies. Legal and technical mechanisms continue playing crucial complementary roles as well.

Summary

This chapter outlined the crisis of public trust currently facing data systems and governance regimes. Controversies around violations of privacy, opaque decision-making, unchecked power, and unintended consequences have steadily damaged public confidence. This trust deficit obstructs realizing the huge potential societal benefits in ethical leveraging of data.

Participatory data stewardship presents a path forward. Engaging beneficiaries as stakeholders in processes for collecting, analyzing, and using data promotes outcomes better aligned with public values. It provides checks and balances to rebalance power asymmetries. Embedding oversight and collaboration tightens feedback loops that enhance data quality and system equity. Rebuilding trust enables expanding secure and responsible data sharing practices.

Realizing participatory stewardship requires concrete mechanisms tailored to context. The next chapters delve deeper into frameworks to map types of engagement, beneficiaries to involve, use cases from data trusts to co-operatives, and policy connections. Meaningful participation ultimately moves from data practices as an imposition to data as a collectively governed resource that empowers the people and communities it impacts.

---

1. *"NHS care.data scheme closed after years of controversy"* by James Temperton for Wired
2. *"Drag queens and Artificial Intelligence: should computers decide what is 'toxic' on the internet?"* by Alessandra Gomes, Dennys Antonialli and Thiago Oliva for the InternetLab
3. *"Who cares what the public think? UK public attitudes to regulating data and data-driven technologies"* by Aidan Peppin for Ada Lovelace Institute

CORE PRINCIPLES OF DATA STEWARDSHIP

Responsible and Ethical Data Management

What constitutes responsible data stewardship in practice? At its foundation, it means implementing careful practices for how data is collected, stored, analyzed, used and shared. This encompasses core principles of sustainability, transparency, security, and intentionality in data management.

1. SUSTAINABLE COLLECTION AND USE

Responsible stewards take a long-term perspective considering future consequences beyond immediate goals. This means conserving data as a precious resource rather than maximizing extraction. It demands questioning what is strictly necessary and avoiding uses with unclear necessity or proportionality. Data minimization matched to specified aims limits potential exposure or misuse.

2. TRANSPARENT PROCESSES

Clear documentation and openness should permeate all data operations. This encompasses cataloging what is collected and how. Data flows between sources and uses should not be hidden. Methodologies for analysis and architectures of data systems should be inspectable rather than black boxes. Such transparency allows oversight and adds context to interpret limitations.

3. SECURITY AND PRIVACY PROTECTIONS

Stewards must safeguard entrusted data through technical protections like encryption alongside access control policies. Higher sensitivity data requires heightened precautions proportional to potential risks of exposure, especially for vulnerable groups. Responsibility includes prompt notification and remediation plans even for breaches with low likelihood of harm.

4. INTENTIONAL STEWARDSHIP CULTURE

Beyond tactical protections, responsible data stewardship relies on promoting organizational cultures and professional norms that treat data as a vital trust rather than solely a commodity. This manifests through data ethics training, empowered roles dedicated to stewardship responsibilities, and leadership emphasizing social license and mission-driven governance. Intentionally nurturing stewardship makes it endure beyond perfect procedures.

Preserving Individual and Collective Data Rights

Responsible data stewardship is not just about technical implementation. It equally depends on governance regimes and practices that honor both individual and collective rights around data. This demands balancing autonomy, representation, public trust, and equity.

1. RESPECTING INDIVIDUAL CONSENT

At the basic level, people retain rights to control use of personal information. This encompasses notice and consent for collection and processing. It also provides ongoing rights of access to view one's data and ability to request changes or deletion. While informed consent alone is limited, preserving some individual agency is an important base.

2. HONORING COLLECTIVE INTERESTS

However, individuals do not exist in isolation. Data practices deeply shape collective conditions around rights, opportunities, and power differentials. Responsible stewards assess community-level interests and involve representative groups in governance decisions influencing them. This could encompass anything from neighborhood impacts to group civil liberties threats.

3. FURTHERING SOCIAL LICENSE

Wider public trust provides the backdrop enabling any data systems to sustainably operate. Cultivating broad transparency, accountability, and perceptions of deservingness to handle data is pivotal. Even if not every single person participates, social license through serving public interests grants legitimacy to necessary data uses.

4. PROMOTING EQUITABLE OUTCOMES

As data permeates decision-making across areas like credit, employment, and public services, ensuring equitable treatment and progress towards justice becomes integral. Responsible stewardship demands proactively assessing and mitigating group-based disparities in both representation and impact. This includes both bias assessments and civil rights law adherence.

Embedding Participatory Approaches

True data stewardship requires participatory governance engaging those impacted by data systems in their design and oversight. This serves both instrumentally to improve practices as well as intrinsically for ethical empowerment. There are interdependent components to embed participation within stewardship.

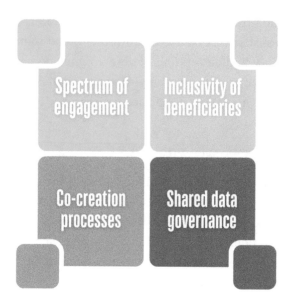

I. SPECTRUM OF ENGAGEMENT

There are multiple modes of engagement depending on goals and contexts. At a minimum, informing and transparency foster understanding. Consulting constituencies gathers feedback. Further involvement empowers collaboratively making trade-offs or even directly shaping decisions in specific cases. Layering approaches addresses different needs.

2. INCLUSIVITY OF BENEFICIARIES

Careful consideration of the populations affected is essential for legitimate participation. This certainly incorporates data subjects directly within datasets. However, governance decisions frequently affect wider publics through policy or products derived from data. Inclusion should encompass marginalized groups at particular risk of impacts.

3. CO-CREATION PROCESSES

Embedding participation means stewards and beneficiaries come together in collaborative processes for shaping data practices. This manifests through participatory forms of technology design, impact assessment, and priority setting. Community-rooted methods tapping local expertise make engagement more meaningful and grounded.

4. SHARED DATA GOVERNANCE

Joint governance forums fostering participatory decision-making provide a infrastructure for sustainability. Models that empower users with real authority over data itself, such as data collectives and trusts, instantiate the concept of data as a common good to be actively stewarded by those affected rather than passive consumers.

Guiding Ethical Frameworks

Responsible data governance further relies on comprehensive mechanisms to assess ethical implications and facilitate oversight. Combining bottom-up participation with top-down structures promotes accountability.

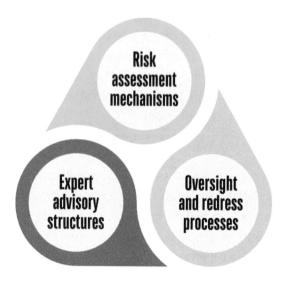

1. Risk assessment mechanisms

Data systems interact in complex ways requiring proactive audit. Privacy impact assessments manage specific risks around personal data usage. Broader algorithm audits surfaced potential biases and harms from machine learning models that stewardship aims to reduce. Embedding ongoing impact monitoring flags emerging issues.

2. Expert advisory structures

Independent ethics boards and panels comprised of diverse specialists lend institutional wisdom to review proposals and policies. They foreground risks and equities that internal teams can overlook. While not replacing inclusive participation, their informed perspective complements other inputs.

3. Oversight and redress processes

Channels for those negatively impacted by data systems to file grievances enable accountability and reform. Documenting complaints feeds continuous improvement. Where disputes arise over data rights or governance decisions, transparent proactive issue resolution processes preserve legitimacy and trust. Remedies should aim to address both immediate issues and root causes.

Robust ethical oversight frameworks guide responsible data stewardship evolving in line with emerging lessons and norms. Interlocking participation mechanisms, expert guidance, and formal accountability together uphold public interests.

Summary

Overall, responsible and ethical data stewardship in service of people and the public good inherently means participatory data governance. The next chapters delve deeper into specific mechanisms and use cases enacting bottom-up empowerment. Examples showcase how data trusts, collaboratives, and other models instantiate participation principles into practice through real structures and decision-making.

18

CASE STUDY: DATA FOR GOOD COLLABORATION

Good Cycles is a Melbourne-based social enterprise that provides employment opportunities for at-risk youth through bicycle repair and other sustainability programs. However, as a non-profit organization, Good Cycles lacked the data analytics capabilities to effectively measure and communicate the impact of its programs.

Approach

To build Good Cycles' data capacity, Swinburne University's Social Innovation Research Institute partnered with them on the "Data for Good Collaboration" project[1]. This initiative:

- Facilitated interactive co-design workshops for Good Cycles staff to navigate using data.
- Created data literacy building webinars.
- Helped analyze organizational data to derive insights into program outcomes.
- Integrated external ABS datasets to supplement understanding of youth education and employment.

Additionally, a collaborative "Data Co-Op" model was used to develop data sharing partnerships between Good Cycles and other non-profits.

Outcomes

Key outcomes included:

- Analysis showed improvements in communication, teamwork and problem-solving skills among youth in Good Cycles' employment training programs.
- Mapping trainee transportation data displayed reduced congestion and emissions due to biking.
- Presenting impact evidence opened opportunities for further data sharing with partners.

The Data for Good Collaboration equipped the Good Cycles team to better leverage its organizational data through capacity building and participatory analysis.

Conclusion

This case study demonstrates how participatory and collaborative approaches can empower non-profits like Good Cycles to more effectively measure and communicate the social impact of their programs through data. Building capacity and data sharing partnerships are key to overcoming barriers faced by resource-constrained organizations.

---

1. *"Good Cycles Data CO-OP"* by DataCoop

19

A FRAMEWORK FOR PARTICIPATORY DATA STEWARDSHIP

Spectrum of Participation

There are a range of approaches to enabling participation in data systems based on the level of engagement and influence afforded to beneficiaries. Consider the mechanisms below as an indicative spectrum.

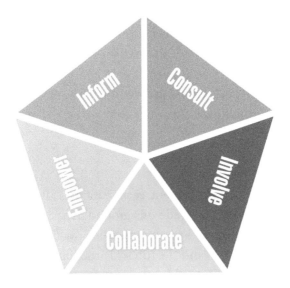

A. INFORM

At the basic level, initiatives can improve transparency and explainability to inform beneficiaries about data practices. This encompasses communication about purposes, protections, and sharing. It also includes explaining particular systems and methodologies in accessible ways. This orientation lays the groundwork for further participation.

B. CONSULT

Many organizations also undertake consultation to gather user perspectives. This can take the form of focus groups, interviews, surveys, and other feedback mechanisms. While not guaranteeing influence, it incorporates public views on priorities and concerns into design choices. The limitation is the extent user centricity remains symbolic without real responsiveness.

C. INVOLVE

Other participatory structures involve beneficiaries more actively such as through long form deliberation. The goal is gathering informed input to challenges requiring collective judgement. Advisory boards are another common technique to channel impacted voices into governance decisions. This weighs public interests transparently against other factors in policymaking.

D. COLLABORATE

At greater levels of engagement, certain models allow beneficiaries to directly negotiate trade-offs around data sharing and use rules. Platform cooperatives empower user-owners with voting rights over policies and features. Participant councils can govern access terms or ethics for research datasets based on collective priorities. This collaboration binds decisions to user direction.

E. EMPOWER

Finally, the most extensive participation establishes user authority and control within governance. Data collectives with shared ownership instantly full participation rights. Patient committees granting case-by-case access to health records centrally apply consent preferences. While rare, these approaches recognize data as a common good for beneficiaries to govern.

The following sections overview applications of this participation spectrum to build empowered, human-centric data stewardship.

Key Questions for Beneficiary Identification

Who specifically should participate in data governance? Defining the beneficiary populations is essential for legitimate and effective engagement. Ask:

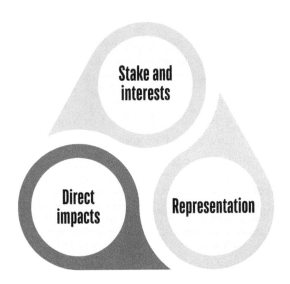

1. STAKE AND INTERESTS

Of course, those with personal information directly in a dataset have a key stake, as do any communities characterized. Start by considering data subjects and then ponder indirect impacts on adjacent groups.

2. DIRECT IMPACTS

Next contemplate who might be most affected by decisions or policies related to data practices in focus. This depends on context but aims to include perspectives actually experiencing consequences, which could unveil issues less proximate technologists miss.

3. REPRESENTATION

Finally assess who remains underrepresented in processes and data itself—the inclusion gaps needing counterbalancing. Seek populations at risk of silencing or bias despite high stakes. Their input surfaces unseen risks and alters power imbalances.

In general, design participation initiatives consciously focused on diversity, equity and inclusion from the outset. Practical barriers prevent many marginalized groups from engaging unless expressly welcomed. There will always be constraints to universal involvement. But responsible stewardship demands conscientiously including beneficiaries beyond just privileged technologists. Tandem legal protection of minorities remains essential even alongside participation.

The next section surveys examples of participatory data governance emerging across sectors that consider this question of representation among beneficiaries.

Emerging Use Cases

How is participatory data governance currently taking shape across contexts? Consider the real-world use cases below that put engagement into practice:

A. GOVERNMENT AND PUBLIC SECTOR

Fairness and representation are pivotal issues for public sector data initiatives because of their expansive societal impacts. Emerging policy innovations demonstrate avenues for accountability.

- **Open data portals:** Platforms publishing government datasets for transparency allow citizens to directly audit underlying information as armchair analysts.

Features like public request processes give civilians Agency to shape release priorities democratically.

- **Algorithmic audits:** Given public concerns over biases in automated decisions, some localities have created participatory algorithm audits. Multidisciplinary community oversight groups review analysis for fairness issues and make reform proposals prioritizing equity.

B. Private sector

Pressures on platforms from regulators and users have spurred some firms to allow greater visibility and consultation into content and data policies:

- **Responsible AI guidelines:** Technology leaders releasing ethics principles solicit diverse public commentary to improve guidelines balancing innovation and responsibility. This feedback helps address blind spots and pressure tests commitments.

- **Ethical data partnerships:** Startups have explored data trust models featuring participant councils governing access approvals ensuring research requests demonstrate direct public benefit with informed consent as a check against exploitation based on collective priorities.

C. Research and academia

Scientific studies centrally relying on human participants grapple with balancing advancing knowledge with avoiding extractive dynamics:

- **Participatory mapping:** Community-based
  participatory mapping engages residents in collectively
  charting local needs and assets with public memory
  and experiences shaping spatial renderings counter to
  top-down views obscuring marginalized histories.

- **Community-based modeling:** Projects modeling
  dynamics with complex societal effects like climate
  change create participatory simulations integrating
  community knowledge and values into scientific
  assumptions and scenarios to make policy more
  responsive to lived realities.

D. CIVIL SOCIETY

Grassroots alternatives reimagine data infrastructure grounded
in empowered cooperation:

- **Data activism:** Initiatives like data unions and data
  justice labs convene impacted constituencies to
  formulate affirmative visions and watchdogs over
  practices through grassroots mobilization tactics that
  restructure basic power relations.

- **Data cooperatives:** Member-owned data co-ops
  govern sharing based on collective approval and ethics
  not just individual consent. They demonstrate
  participatory data governance in action through
  democratic oversight mechanisms purpose built
  around constituencies.

The constraints facing these examples reveal tensions in
expanding participation as the next section summarizes.

Challenges for Participation

While rich in promise, participatory approaches confront hurdles requiring navigation:

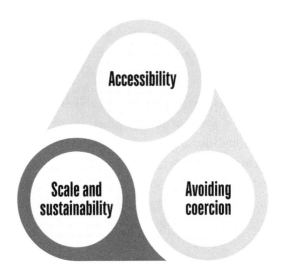

A. ACCESSIBILITY

Participation often further empowers those with time, capacity, knowledge and other privileges to engage unless consciously designed for inclusion. Meetings or complex policy issues impose high barriers preventing marginalized people from shaping decisions affecting them. Proactively investing to address accessibility gaps remains vital.

B. SCALE AND SUSTAINABILITY

Participatory initiatives also struggle to achieve the scale and resources for durability of institutions relying on extraction or coercion. The pressures of funding models and growth expectations deposited alternative data platforms before. Avoiding replication means acknowledging trade-offs.

C. AVOIDING COERCION

As data permeates services and opportunities, measures to encourage people donate or share data risk unintended coercion or removal of meaningful choice. Ensuring ongoing consent and exiting data sharing remains essential even amidst pursuit of social goods to avoid manipulated participation.

Despite challenges, participatory data stewardship offers a compass heading for reorienting practices toward empowerment. With thoughtful design and leveraging complementary collective rights and expert guidance, participatory processes can realign data with public values and priorities. The question becomes how to scale pathways and coalitions for getting there.

Summary

This chapter mapped a spectrum of participatory approaches to embed engagement within data systems:

- Informing around purposes and practices.
- Consulting on perceptions and priorities.
- Involving in governance policymaking.
- Collaborating around data sharing decisions.
- Empowering for user ownership and control.

It also highlighted how careful inclusion of beneficiaries should consider direct stakes, likely impacts, and representation gaps needing redress.

Use cases illustrated diverse real-world techniques in action from municipal algorithmic audits to grassroots data cooperatives:

- Government open data and oversight bodies.
- Private sector self-regulatory consultation.
- Academic participatory mapping and modeling.
- Civil society data activism hubs and alliances.

Each comes with trade-offs around accessibility, scale, and avoiding potential coercion requiring navigation.

This participation toolkit aims to complement other essential policy interventions like data rights laws. The following chapter connects participatory stewardship to necessary governance infrastructure for enacting bottom-up empowerment. Together human-centered, ethical data systems relying on consent and public oversight can unlock data for good.

20

KEY ACTORS IN DATA STEWARDSHIP

This chapter covers the main actors in data stewardship:

Data Subjects

The most direct stakeholders in data governance are people whose personal information comprises datasets and algorithmic systems. How are rights and interests of data subjects central to participation?

Data subjects refer to the individuals about whom data is actively recorded, such as profiles, behaviors, locations, biometrics and more. They possess innate interests in determining what is collected, how it is analyzed, whether it is retained, and how it might shape automated decisions or service delivery concerning them.

Participation empowers data subjects to better control use of their information in line with expectations around privacy as well as broader interests. This demands mechanisms providing transparency, consent choice, access to their data, and opting-out. Individual agency remains a vital counterweight to organizational self-interest.

In particular, people have diverse risk tolerances and personal benefit-harm calculations around data sharing that warrant reflection through participatory policymaking. Research shows distinct segments among public attitudes. Enabling participatory governance means representing plurality.

There are also inherent limits to isolated individual action within data systems structured to leverage people's data. This points to establishing collective participation mechanisms balancing autonomy and scale through pooling consent or representation.

Wider Publics

Beyond those directly in datasets, data practices shape collective conditions making wider publics also vital stakeholders for participation.

Governance decisions around data use often impact citizen experiences of technology, urban environments, social media polarized discourse, and other domains well beyond direct data subjects alone. This argues for broadening who participates.

Datafication links closely to issues with diffuse public effects such as surveillance infrastructure enabling state control or research gaps slowing public health advances. Since steward-ship choices cascade, input should represent community interests.

Extending engagement widens oversight helping flag potential externalities or representing common concerns of justice and equity otherwise marginalized by technical design thinking. Deep public impacts argue for democratizing data.

Wider social contexts also produce populations made more vulnerable by data practices due either to likelihood of exclu-sion/erasure from datasets or reliance for services on accurate representation. Centering these groups within participatory regimes offers self-determination.

In summary, data issues transect society so those impacted require voice in governance beyond direct data subjects alone —especially officially disempowered communities.

Underrepresented Groups

Data and technical systems built on demographic exclusion further collective harms highlighting the need for participatory inclusion of marginalized groups.

Ubiquitous findings of non-representative training data or algo-rithmic performance gaps reveal patterns of exclusion by race, gender, disability status and other characteristics with inequality effects. The ubiquity argues this stems from struc-tural biases rather than incidental oversights.

Whether included in datasets or evaluating system perfor-mance directly on minorities, data practices still impact the interests of excluded groups through their proxy effects calibrating societal policies, opportunities, stereotypes and environments. They cannot opt-out of influence.

The real-world consequences range from hindering access to credit, housing or jobs to enabling expansion of discriminatory state surveillance. Data exclusion enables the public sector equivalent of redlining. This infringes on civil rights and liberties requiring redress.

Participation specifically offers the possibility for underrepresented groups to rectify harms created by exclusion at multiple levels—surfacing exclusion; shaping collection to improve representation; steering governance choices balancing competing priorities to promote their interests; and directing distribution of benefits and value.

In essence, inclusive participation begins redistributing disproportionate power. By the nature of marginalization, this requires intentional empowerment mechanisms rather than waiting for emergent involvement.

Technology Workers

Frontline technology practitioners play an influential yet complex role situated between senior management and user experiences. What is their stake and how might participation empower positive change?

Engineers, designers, coders, analysts and other technology workers directly build, deploy, maintain and improve data and algorithmic systems. Their choices instantiate intent and ethics into code, defaults, metrics, and business practices with impacts cascading across operations.

Despite depictions as rote implementers, tech workers exercise considerable discretion mediating between institutional incentives and professional norms. Typically, closer connections to user needs also shape a sense of purpose and modules although constrained by structural realities of firms and markets.

Recognizing their power, technology labor organizing leverages solidarity around ethics and social responsibility to counter excessive commercial motivations. Collective participation can force improvements in areas like military contracting, diversity, or environmental sustainability.

As insiders, even individual conscientious objections or whistleblowing shape public discourse on controversial areas like moderation rules or algorithm harms. Tech worker participation is thus pivotal to raising issues otherwise siloed behind non-disclosure agreements and lobbying resources.

In summary, technologists form a key constituency for participatory stewardship to raise alternate priorities within institutions yet require empowerment against constraints on individual risk and speech.

Policymakers

Governments play central stewardship roles regulating private data systems and harnessing public data for services. How does participation connect top-down legal authority with ground-up advocacy?

Administrators, regulators, and legislators shape data governance through statutory powers and funding research and digital infrastructure modernization. Their choices codify rights, incentives and access frameworks that bound what models seem viable.

Governance also demands coordinating complex bureaucratic portfolios for alignment from privacy regulations to non-discrimination oversight to industry partnership programs. This benefits from tapping wider expertise navigating change.

Ultimately accountable to citizen electorates, the unique levers of state lie in the ability to mandate legally binding reforms, industry reporting, empower new authorities, and redirect spending towards oversight bodies—exercising sovereignty.

Integrating participatory input from those governed operationalizes responsiveness allowing policies to better reflect collective interests versus just industry lobbying or government assumptions. It makes the system more democratic.

In essence participatory governance makes state stewardship of data infrastructure better calibrated to serve public values through bureaucratic transformation towards responsible innovation centered on human rights.

Responsible Institutions

Lastly, private and social sector organizations play essential roles as data stewards collecting, analyzing, and building services around information that requires internal transformations to enact participatory governance.

Everything flows from cultural values established at the highest levels regarding purposes, competing incentives, whose interests matter and why participation advances missions. This determines resourcing and risks empowered product teams can take engaging beneficiaries.

Participatory processes certainly create short-term uncertainty, delays, and constraints on data leveraging anathema to growth obsessions. But this trades off against long-term legitimacy, sustainability, quality, and impact. The mindset shift is seeing participation as R&D integral to responsible innovation.

With leadership backing, institutions can embed bespoke participation through multiple avenues—informing product design research, consulting advisory boards, collaborating around dataset access, conducting joint impact assessments, or even empowering community governance over projects. This sees beneficiaries as partners rather than just users throughout operations.

Finally, a major organizational impact lies in modeling reforms that help mature the broader accountability ecosystem of norms, expectations, regulations, and review forcing the industry as whole to raise standards over time. Anchor institutions demonstrate possibilities to others.

Fundamentally participatory data governance requires institutions adopt responsibility for stewardship as fundamental to their social performance and licenses rather than risk or crisis management.

Conclusion

There exists alignment in interests across these constituencies —from direct individual control, to restraining externalities, to providing democratic checks all argue for increasing bottom-up participation. Coalition power combining advocacy and formal regulation can drive change.

Of course, vastly different motivations and constraints act on private companies versus regulators versus grassroots advocates. But coordination of complementary forms of participation tackling issues from different vantage points reinforces efforts through a separation of powers. Distinct mechanisms create accountability.

21

PARTICIPATORY MODELS

Data Trusts

Data trusts offer one infrastructure for participatory data governance with public interest stewardship.

We believe data trusts can help support crucial health data research into pregnancy and childhood development, while at the same time providing enhanced participation and more robust safeguards for data and data rights.

Jessica Bell, *Born in Scotland* Data Trust[1]

A. DEFINING CHARACTERISTICS

Data trusts[2] are legal structures governing datasets separating use decisions from commercial interests. Multi-stakeholder boards align data sharing with democratically determined ethical conditions. This oversight curates access often paired with perturbation for privacy.

B. MODELS AND EXAMPLES

Municipal data trusts manage public asset connectivity data including cameras or sensors. Health data trusts enable research access based on patient interest determinations of acceptable areas balancing privacy risks against social goods. More open models host crowdsourced information as common pools.

C. BENEFITS

Proponents argue data trust participation mechanisms address problems of exploitation, bias, and exclusion associated with public or private data monopolies. Board oversight deliberates representing diverse groups. Decentralized curation limits centralized surveillance risks. The trust vehicle also sustains projects as self-funding once operational unlike one-off initiatives.

D. LIMITATIONS

However, resourcing complex legal setups remains challenging. Questions persist around appropriate board configuration avoiding governance captured by narrow interests. ambivalence about truly relinquishing centralized data ownership also hinders adoption. And scale presents daunting coordination puzzles regarding fragmentation versus consolidation across trusts.

In essence, data trusts offer intriguing civic infrastructure yet still face obstacles to system transformation without surmounting steep learning curves about participation.

Data Cooperatives

As an alternative model, data cooperatives look to collective shared governance grounded in member empowerment.

A. DEFINING CHARACTERISTICS

Data co-ops are member-owned structures for pooling personal data securely as a common resource. This grants members joint control over collective data use based on shared ethics and priorities instead of limited individual privacy. Data becomes a community asset democratically managed.

B. MODELS AND EXAMPLES

Platform co-ops appropriate the platform business model but with user ownership disrupting extractive ad models with rights and equity. Health data co-ops enable members to allow vetted research access on ethical conditions members shape around priorities like public benefit requirements. And smart city co-ops reorient the centrality of community needs in technology infrastructure decisions by becoming infrastructure co-owners.

C. BENEFITS

Cooperative participation means data contributors govern use centrally through oversight mechanisms like elected boards and member voting procedures. This provides self-determination regarding ethical limits, commercial influences, and distribution of benefits according to collective priorities. It embeds participation within the business structure.

D. Limitations

However, as small-scale startups typically, resourcing complex technology development and navigating regulatory barriers proves challenging without outside philanthropic support. Generating mass cooperative consciousness that motivates participation takes sociopolitical organizing rather than technical solutions alone. There also remain open questions about translating broad representation into equitable governance designs avoiding the tyranny of the majority.

At their best, data cooperatives demonstrate the art of the possible in participatory paradigms even if challenging to replicate at scale under status quo constraints.

Participatory Algorithms

Rather than data itself, the sphere of algorithms offer another frontier for participatory oversight in stewardship.

A. Defining characteristics

As societal decision-making depends more on coded models, participatory approaches have focused on auditing algorithms by empowering beneficiaries and external reviewers to analyze functionality based on transparent performance indicators relative to democratically determined criteria.

B. Models and examples

Municipal participatory audits assess procurement algorithms against racial equity metrics with community task forces. Worker review boards evaluate workplace management algorithms balancing productivity and conditions. And product testing seals certify software algorithms were screened for discrimination by consumer protection committees.

C. Benefits

This accountability ecosystem inserts impacted voices and public interest guardrails against isolated engineering design choices and performance gaming. It also leverages tools making model behaviors more inspectable by lay participants. Expanding participatory algorithm oversight beyond direct producers to empower wider collectives increases beneficial outcomes.

D. Limitations

However, transparency alone remains insufficient without enforcement mechanisms compelling responsible design choices around known issues. Technical or statistical fluency poses barriers to inclusive participation for many. And questions persist around appropriately mapping distinct interpretive communities onto judgment calls requiring adjudication of competing interests and definitions of fairness.

In total, participatory algorithms progress civil oversight yet achieving change still depends on complementary policy and market pressures for leverage.

Open Data Initiatives

Participation regarding public sector data also operates through open government data programs espousing transparency.

A. Defining Characteristics

Open data initiatives publish government datasets online for public reuse aiming to enable independent analysis, innovation, and accountability. This shifts control over public asset data use from closed bureaucracies towards democratized access as infomediaries transform raw information into legible insights with agency.

B. MODELS AND EXAMPLES

At the vanguard, data portals release transport timetables to improve mobility apps or restaurant inspection results reshaping consumer markets through crowdsourced food safety tools. More advanced community engagement allows residents to request analytics on issues from pandemic recovery to police force equity that shape participatory policy responses grounded in lived experiences.

C. BENEFITS

In theory participatory open data provides for decentralized public audit and oversight. Granular visibility into government operations allows unofficial accountability investigations assessing effectiveness. Enabled reuse also boosts economic activity for entrepreneurs serving information needs bureaucracies missed. And public prioritization of releases influences data transparency.

D. LIMITATIONS

However, issues arise around truly inclusive participation given required expertise. Under resourcing also hinders government capacity assisting community data projects. Plus, questions remain regarding where transparency fails when it reveals problems without empowering reform. This limits impact without mobilized change movements.

Ultimately open data fosters counter power through enabling rather than guaranteeing participatory governance. Public agency depends on building countervailing organization not just data.

Responsible Data Partnerships

Private sector data sharing initiatives also increasingly employ participation for governance based on research showing its benefits.

A. DEFINING CHARACTERISTICS

Projects from medical trials to mobility services centrally rely on accessing user data necessitating consultative design of sharing and oversight rules. Responsible partnerships convene stakeholders co-creating governance based on transparent deliberation over ethical risks and mitigations.

B. MODELS AND EXAMPLES

Patient advisory boards determine acceptable secondary health data uses considering needs and expectations of communities donating data through participatory meetings and focus groups. Data labeling institutions allow workers crowdsourcing data training set annotations to set pay and labor policies via elected councils. And urban pilots of smart city technologies like responsive traffic signals incorporate resident polling and participatory budgeting determining neighborhood infrastructure priorities reflective of lived mobility needs.

C. BENEFITS

At their best, these responsible data partnerships demonstrate how participation converts zeros-sum antagonisms between institutions and constituencies into positive-sum collaboration expanding shared value. They illustrate how including beneficiary voices strengthens systems against overlooking harms, meeting latent needs, and focusing narrow measures losing public goodwill. The processes also sustain engagement enabling updates as technology and uses evolve with context.

D. Limitations

However, skeptics argue limited participation remains mostly an add-on controlling only narrow parameters failing to transform underlying commercial motives or structures of profit maximization externalizing negative externalities. Critics suggest current responsible data partnerships thus function more as ethical cover for reputation management than meaningful accountability and empowerment. And, questions persist around consistent application and scope limiting compartmentalized programs.

On balance responsible data partnerships highlight possibilities for improving status quo practices but require reinforcing policies like data rights legislation and incentives realignment towards fuller participation ecosystems.

Comparison of Models

How do these varied participatory data governance models compare and contrast? Examining across key dimensions clarifies strengths and weaknesses.

A. Levels of participation

The participation depth spans consulting members on policies, collaboratively governing access decisions in trusts, to cooperatives directly empowering member ownership. Each model offers rungs on the participation ladder appropriate to different starting points and appetites.

B. Types of data uses

Similarly, models differentiate based on public, private, personal, commercial and other data use cases each raising distinct concerns, stakeholders and risk pressures requiring tailored oversight. One size rarely fits all data ecosystems.

C. Scalability

Tensions clearly persist between principles grounded participatory designs and realities of technology scaling under dominant funding models not inherently incentivizing empowerment. This helps explain very few cooperatives yet proliferation of limited partners programs. Existing legal infrastructure enables trusts more readily if still incrementally.

D. Key challenges

And all participatory data governance contends with risks of exclusion absent proactive representation policies and resourcing access especially for marginalized groups. Power imbalances do not automatically disappear through participation without structural change. But incremental widening forums for oversight planted seeds help mature more accountable ecosystems.

There are no perfect models but rather possibilities demonstrated for advocates to advance participation fitting context.

Cross-Cutting Learnings

Stepping back, what overarching lessons emerge across participatory data governance innovations?

A. Context-specific design

No one-size-fits-all participation solution exists. Responsible models require bespoke, community-centered design choices driven by their setting, data types, and cultural histories. Off the shelf transplantation often flounders lacking this grounding. Meaningful participation fundamentally grows from lived soil.

B. Resource constraints

Certainly, any participatory shift contends with engrained incentives and assumptions perpetuating data 'extractivism'. However equal attention must focus on overcoming very real material barriers excluding many from shaping governance like lack of time, money, access, and skills for engagement. Systems change requires resourcing participation as integral not extra.

C. Risks of exclusion

This demands emphasizing participatory initiatives centered on constituencies vulnerable to marginalization given ubiquity of exclusion dominate existing data ecosystems. Responsible governance means the most impacted people help decide policies and priorities, not already empowered voices further monopolizing debates.

D. Feedback loops

Doing this well creates positive feedback loops where effectively participating then builds capacities, trust, and momentum for further participation. But legitimacy crucially depends on visible policy and practice changes responsive to input less processes become empty rituals breeding deeper cynicism. Outcomes demonstrate values.

Fundamentally, inclusive participation offers guide rails towards data systems reflecting collective interests but requires transparent, accountable follow through matching good faith with changed power.

---

1. datatrusts.uk/pilot-bis
2. "Data Trusts: from theory to practice" by the Data Trusts Initiative UK

CASE STUDY: PARTICIPATORY APPROACH TO ALGORITHM DESIGN

412 Food Rescue is a non-profit based in Pittsburgh, PA that coordinates an on-demand food donation pick-up and delivery service. Volunteers transport donations of excess fresh food from grocery stores, restaurants, and other businesses to local food banks, shelters, and community organizations serving people in need.

As the service grew, 412 Food Rescue struggled to equitably and efficiently match their rapidly increasing stream of incoming food donations to recipient organizations in real-time. Their human dispatchers' allocation decisions were often skewed towards larger organizations in convenient locations, resulting in inequitable distribution.

412 Food Rescue wanted to develop an algorithmic system to recommend donation-recipient matches but recognized the ethical complexity of codifying fairness and efficiency tradeoffs. To address this, they decided to take a participatory approach to designing the matching algorithm.

Approach

412 Food Rescue implemented the WeBuildAI participatory algorithm design framework[1] over a one-year collaboration. This involved:

1. Recruiting a small but diverse group of stakeholder volunteers including donors, volunteers, food bank staff, and 412 Food Rescue employees.

2. Having stakeholders complete over 40 pairwise comparisons between hypothetical matches and explicitly set matching priority rules. This allowed 412 Food Rescue to build computational models representing each stakeholder's unique priorities and beliefs regarding an ideal match.

3. Aggregating the individual models using a voting system to create an overall matching algorithm reflecting the collective priorities.

4. Explaining the algorithm's top 12 recommended matches to stakeholders and administrators through visualizations conveying how different priorities are balanced.

Outcomes

The participatory approach increased stakeholders' perceived fairness and trust in the resulting matching algorithm. Testing the collectively-designed algorithm on 412 Food Rescue's historical data showed it improved equity in food distribution without sacrificing efficiency compared to human dispatchers.

The participation process also made stakeholders more appreciative of the difficulty in making these allocation decisions and increased their empathy for 412 Food Rescue's work. Additionally, comparing differences between 412 Food Rescue employees' own models revealed inconsistencies in their assumptions about stakeholders' preferences.

Conclusion

This case demonstrates how participatory algorithms allowed 412 Food Rescue to develop an algorithmic system that was perceived as fair and trustworthy by their community. The cooperative design process provided mutual benefits through educational insights that supported organizational learning.

---

1. *"WeBuildAI: Participatory Framework for Algorithmic Governance"* by Min Kyung Lee et al.

23

CONCLUSION

Across sectors, uses of data and algorithmic systems continue growing in scale and societal influence. But a trail of controversies make clear that leaving governance solely to isolated technical or business imperatives leads to exploitative, opaque, and unjust outcomes eroding public trust.

Only by recentering participation—of diverse beneficiaries, impacted groups, practitioners, and advocates—can data infrastructure design and oversight instead empower people collectively stewarding data as a common good. Participatory data governance offers the missing catalyst for legitimacy.

Part IV has charted an expansive canvas of real-world innovations pioneering the shift in paradigm. From municipal algorithmic audits committees, to data cooperatives owned and run directly by those contributing intimate personal data, to hybrid public-private trusts stewarding communal information access, models exist constructing data systems accountable around inclusive democracy and equity.

They provide living proof of concept while confronting daunting challenges still requiring maturing participatory practice. We distilled cross-cutting takeaways like tailoring engagement to community context, tackling uneven accessibility barriers excluding many voices, and above all rewarding participation through procedural and distributive change demonstrating credible influence.

There exist no perfect solutions, no singular law or technology or campaign alone suddenly ushering complete networked citizen sovereignty. But through sustained, coordinated affinities across difference for advancing both bold visions and near-term, incremental disruptions in dialectical tension, socio-technical systems can come to reflect democratic public values.

PART V

AI TRANSPARENCY AND ALGORITHMIC AUDITING

24

INTRODUCTION

Algorithms, or step-by-step procedures for solving problems or accomplishing tasks, underpin an ever-increasing number of automated decisions in both public and private sectors. Algorithms determine everything from the ads we see online to whether we qualify for loans or social services.

However, algorithms can entail risks of bias, discrimination, opacity, and unintended harms if not developed responsibly. High-stakes algorithmic decisions made by complex machine learning systems present particular accountability and ethical challenges.

Algorithm auditing has emerged as a critical governance mechanism to evaluate algorithmic systems, assess their impact, and remedy issues. Audits aim to determine if automated decisions comply with ethical, social and legal norms by examining their purpose, logic, data, functionality and effects.

Well-designed audits promote:

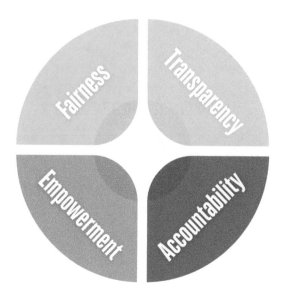

- **Fairness**—Identify and mitigate discrimination, bias and unfair outcomes
- **Transparency**—Increase system legibility and explainability to stakeholders
- **Accountability**—Enable oversight and attribution of responsibility
- **Empowerment**—Help affected individuals understand, question and contest decisions

Auditing encompasses various technical and social scientific methods, both quantitative and qualitative. Key techniques include:

- Inspecting source code, objectives and data.
- Testing functionality and accuracy.
- Surveying end user experiences.
- Evaluating metrics, assumptions and social impacts.
- Organizing participation of affected communities.

To be effective, audits must be independent, technically rigorous, holistic and iterative throughout an algorithm's lifecycle. Tailoring transparency to stakeholders' needs while avoiding fatigue is critical.

We examine algorithm auditing in depth, including motivations, methods, case studies, challenges and recommendations. Our goal is to chart a path towards reliable, empowering algorithmic accountability.

Importance of Transparency for Responsible AI

Transparency is a cornerstone of responsible AI development and deployment. Without adequate transparency, it is nearly impossible to fully assess algorithmic systems or remedy issues.

Transparency serves multiple interrelated aims:

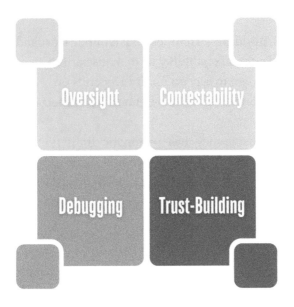

- **Oversight**—Enables regulators, auditors and watchdogs to evaluate AI systems, check accuracy, and investigate problems. This requires comprehensive information on system design, objectives, training data, monitoring practices, etc.

- **Contestability**—Empowers affected individuals and communities to understand decisions, lodge complaints, appeal outcomes and exercise rights. Necessitates clear communication channels and tailored explanations.

- **Debugging**—Allows developers to identify model shortcomings, performance drifts, emerging biases and other technical issues requiring correction. Requires access to monitoring data from production systems.

- **Trust-Building**—Helps establish public trust and organizational credibility by demonstrating commitment to accountability. Depends on transparency applied throughout the AI lifecycle.

However, transparency has pragmatic limitations and risks. Revealing too much system information can compromise efficiency, innovation, intellectual property or security. Complex transparency can overwhelm consumers and erode trust.

These dilemmas require "meaningful transparency" carefully tailored to meet stakeholders' needs within context. Elements may encompass purpose, data provenance, explanatory tools, impact assessments, monitoring policies and dispute processes.

Technical methods[1] like privacy-preserving statistics, zero-knowledge proofs and trusted research environments can enable transparency without full disclosure. Communication methods should empower diverse stakeholders while avoiding fatigue.

True transparency is intrinsic to AI development, not an afterthought. By deeply integrating transparency and accountability, we can realize AI's benefits while regaining public trust and promoting justice.

Challenges in Achieving Meaningful Transparency

While transparency is essential for accountable AI, implementing meaningful transparency that serves stakeholder needs poses multifaceted technological, business and social challenges.

Technical Barriers:

- Complex, opaque models like deep neural networks defy simple explanation and resist full elucidation even for experts.

- Lack of developer skills, literacy and training in emerging explanatory tools. Proliferation of largely unproven methods leads to uncertainty.

- Immature, inconsistent performance of many explanation techniques paired with limited applicability across model types.

- Privacy preserving methods add complexity; fully anonymizing data can diminish utility.

Business Constraints:

- Perceived competitive risks of revealing system details beyond the minimum required. IP protection often prioritized over transparency.

- Lack of leadership prioritization and incentives. Transparency largely not demanded by customers or conditioned by regulation.

- Resource intensive. Customized transparency requires cross-functional collaboration, platform changes, policy development and dedicated staff.

Social Considerations:

- Diverse literacy levels complicate communications. Explanations useless or misleading if outpacing users' context and ability to act.

- Potential to overwhelm consumers, erode trust, or enable system gaming with excess transparency. Requires careful stage-gating.

- Hard to define "right" level of transparency upfront and difficult to iterate quickly within commercial constraints. Customization is key.

By acknowledging rather than downplaying these obstacles, AI practitioners can make pragmatic transparency decisions while pushing boundaries and advocating change.

With concerted, collaborative effort, a culture shift placing transparency at the heart of AI development is achievable over time. The stakes warrant persistent progress.

1. "*UN Handbook on Privacy-Preserving Computation Techniques*" by the Privacy Preserving Techniques Task Team for the United Nations Global Working Group (GWG) on Big Data

UNDERSTANDING AI TRANSPARENCY

Distinction Between Transparency and Explainability

Transparency and explainability are closely related in AI accountability, but they are distinct concepts[1]. Transparency is an overarching principle concerned with increasing the visibility and understanding of AI systems through whatever methods are most appropriate. Explainability refers specifically to techniques for elucidating how an AI model works—interpreting the mechanics behind inputs, weights, neural connections etc. that determine outputs.

In other words, explainability focuses inward on demystifying the "black box" through granular elucidation of model aspects and individual decisions. Transparency looks outward at higher-level communication of AI meaning, effects, risks, and redress to affected communities. Explainability serves transparency by revealing model information, but many transparency elements go beyond intricate model explanations.

Elements Beyond Explainability: Purpose, Metrics, Data Provenance, Social Impact

Transparency entails more than just explainability of how AI models work internally. Additional critical elements of transparency include:

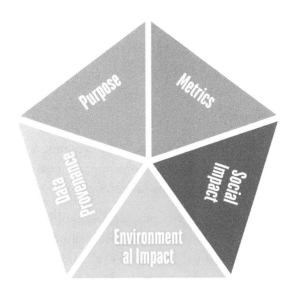

PURPOSE

Stating the intended function and uses of an AI system openly allows stakeholders to contextualize decisions and query appropriateness. Ambiguity around objectives undermines accountability.

METRICS

Detailing metrics like accuracy levels, speed, return on investment or other factors optimized for sheds light on priorities and tradeoffs relative to consumer needs or social goods.

DATA PROVENANCE

Understanding data sources, collection methods, processing, feature selection and training procedures surfaces potential biases and limitations baked into models. Data histories profoundly influence system outputs.

SOCIAL IMPACT

Assessing project and potential risks of harm spanning discrimination, addiction, polarization, economic injustice allows mitigation. Auditing impact on vulnerable groups is key for just AI.

ENVIRONMENTAL IMPACT

Quantifying extensive computing requirements, energy use, carbon emissions and resource consumption enables sustainability improvements critical as AI scales exponentially.

Taken together, these pieces provide stakeholders a comprehensive view of an AI system's purpose, parameters, assumptions and effects essential for sound evaluation and oversight. Explainability of model mechanics alone conveys little about real-world fitness without this contextualization. Whether transparency translates into empowerment and accountability relies upon holistic communication of these critical system attributes.

Role of System Design Perspective: Data, Features, Objectives

Fundamentally, transparency requires understanding an AI system's design goals and construction:

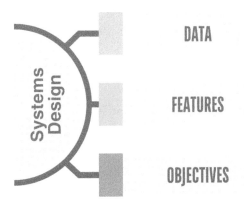

DATA

The data used to train machine learning models impart key characteristics. Data may bias systems towards partial worldviews if narrowly sourced or reflect inequitable social structures via distorted feature representation of marginalized groups. Auditing and disclosing data provenance aids accountability.

FEATURES

Feature engineering, or how machine learning datasets are structured, encodes assumptions about meaningful information made by developers. Choices drive model focus—direct encoding of protected attributes like race and gender versus seemingly neutral phenotypic variables carrying demographic inferences. Feature selection should consciously balance utility and ethics.

OBJECTIVES

AI systems optimize for quantifiable targets set by engineering teams, whether revenue, engagement or predictive accuracy. Metrics chosen incentivize algorithmic focus on desired

outcomes yet may neglect important human values. Understanding metrics clarifies actual vs stated priorities and allows
debate.

Taken together, these choices comprise a system's purpose as
manifest in design decisions and functionality. Without oversight of engineering choices around data, features and metrics
in context, developers evade accountability for potentially
problematic AI behavior. Transparency fosters external scrutiny of these fundamental drivers of algorithmic outputs central
for recourse.

Ideally, transparency commences at initial development
phases, laying system foundations amendable to public
accountability. Attempting retroactive transparency often
proves inadequate absent technical mechanisms enabling
trustworthy disclosure. Responsible innovation requires
concurrent system design and reporting frameworks to actu-
alize AI for societal benefit.

"Meaningful Transparency" Tailored to Stakeholders

True transparency is user-centered, not technology-centered.
Meaningful transparency provides stakeholders customized
insights enabling comprehension and agency rather than
perfunctory disclosure of technical minutiae. Tailoring transparency to literacy levels and use cases while mitigating fatigue
is essential.

For example, regulators may require extensive documentation
of data flows, feature engineering, model validation results, key
metrics and monitoring policies to perform audits. Individuals
affected by AI systems likely need entirely different transparency—perhaps notifications of automated decision making,

straightforward explanations of model factors influencing certain outcomes paired with convenient recourse mechanisms to contest determinations.

Meaningful transparency delivers the right information through appropriate channels at suitable times to satisfy specific stakeholder objectives, such as:

- **Regulators & Auditors**—Perform effective oversight and investigations to uphold laws.
- **Clients & Expert Users**—Interpret model behaviors, validate against use cases and fix issues for improved service quality and safety.
- **End Users & Product Consumers**—Understand why content or recommendations were shown; assess relevance and personalize experiences.
- **Individuals Subject to Algorithmic Decisions**— Contest determinations, resolve issues, remedy errors.
- **Impacted Communities**—Evaluate collective risks and benefits; organize participation.
- **The Public**—Instill confidence in institutions applying AI and gauge accountability.

Technical methods like interactive visualizations, natural language model explanations and contextual performance dashboards tailored for non-expert users exemplify meaningful transparency. But no singular approach serves every audience and use case—customization is imperative, as is a philosophy placing human empowerment over raw data salience. The ends (stakeholder agency) supersede the means (selective transparency modalities).

---

1. *"Stop Explaining Black Box Machine Learning Models for High Stakes Decisions and Use Interpretable Models Instead"* by Cynthia Rudin

26

THE PERILS OF TRANSPARENCY: AN ORGANIZATIONAL CASE STUDY

Tapestry Inc. is a multi-billion-dollar fashion conglomerate operating renowned brands like Coach, Kate Spade, and Stuart Weitzman. It employs algorithms to guide employees in product allocation decisions—determining optimal inventory distribution across retail stores.

Allocators make judgement calls on the number of specific products to send to hundreds of locations—a complex process benefiting from data-driven algorithmic recommendations. The company tested[1] how employees respond to advisories from two different algorithms:

ALGORITHM 1: INTERPRETABLE

A simple "weighted moving average" model averaging historical sales data from the past 3 weeks. Explicitly shows input variables and recommendation logic.

ALGORITHM 2: UNINTERPRETABLE

An opaque machine learning model referencing sales data from the past 16 weeks plus additional variables like promotions and holidays. Pattern-based and highly complex with no visibility into workings.

Research Question

How does the interpretability of an algorithm's recommendation logic affect the likelihood of human decision makers trusting and accepting the algorithm's suggested course of action?

Method

Product allocators made judgement calls on inventory distributions, with each decision randomly either supported by Algorithm 1 or Algorithm 2. Researchers compared human agreement rates between the two algorithms when suggestions conflicted with original employee judgements.

Additionally, through interviews and surveys, researchers investigated why allocators agreed with each algorithm's recommendations.

Key Findings

Despite lower complexity, allocators were more likely to distrust recommendations from the interpretable Algorithm 1 compared to the uninterpretable Algorithm 2:

- When they could scrutinize Algorithm 1's reasoning, allocators often overconfidently second-guessed recommendations by speculating flaws. This "overconfident troubleshooting" eroded trust in the interpretable algorithm.

- In contrast, allocators couldn't interrogate Algorithm 2 but knew respected peers helped develop it. This "social proof" of a trusted development process increased acceptance of the uninterpretable algorithm's opaque outputs.

Implications

The findings reveal unintended consequences of algorithmic transparency—visibility into an algorithm's reasoning process can undermine trust compared to social validation. As businesses embrace AI, leadership should be cognizant of this psychological effect and strategically communicate developmental rigor plus involve respected colleagues in design processes—even for seemingly "self-explanatory" algorithms.

---

1. "Why Providing Humans with Interpretable Algorithms May, Counterintuitively, Lead to Lower Decision-making Performance" by Timothy DeStefano et al. for MIT Sloan Research

27

STAKEHOLDERS AND THEIR TRANSPARENCY NEEDS

AI transparency requires understanding distinct needs across stakeholder groups:

Builders

Developers, data scientists, engineers. Require internal transparency on model debugging, accuracy, monitoring data to improve core functionality.

Clients & Expert Users

Paying customers operating AI systems as a service. Depend on transparency around intended uses, limitations, security to ensure quality provision.

End Users

Product consumers and content generators. Need transparency enabling personalization and assessment of relevance vis a vis preferences.

Individuals Subject to Algorithmic Decisions

People directly impacted by AI systems. Vital transparency around logic, contestation channels, responsible parties to dispute outcomes.

IMPACTED COMMUNITIES

Demographics collectively affected. Transparency aids evaluating risks, benefits and organizing participation.

PUBLIC

Society at large. Requires transparency instilling confidence in AI providers and confirming accountability.

NGOS & WATCHDOGS

Public interest groups. Need transparency to investigate issues and advocate on behalf of vulnerable communities.

REGULATORS & AUDITORS

Government agencies, independent auditors. Depend on extensive transparency across data, design, metrics, equity impact etc. to ensure legal compliance.

The right transparency empowers stakeholders by serving their distinct interests rather than taking a one-size-fits-all approach. Customization requires understanding evolving needs, literacy constraints and ethical imperatives across constituents.

Determining If Transparency Enables Informed Decisions

Meaningful transparency provides stakeholders useful, actionable insights to further their interests—not data for its own sake. We must determine whether transparency translates into agency, enabling stakeholders to make better decisions given their position and abilities.

For example, comprehensive model documentation aids developers in debugging but overwhelms end users. Exposing monitoring dashboards enables watchdog auditing but risks unintended gaming. Transparency around high-level system design choices clarifies values for the public while possibly eroding competitive advantage.

To gauge if transparency proves empowering versus perfunctory, we must evaluate:

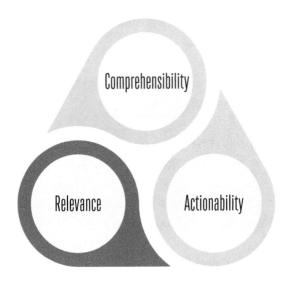

- **Comprehensibility** – Does transparency accommodate stakeholders' background, fluency with technical concepts and ability to act on new information? Overly complex transparency disempowers.

- **Relevance**—Does transparency address stakeholders' key questions and concerns? Irrelevant information frustrates more than assists.

- **Actionability** – Can stakeholders leverage
  transparency to pursue interests and objections,
  whether contesting decisions, conducting
  investigations or pushing reforms? Transparency
  enables change, not just comprehension.

Additionally, we must confirm transparency translates into
accountable AI overall by determining whether stakeholders
can:

- Understand automated decisions and how they are
  made, including data use.

- Effectively query, appeal or consent to specific
  algorithmic determinations.

- Obtain formal review by a principal designer and push
  corrective model changes.

- Request human intervention in preference to solely
  automated choices.

- Submit complaints to an internal team charged with
  reconciliation and response.

If thoughtfully implemented transparency fails to shift power
dynamics and outcomes in stakeholders' favor, the mechanisms
likely demand adjustment or supplementation with policy and
legal channels for recourse. Progress requires candidly evaluating efficacy too.

TRANSPARENCY IN PRACTICE

Research into existing transparency efforts[1] reveals common themes:

ACCURACY & DEBUGGING PRIORITIZED

Most organizations focus transparency internally on maximizing accuracy and debugging model issues. Techniques aim to help developers refine performance, quantify uncertainty, and prevent errors compromising service quality. External transparency gaining consumer trust remains secondary.

EXPLANATIONS FOR EXPERT USERS

Current transparency also centers explanations on expert clients directly employing AI systems, not impacted communities. These build necessary domain fluency to properly apply models. But individuals subjected to automated decisions stay disempowered by marginal gains in system legibility.

MINIMAL LEADERSHIP PRIORITIZATION

Limited transparency dominates partly due to low prioritization from leadership lacking market, regulatory or social pressure. Voluntary transparency initiatives fight for resources as businesses emphasize scalability, efficiency and return on investment. Compliance rarely constitutes competitive advantage absent strong governmental guardrails.

In sum, prevailing transparency practices privilege accuracy gains for organizations over accountability to affected people. Leadership incentives must make consumer trust, equity and contestability competitive differentiators before firms self-actualize transparency central to AI development lifecycles rather than an add-on. Signs point to increasing external pressures reshaping motivations over time as stakeholders find their voice.

Explaining Research

Explainable AI (XAI) as a research field has blossomed, yielding new methods for interpreting opaque models like deep neural networks defying human scrutiny. However, traction lags regarding real-world tool integration. Research reveals a deployment gap hampering accountability:

Proliferation Without Confidence

Developers hesitantly adopt novel XAI techniques lacking evidentiary confidence in consistency and quality of explanations generated. Faced with a glut of largely unvalidated methods, most builders opt to not implement rather than risk inaccurate insights eroding consumer trust.

Customization Over Complexity

Where explanation tools do integrate, simplicity and alignment to use cases takes precedence over intricate elucidations of model mechanics. Stakeholders demand digestible, actionable logic communicating model behaviors and decisions factors relatable to their experience.

POST-HOC PITFALLS

Reliance on post-hoc explanation techniques retrofitted to inscrutable models forces tensions between accuracy and accountability. Architecting human centered design and domain expert fluency from inception reaches transparency objectives more assuredly for high stakes use cases.

INCOMPLETE SOLUTION SET

An array of model families and data types frustrates one-size-fits-all technical solutions, especially in cutting edge generative AI. Tailoring composable solutions to particular challenges remains ongoing exploration needing stakeholder participation.

In response, we must set reasonable expectations for XAI's state of possibility, emphasize software engineering incorporating transparency early, and acknowledge enduring tradeoffs around accuracy versus explainability in complex commercial systems.

Little Transparency Beyond Data Bias; Limited Social/Environmental Focus

Organizations make fledgling attempts at transparency around potential data issues like bias and accuracy. However, transparency rarely extends to evaluating social impacts, environmental externalities or providing comprehensive system information.

DATA METRICS DOMINATE

Most transparency sharing focuses on quantification of training data properties (volume, demographic makeup, label quality) and output metrics like precision. This aids debugging but reveals little about real-world performance.

Limited Social Impact Assessment

Few organizations audit risks of collective harm across vectors like economic injustice, reputation damage, youth wellbeing or political polarization. Responsible innovation requires impact assessment to catch unintended consequences.

Minimal Environmental Accounting

In transparency documentation, minimal organizations detail intensive computations required, energy consumed, or emissions resulting from resource-greedy AI systems. Tracking environmental impact is critical as AI scales exponentially.

Narrow View Obscures Big Picture

Current emphases on data and accuracy metrics obscure wider considerations of ethical purpose, key trade-offs, sustainability and community participation constituting comprehensive accountability.

While incremental progress makes flawed systems legible, focus must elevate to transparent holistic life cycle assessment quantifying socio-technical impacts—both realized and potential. One-dimensional transparency begets myopic AI unfit for complex social realities. We need multifocal lenses revealing wider pictures.

---

1. *"AI Transparency in Practice Report"* by Ramak Molavi Vasse'i, Jesse McCrosky and Mozilla Insights

29

DELIVERING TRANSPARENCY

Guidelines for Transparency to Clients, End Users, Regulators, Public

Transparency initiatives must align disclosure to the distinct needs of stakeholder groups. Failing customized transparency overwhelms audiences, seeds confusion and erodes organizational trust. We explore tailored transparency guidelines for key constituents:

CLIENTS & DOMAIN EXPERTS

Expert users demand situational transparency explaining behaviors within applications and prescribing adjustments meeting specialty requirements. This requires apt translations of model factors and logic.

END USERS & PRODUCT CONSUMERS

Individuals seek understandable systems logic clarifying personal impacts and options to correct undesired algorithmic treatments. This requires clear communication channels and convenient recourse mechanisms.

REGULATORS & AUDITORS

Stringent transparency furnishing extensive documentation
and reporting supports regulator audits assessing statutory and
ethical compliance. However, transparency degrees must scale
appropriately across organization sizes and risk levels.

GENERAL PUBLIC

Public transparency warrants digestible reporting on benchmark performance, procedures ensuring fairness, intended
societal benefits and contact channels to strengthen collective
confidence and discourse around AI.

Transparency approaches remain works in progress needing
stakeholder collaboration. However, by tailoring methods to
community needs and abilities, organizations can aid accountability lacking today. The following sections explore directions
and dilemmas in transparent AI delivery.

Right Level and Type of Information for Literacy and Needs

Effective transparency requires meeting stakeholders where
they stand—accommodating backgrounds, questions and
channel preferences. Both information type and delivery mechanisms must align with audience literacy and aims.

For example, an expert clinical user needs nuanced explanatory visualizations revealing relationships between influential
features in medical imaging algorithm outputs. This elucidates
behaviors aiding sound diagnoses. Consumer patients expect
understandable logic around disease risk scoring, not technical
descriptions better serving specialists.

Likewise, community groups need transparency and participation mechanisms different than individual consumers. Regulators require extensive documentation and audit data streams

versus public reporting summarizing key indicators like accuracy, contestation rates and progress toward quantifiable ethical metrics.

Rules of thumb for right-sizing transparency include:

- Seek direct input from user groups on utility of information provided.
- Use plain language explanations augmented by technical detail.
- Layer information allowing variable depth per audience interest and ability.
- Convey logic in context of familiar use cases and decision factors.
- Clarify data usage and origin stories shaping model perspectives.
- Outline action paths for problem reporting, contesting decisions and voicing concerns.

Of course, stakeholders themselves often struggle articulating transparency needs absent experience. Thus, transparency initiatives should incorporate feedback loops, user testing and community engagement to iteratively fit evolving literacy and objectives surrounding AI systems permeating daily life. The first edition need not be final—but it must begin somewhere.

Avoiding Transparency Fatigue Versus Deceptive Transparency

Organizations must strike an elusive balance making AI systems sufficiently transparent without overburdening consumers. Both fatigue from excess disclosure and deception from orchestrated opacity constitute pitfalls eroding confidence.

TRANSPARENCY FATIGUE

Lengthy legalistic privacy policies, obtuse cookie consent flows and myriad app permission requests have conditioned people to instantly dismiss or blindly authorize opaque systems. Organizations must fight insidious "transparency theater" exhausting consumers with vacant disclosures ignored.

DECEPTIVE TRANSPARENCY

However, calculatedly hiding transparency complexity to not alienate users risks deceptive design sidelining accountability. Omitting uncomfortable details like monitoring practices, retention periods or worst-case scenario risks betrays user agency.

CRAFTING THE GOLDILOCKS ZONE

The solution lies between vapid verbosity and deceptive simplicity—the Goldilocks Zone of meaningful transparency respecting attention as a scarce resource while upholding consent duties. Getting incentives right matters too—seeing transparency as opportunity, not imposed burden. Signposting and progressive disclosure help strike balance. But the north star stays empowering humans touched by AI, not systems. Through this lens, we can design AI and governance interactions that earn trust through transparency implemented thoughtfully.

30

AI TRANSPARENCY: CHALLENGES AND RECOMMENDATIONS

Multiple reinforcing factors impede transparency traction:

WEAK MOTIVATION

Absent bottom-up pressure from concerned consumers and communities or top-down legislation mandating disclosures, most organizations lack sufficient incentives prioritizing transparency. Leaders rationally prioritize innovation velocity, efficiency and returns above abstract benefits of accountability.

NO STANDARDS

A vacuum persists around practical standards establishing appropriate transparency guardrails spanning data, model monitoring, algorithmic justice, environmental impact and more. Technologists desire reference implementations to avoid poor practice or wasted efforts recreating wheels.

TOOTHLESS OVERSIGHT

While the EU AI Act promises to drive change in the upcoming years, regulatory capacity promoting algorithmic accountability is still embryonic with little appetite enforcing even existing statutes in AI services, let alone trailblazing new oversight regimes keeping pace with tech transformation. Nonbinding guidance solicits voluntary transparency. For now, lighthouses shine across an unchecked sea where self-governance passes as shipshape.

Progress navigating these headwinds falls upon organized consumer pressure, high-profile controversies crystallizing harms and internal advocates seeding culture shifts positioning transparency as central to innovation excellence, not adjacent. But swift currents sweep many upstream. Those riding waves at will stand exception, not the rule—for the moment.

Emphasize Stakeholder Empowerment Over Illusion of Control

Beware transparency mechanisms implying agency they do not practically confer through selective or superficial disclosures. As in deceptive design manufacturing consent via cookie banners, transparency can camouflage more than illuminate if misapplied.

We must emphasize genuinely empowering people, not feigning user control over inherently opaque systems. Beyond factual information accuracy, transmission efficacy means enabling stakeholders to act congruent with interests and ethical concerns whether opting out of surveillance advertising, contesting unfair algorithmic determinations or rallying collective pressure against exploitive industry plays.

Examples of empowering transparency include:

- Conspicuous opt-out controls unconditionally revoking tracking and behavioral customization.

- Independent audit mechanisms assessing algorithmic equity with teeth.
- Required response protocols for investigating contested algorithmic decisions.
- Published commitments governing appropriate feature evolution scoped by explicit ethical system purposes and uses.

Where full transparency proves implausible, policy mandates can partially compensate through judicious process obligations. However, technologists retain responsibilities upholding precaution and moral imagination regarding potential harms from unleashed generative models outpacing foresight.

While constraints breed resentment and subtle subversion, rallying diverse teams around serving vulnerable communities often seeds self-sustaining cultures embracing transparency as gateway to equitable innovation. We must prioritize people, not technology marvels—however wondrous.

Develop Empathy for Subjects; Consider Unintended Consequences

Well-intentioned builders often overlook people directly touched by algorithmic systems during design phases obsessed with data and technical architecture. But relating transparency to lived experiences grounds accountability.

Technologists should participate in immersive simulations navigating high stakes automated decisions like welfare benefits determinations or pre-trial risk scoring as requesters. These sensitize developers to feared obscurities and dire frustrations from opaque algorithms determining life trajectories.

Engineers should also convene participatory workshops with affected communities revealing solidarity more than explaining mystifying models. Seeing fears, confusion and desires in subjects' eyes sparks realization no dashboard designer could know. And impacted voices should participate in planning potentially risky system uses with precaution rather than after protest.

Ongoing controversies around generative AI releasing untested societal experiments highlight studying precedents and proactively self-reflecting on potential harms. Envisioning worst cases and mitigations before product ideation commences can prepare and prevent.

Considerations include:

- Systemic risks of misuse beyond stated intentions.
- First order capabilities leading indirectly to unacceptable applications.
- Economics incentivizing harmful effects from engagement maximizing optimization.

No solution set fully contains consequences from exponentially growing information hazards. But incorporating diverse perspectives, contestability by design and ethical sensitivity helps craft AI furthering human potential on balance.

Use Interpretable Models Where Possible

Perfect explainability of complex AI like neural networks will remain practically unattainable. However, in contexts demanding accountability, interpretable models aligned to use cases minimize opaque components propagating risks and inhibiting oversight.

By choosing architectural simplicity fitting core needs over maximizing accuracy, stakeholders attain pragmatic transparency. Example families of interpretable models include:

- Decision trees conveying clear logic gates from inputs to outputs.
- Linear regression revealing relative influence of explanatory variables.
- Relational rule-based systems codifying human knowledge.
- Ensemble approaches blending interpretability with limited complexity.

Interpretability exists in service of managing complexity, not eliminating it. Augmenting interpretable cores with selective opaque components adds functionality while maintaining scrutiny. This future-proofs retraining data dependencies and upgrades for accountability absent in some end-to-end black boxes.

Additionally, inherently interpretable models simplify key model governance factors noted below which enable meaningful transparency in deployment:

- Auditing and debugging model behaviors.
- Monitoring and promptly addressing performance drift.
- Understanding tradeoffs made from accuracy maximization.
- Discovering proxy encodings potentially introducing bias.
- Clarifying roles and expertise domains to establish responsibility.

- Explaining model factors and logic for affected stakeholders.
- Bounding risks from inherent subjectivities in the modeling.

Transitioning complex commercial systems raises challenges. But interpretable foundations uphold transparency and trust where it counts—in high stakes decisions denying opportunities or determining access. Interpretable AI should be the rule, not exception.

Conclusion

Meaningful transparency represents a pivotal component of responsible innovation, not an elective accessory.

As revealed however, transparency has inherent constraints unlikely disappearing completely despite advances:

Tensions between accuracy maximization and interpretability persist for intrinsically inscrutable models, requiring choices and multifaceted transparency approaches spanning tools, documentation and participatory assessment.

Rigorously auditing complex models requires interdisciplinary skill sets, significant compute resources and access controls balancing confidentiality—capacities presently scarce. Democratizing oversight needs governmental support and private sector shifts.

Prevailing business economics incentivize productivity over accountability absent strong consumer pressure and regulation valuing equity. Leadership bravely redefining competitive differentiators can transform cultures to make transparency indispensable.

Thus, transparency constitutes one instrument within a broader orchestra required for AI accountable to civil rights, moral values and human development in coming decades of machine intelligence ubiquity. But well-coordinated, the symphony holds promise.

Through understanding possibilities, dilemmas and assumptions in novel socio-technical systems, we gain agency crafting wise governance and oversight instilling trust. We must proceed judiciously, neither hastily nor hesitantly into an algorithmic age with transparency lighting pathways ahead.

Tailor Carefully to Empower Stakeholders Without Overwhelming

Meaningful transparency requires nuanced understanding of diverse users and uses for empowerment, not just factual accuracy. We must match information types, degrees and delivery mechanisms to stakeholder competencies and aims without overwhelming or distracting.

For example, an expert physician needs explanatory visualizations revealing clinical decision factors. But quantifying confidence intervals risks fostering false precision for consumer patients better served by clear logic explaining disease risk scores. multi-layered transparency suits the specialist; simplicity and clarity aids the citizen.

Likewise, community groups need mechanisms facilitating participation different than consumers expect individual recourse. And regulators require extensive disclosures including code auditing and impact assessments varying by risk level. Tailoring transparency avoids one-size-fits all folly.

Rules of thumb include:

- Seek direct user input on utility of information provided.
- Use plain language explanations augmented by technical detail.
- Layer information allowing variable depth per audience.
- Outline clear paths for problems reporting and voicing concerns.

Of course, finding the "right transparency" challenges even the most conscientious organizations. But the solution lies not in transparency theater checked boxes satisfying none. Through inclusive design practices, stakeholder engagement and iterative delivery, we can build AI serving society responsibly—but only if we listen first to the people it touches.

Focus on System's Purpose More Than Pure Explainability

Preoccupation with intricate model mechanisms and post-hoc explanation techniques often distracts from transparently conveying an AI system's intended purpose and key drivers of behavior central for governance. We must broaden focus beyond pure explainability to full accountability.

Engineering teams control choices on data collection, feature representation, model family selection and accuracy metrics ultimately dictating outcomes. These amount to baked-in value judgments requiring daylight. Vetting purposes, variables and plans for redressing harms outrank grasping neural network weights or tree ensembles.

For example, comprehensively documenting properties of training datasets, taxonomic categories inferred and real-world usage constraints aids oversight more than inconsistent local explanations around image labels or loan default predictions.

Similarly, qualifying environmental costs from computational resource consumption quantifies sustainability.

That is not dismissing explanatory tools. Their role continues expanding usefully. However, explainability serves the wider end of accountability; it constitutes means, not ends alone. And narrowly fixating explainability as surrogate for full transparency risks unintended blindness spotting systemic pitfalls.

By elevating the purpose animating systems from abstraction into shared commitments governing engineering tradeoffs and ethical responsibilities, we ground transparency where it counts. If AI should aid humanity, defining aid's scope and success remains imperative—however inelegant to datums dancing audaciously today.

31

UNDERSTANDING ALGORITHMIC AUDITING

Algorithmic auditing refers to the systematic assessment of automated decision-making systems to determine if they meet key standards around transparency, fairness, safety and effectiveness.

As algorithmic systems grow more complex and consequential, audits provide a vital accountability mechanism enabling oversight bodies, impacted communities and the general public to understand AIs and remedy issues.

Well-designed audits promote:

- **Transparency & Explainability:** Elucidate system logic, reveal biases, clarify data usage.
- **Fairness & Justice:** Uncover discrimination, ensure equitable treatment of individuals.
- **Effectiveness & Accuracy:** Validate intended functionality, quantify uncertainty, prevent errors.
- **Attribution of Responsibility:** Establish provenance, facilitate recourse for problems.

- **Empowerment Through Participation:** Engage affected communities to evaluate outcomes.

Robust algorithmic auditing requires expertise spanning computer science, statistics, social science and law. Technical audits assess software functionality while participatory audits engage affected populations. Combined, these further accountability on core questions of whether systems work as intended and if they promote societal values.

As artificial intelligence grows more impactful, independent algorithmic auditing constitutes a linchpin for ensuring AI responsibly serves broad public interests. Understanding motivations and mechanisms of audits empowers advocates calling for and conducting rigorous, regular oversight.

Promoting Transparency, Explainability and Recourse

Core focuses for algorithmic auditing include scrutinizing transparency, explainability and provisions for individual or group recourse. Audits probe whether systems offer adequate information and measures upholding user rights.

Transparency & Explainability

Audits evaluate the degree to which organizations open architectures, data flows, metrics, assumptions and monitoring practices to oversight bodies or consumers. Key questions include:

Are objectives and design choices sufficiently explained?

Do explanations convey multifaceted logic in clear terms?

Is uncertainty quantification candid yet constructive?

Are social scientists partnering with engineers for holistic evaluation?

As previously discussed, excessive transparency risks over-whelming consumers or compromising intellectual property. But selective disclosures strain credibility absent supporting audit trails demonstrating claimed safeguards.

RECOURSE

Audits determine if impacted individuals and groups can effi-ciently appeal algorithmic decisions or address emerging issues. This needs institutional responsiveness. Elements promoting recourse include:

- Published metrics quantifying complaint rates by category over time.
- Service level agreements for resolving appeals of automated determinations.
- Accessible interfaces for registering concerns and suggesting improvements.
- Notification protocols for significant changes potentially affecting user experiences.

Effective algorithmic auditing constitutes both a technological capability and a leadership commitment prioritizing user empowerment. Annual transparency reports meeting bare minimums evade the spirit of reform which regular, rigorous audits manifest.

Evaluating Bias, Fairness, Safety and Effectiveness

In assessing complex algorithmic systems, audits probe across critical dimensions including fairness, bias mitigation, safety and real-world performance.

FAIRNESS & BIAS

Audits determine whether organizations sufficiently guard against biases skewing automated decisions. Factors examined include:

- Representativeness of training data relative to deployment scope.
- Proxy variables encoding demographic attributes directly or indirectly.
- Testing for disparate impact across gender, ethnic and age groups.
- Participation of diverse user populations in design and pre-deployment trials.

SAFETY & SECURITY

As algorithms guide increasingly sensitive decisions, sound audits interrogate precautions ensuring decisions minimize risks of harm.

Considerations include:

- Secure computing infrastructure resistant to data breaches.

- Validation tests safeguarding against catastrophic model failures.
- Monitoring production systems for emerging reliability issues.
- Crisis response plans addressing worst-case spill-over effects.

ACCURACY & EFFECTIVENESS

Ultimately, algorithmic effectiveness undergirds safety. Yet metrics like predictive precision do not guarantee suitability across varied contexts. Thus, auditing probes:

- Benchmarks for quantifying uncertainty to support robustness.
- Processes continuously monitoring real-world performance per use case.
- Mechanisms incorporating user feedback into model refinement.
- Qualitative surveys gauging utility and problem incidence.

Regular auditing provides the evidence to diagnose when algocratic systems demand remedy—or recalibration on ethical grounds.

Algorithmic Audits: Study Highlights Current State

A recent study provides the first comprehensive overview of the growing field of algorithmic auditing, based on interviews with industry leaders and a survey of over 150 practitioners[1]. The study had five key findings:

1. Auditors focus more on quantitative assessments of accuracy and data quality rather than qualitative evaluations of

processes and impacts. Over 75% assess technical aspects, while less than half examine harm reporting systems or team diversity.

2. Standards are limited and 93% of auditors use custom methods rather than standardized frameworks. However, there is broad agreement that audits require both technical and qualitative analyses.

3. Major barriers include lack of buy-in from companies to conduct audits and limited auditor powers to mandate changes. Over 80% of auditors have made unimplemented recommendations.

4. Consideration of real-world harms and involvement of affected communities is limited. Only 41% of auditors say stakeholder participation is critical and just 4% shared documentation of this occurring.

5. While 95% agree audits should be legally mandated, details like scope, disclosure rules and auditor accreditation standards remain contested.

Based on these findings, the study outlined policy recommendations including: legally requiring independent audits against defined standards; notifying individuals subject to automated decisions; mandating disclosure of some audit results; incorporating harm incident reporting into audits; ensuring participation of affected communities; and developing auditor evaluation or accreditation systems.

Overall, this research indicates algorithmic auditing is a rapidly evolving practice that requires additional regulatory and professional guidance to ensure audits effectively assess AI systems and mitigate harms. Further domain-specific research and policy development is still needed in this critical area of algorithmic accountability.

1. "Who Audits the Auditors? Recommendations from a field scan of the algorithmic auditing ecosystem" by Costanza-Chock, Harvey, Raji, Czernuszenko, and Buolamwini for the 2022 ACM Conference on Fairness, Accountability, and Transparency (FAccT '22)

32

METHODS AND TOOLS FOR ALGORITHMIC AUDITING

Reviewing Source Code, Objectives, Data and Design Choices

A foundation of rigorous algorithmic auditing is carefully reviewing system source code, engineering objectives, training data and key design choices underpinning functionality.

Elements reviewed may include:

SOURCE CODE

- Inspecting software source code and architecture.
- Static analysis of code structure and key dependencies.
- Dynamic testing examining functionality on sample data.

ENGINEERING OBJECTIVES

- Model priorities implied by accuracy metrics optimized.

- Benchmark thresholds targeted on key performance indicators.
- Processes ensuring objectives align with organizational values.

Training Data

- Provenance including initial sources and aggregation flows.
- Understanding sampling methodology and coverage gaps.
- Identifying processing stages influencing output patterns.

Design Choices

- Architectural commitments and feature engineering rationales.
- Model family selections and tuning methodologies.
- Analyzing tradeoffs made regarding accuracy versus. explainability

Supplemented by monitoring production systems and user interviews, reviewing foundational building blocks clarifies assumptions and values driving outcomes. However, access to proprietary platforms remains a barrier; auditors need sufficient legal backing to understand modern algorithmic systems. Partnership is ideal, but transparency mandates loom if cooperation lags.

Functionality Testing

In addition to reviewing foundational system elements, rigorous algorithmic auditing requires robust functionality testing across development, staging and production environments.

Approaches to technical testing include:

UNIT TESTING

Validating performance of isolated model components like neural network layers on controlled sample data.

INTEGRATION TESTING

Quantifying end-to-end model behavior upon integrating modules during architectural prototyping using simulated workloads.

USABILITY TESTING

Engaging trial user groups to operate beta systems on representative tasks, noting areas of confusion suggesting design refinement.

LOAD TESTING

Quantifying model latency, stability and output consistency given variable production-scale request volumes and mixtures exercising infrastructure.

EXCEPTION TESTING

Intentionally feeding edge-case, illegal and malformed inputs to gauge system security, safety prevention and failure handling mechanisms.

Together these tests evaluate algorithms technically on criteria spanning correctness, resilience, ease-of-use and reliability metrics vital for complex software applications. However, ultimately algorithms serve human purposes; technical efficacy requires alignment with ethics and values beyond engineering.

Thus accountability requires cultural and power audits in addition to functionality tests.

Monitoring Production Systems

Rigorous algorithmic auditing requires monitoring real-world production systems surfacing model limitations needing redress. Yet many organizations currently minimize operational transparency once models deploy.

Elements production monitoring enables include:

PERFORMANCE ANALYTICS

- Tracking key accuracy indicators over time filtered by subpopulations reveals uneven model degradation or emerging bias.
- Matching effectiveness to original benchmarks flags underperformance informing model retraining cadences.

USER BEHAVIOR ANALYTICS

- Aggregate measures of engagement, complaints and inquiries gauge product appropriateness across use cases and consumer groups.

COMPLIANCE REPORTING

- Ongoing exception monitoring identifies violations of policies for escalation procedures while producing compliance audit trails.
- Tracking disputes lodged and resolutions reached indicates proper functioning of recourse mechanisms.

- Analyzing patterns in reliability incidents, security events, ethical breaches and liability claims highlights areas for mitigating actions.
- Forensic data supports root cause investigations, crisis communication and impact remediation.

Viewing production transparency as opportunity rather than obligation begets more just societies. Responsible innovation requires continuous review—and willingness correcting course given evidence. This mandate exceeds regulations; our shared algorithmic future depends on science and systems advancing equitable human thriving.

Organizational Governance Audits—Policies, Standards, Controls

Beyond examining algorithmic models themselves, comprehensive auditing evaluates organizational governance, policies and controls steering the adoption of artificial intelligence.

Areas scrutinized through governance auditing include:

VALUES & POLICIES

- Reviewing processes formulating ethical codes of conduct, model risk principles and AI standards contextualizing programs.
- Assessing awareness and comprehension of guidance across management, engineering and adjacent staff.

DEVELOPMENT LIFE CYCLES

- Evaluating rigors instituted in solution ideation, data gathering, model prototyping, testing and deployment phases.
- Auditing accommodations made for participated design, pre-launch auditing and post-deployment monitoring.

RISK MANAGEMENT

- Inventorying processes for surfacing and mitigating foreseeable dangers of AI projects prior to launch using techniques like red teaming.
- Assessing responsiveness and adaptability addressing unanticipated issues arising after deployment.

Together these gauges measure institutional readiness responsibly wielding AI's rising influence. Deficiencies demand investment elevating accountability capabilities. Leadership requires internal transparency and commitment toward external opening wherever possible weighing each revelation judiciously.

Impact Evaluations—Unintended Consequences

Even ostensibly sound algorithms steering automated decisions risk unpredictable ripple effects undermining social cohesion or amplifying inequality. Responsible oversight requires monitoring deployment impacts with an eye towards safeguarding public welfare.

Areas of algorithmic impact assessment include:

DISCRIMINATION ANALYSIS

Quantifying group experiences stratified by protected attributes reveal fairness issues or homogenizing effects overriding ethical individualization.

OPPORTUNITY EQUITY

Measures of wealth, health and socioeconomic mobility shine light on self-reinforcing cycles of advantage concentration or exclusion demanding intervention.

COMMUNITY INTEGRITY

Indicators around belonging, empowerment and polarization map AI influence on civic fabrics determining psychological wellbeing at scale for targeted redress.

Technologists focused purely on model accuracy neglect the broader context determining if socio-technical systems prove beneficial on the whole. We must steward algorithmic infrastructure upholding equitable access to sustainable thriving futures for all people, not optimization devoid of conscience. Impact auditing provides tools awakening this calling.

33

THE IMPORTANCE OF AI USE CASE REGISTRIES: LESSONS FROM CALIFORNIA'S EXECUTIVE ORDER

As the adoption of AI and automated decision systems (ADS) continues to accelerate across various sectors, including government agencies and private enterprises, the need for responsible AI governance has become more pressing than ever. One critical aspect of effective AI governance is the establishment and maintenance of comprehensive AI use case registries. These registries serve as a centralized inventory of all AI and ADS deployments within an organization, enabling better risk management, transparency, and accountability.

California's Executive Order N-12-23 relating to the use of Generative AI by the State and the subsequent passage of Assembly Bill 302 (AB-302) titled "Department of Technology: high-risk automated decision systems: inventory" provide a compelling case study on the importance of AI use case registries in promoting responsible AI use and procurement. By mandating the creation of a comprehensive inventory of all high-risk automated decision systems used, developed, or procured by state agencies, California has set a powerful precedent for other jurisdictions and organizations to follow.

The Value of AI Use Case Registries

AI use case registries offer several key benefits for organizations seeking to govern their AI and ADS deployments responsibly:

1. RISK IDENTIFICATION AND MITIGATION

By maintaining a comprehensive inventory of all AI and ADS use cases, organizations can better identify and assess the potential risks associated with each deployment. This includes risks related to bias, fairness, privacy, security, and other ethical considerations. With a clear understanding of the risks involved, organizations can develop targeted mitigation strategies and implement appropriate safeguards to minimize potential harms.

2. TRANSPARENCY AND ACCOUNTABILITY

AI use case registries promote transparency by providing a clear and accessible record of an organization's AI and ADS deployments. This transparency is crucial for building public trust and ensuring that organizations are held accountable for their use of these technologies. By disclosing information about their AI and ADS use cases, organizations demonstrate their commitment to responsible AI governance and enable stakeholders, including regulators, auditors, and the public, to scrutinize their practices.

3. COMPLIANCE WITH EMERGING REGULATIONS

As governments around the world begin to introduce regulations and guidelines for AI and ADS, maintaining an up-to-date AI use case registry will become increasingly important for compliance purposes. The EU AI Act, California's Executive Order and AB-302 are prime examples of this trend, requiring public and private sector entities to disclose information about their high-risk AI and ADS deployments. By proactively establishing and maintaining an AI use case registry, organizations can stay ahead of the regulatory curve and ensure they are well-positioned to meet emerging compliance requirements.

4. FACILITATING RESPONSIBLE PROCUREMENT

AI use case registries can also play a crucial role in promoting responsible AI procurement. By requiring vendors and suppliers to disclose information about their AI and ADS products and services, organizations can make more informed decisions about which technologies to procure and deploy. This transparency enables organizations to assess the potential risks and benefits of different AI solutions and select those that align with their responsible AI governance principles and standards.

Lessons from California's Executive Order and AB-302

California's Executive Order N-12-23 and AB-302 offer several valuable lessons for organizations seeking to establish effective AI use case registries:

1. DEFINING HIGH-RISK AI AND ADS

One of the key challenges in creating an AI use case registry is determining which deployments should be included. California's legislation provides a clear definition of "high-risk automated decision systems" as those that assist or replace human discretionary decisions with legal or similarly significant effects, such as decisions related to housing, education, employment, credit, healthcare, and criminal justice. By focusing on high-risk deployments, California has prioritized the most critical use cases while avoiding an overly burdensome reporting requirement for lower-risk applications.

2. ESTABLISHING COMPREHENSIVE INVENTORY REQUIREMENTS

AB-302 sets out detailed requirements for the information that must be included in the AI use case registry, such as a description of the automated decision system, its purpose, the data it uses, the measures in place to mitigate risks, and the potential impacts on vulnerable communities. These comprehensive inventory requirements ensure that the registry provides a thorough and meaningful record of each AI and ADS deployment, enabling effective risk assessment and mitigation.

3. SETTING CLEAR DEADLINES AND RESPONSIBILITIES

California's Executive Order and AB-302 establish clear deadlines for the development of guidelines, the creation of the AI use case registry, and the submission of annual reports. They also assign specific responsibilities to key state agencies, such as the Department of Technology and the Office of Data and Innovation, for overseeing and implementing these requirements. By setting clear timelines and accountability mechanisms, California has ensured that the AI use case registry will be developed and maintained in a timely and effective manner.

4. FOSTERING A CULTURE OF RESPONSIBLE AI GOVERNANCE

Perhaps most importantly, California's Executive Order and AB-302 send a strong signal about the state's commitment to responsible AI governance. By mandating the creation of an AI use case registry and requiring state agencies to consider the risks and impacts of their AI and ADS deployments, California is fostering a culture of transparency, accountability, and ethical responsibility in the use of these technologies. This culture shift is essential for ensuring that AI and ADS are developed and deployed in a manner that benefits society as a whole.

Implications for Government Agencies and Enterprises

The lessons from California's Executive Order and AB-302 have significant implications for both government agencies and private enterprises seeking to govern their AI and ADS deployments responsibly:

1. PROACTIVE AI GOVERNANCE

Organizations should take a proactive approach to AI governance, establishing AI use case registries and other responsible AI practices before they are mandated by law. By getting ahead of the regulatory curve, organizations can ensure they are well-positioned to meet emerging compliance requirements and build trust with stakeholders.

2. RISK-BASED APPROACH

Organizations should adopt a risk-based approach to AI governance, prioritizing the identification and mitigation of risks associated with high-impact AI and ADS deployments. By focusing on the most critical use cases, organizations can allocate their resources effectively and ensure that the most significant risks are addressed.

3. COLLABORATION WITH STAKEHOLDERS

Organizations should collaborate with a wide range of stakeholders, including regulators, industry partners, civil society groups, and the public, in developing and implementing their AI governance practices. This collaboration can help ensure that AI use case registries and other responsible AI practices are informed by diverse perspectives and align with societal values and expectations.

4. CONTINUOUS IMPROVEMENT

Organizations should view AI governance as an ongoing process of continuous improvement, regularly reviewing and updating their AI use case registries and other responsible AI practices in light of new developments, risks, and best practices. By adopting a culture of continuous learning and adaptation, organizations can ensure that their AI governance practices remain effective and relevant in a rapidly evolving technological landscape.

Conclusion

The establishment and maintenance of AI use case registries is a critical component of responsible AI governance. By providing a comprehensive inventory of an organization's AI and ADS deployments, these registries enable better risk management, transparency, and accountability in the use of these technologies.

34

OPERATIONAL CONSIDERATIONS

Internal Assessment vs. Independent External Auditing

Organizationally, audit authority over artificial intelligence systems can be structured across a spectrum spanning purely internal assessment to fully independent external examination.

Internal assessment offers familiarity advantages with the cost of objectivity. Meanwhile, outsider evaluations gain independence while sacrificing infrastructural comprehension. Thus, blended authority balances tradeoffs.

INTERNAL ASSESSMENT

Pros:

- Leverages intrinsic comprehension of complex, ever-changing systems.
- Enables embedding ongoing oversight into development cycles.
- Instills accountability intrinsically through organizational culture.

Cons:

- Lacks public credibility around independence without external validation.
- Inhibited scrutinizing leadership decisions or surfacing unflattering truths.
- Rarely prioritizes user empowerment over business prerogatives.

Independent External Auditing

Pros:

- Maximizes impartiality probing potentially uncomfortable questions.
- Confers legitimacy by elevating diverse community participation.
- Grounds recommendations in lived experiences of affected stakeholders.

Cons:

- More costly, slower and difficult coordinating beyond corporate walls.
- Hampered by limited visibility into proprietary or classified systems.
- Potentially seen as antagonistic rather than collaborative.

While internal assessment offers efficiencies, independence proves pivotal for accountability. Thus, policymakers should enable mixed authority while boosting public auditing capacity and algorithmic transparency aid it.

Audit Accessibility—Legal Mandates, IP Protections, Public Interest

Access poses barriers for algorithmic auditing, as tightly-guarded proprietary systems resist scrutiny. Trade secrecy must balance against oversight necessities in the public interest.

INTELLECTUAL PROPERTY RESTRICTIONS

Organizations increasingly invoke legal intellectual property protections and contractual non-disclosure agreements to deny auditors visibility into AI system data, design or training procedures. Yet opacity inhibits accountability.

Policymakers should enable limited reviewer access, bound by strict confidentiality when essential. Precedent lies in drug development, where regulators access confidential pharmaceutical trial data ultimately published in aggregate. The public interest deserves analogous transparency.

PUBLIC INTEREST REQUIREMENTS

Mandatory algorithmic impact assessments for domains like finance, healthcare and transportation would foreground public welfare over corporate secrecy. Graduated transparency requirements should ascend with societal risks.

Extending accreditation infrastructure for trusted auditors ensures impartiality. Secure data rooms provision compartmentalized system visibility. Together creative policy solutions can provide daylight—while respecting innovation incentives that fuel economic growth. The balance lies in recognizing corporate stewardship of shared algorithmic infrastructure upon which civil rights depend.

Audit Frequency—Discrete, Continuous, Triggered by Incidents

Audit authority requires calibrated presence balancing organizational burdens against the dynamism of software constantly evolving post-deployment. Three models guide oversight scaling.

DISCRETE AUDITS

Periodic audits on fixed schedules (e.g. annually) allow anticipation and audit preparation. However, gaps risk drifts. Costs include staff diversion and compliance delays.

CONTINUOUS AUDITING

Embedded routine oversight surfaces issues early with less disruption. Observer effects inspire accountability intrinsically. However continuous access risks normalizing surveillance while probing cultural blind spots.

INCIDENT-TRIGGERED AUDITING

Isolating reviews until crises strike balances costs but inhibits ex ante harm prevention. Trigger criteria should be public; pattern analysis guides investigation scopes. Lower burdens enable wider initial deployment. But lagging indicators signal failure after-the-fact.

In practice blended approaches respond proportionally. Graduated requirements should mandate:

- Discrete audits periodically
- Ongoing monitoring at suitably anonymized levels
- Incident response protocols formalizing escalation

Right-sizing audit governance for organizational maturity and use case risk promotes innovation in service of human dignity.

35

CHALLENGES FOR EFFECTIVE AUDITING

Defining Appropriate Risk-Scaled Audit Rigor

Establishing suitable algorithmic audit intensity requires reconciling organizational burdens against ethical stakes. Graduated escalation responds proportionally to use cases based on human rights impacts.

Risk Factors Considering:

- **Population Exposure**—Heightened scrutiny applies for widely deployed AI touching entire classes.
- **Decision Criticality**—Greater rigor fits areas determining access to fundamental needs like loans and parole.
- **Information Sensitivity**—Safeguarding medical or financial data warrants elevated assurance.
- **Compliance Requirements**—Sectoral laws may mandate assessments in domains like employment.
- **Financial Scale**—Larger firms withstand heightened resources requirements monitoring AI ethics.

To calibrate appropriate oversight, consult affected communities surfacing experienced concerns then trace to technical roots requiring transparency. Justify rigor by tangible rights in potential violation, not arcane software details alone. Standards should map audit expectations to risk factors so requirements scale appropriately across use cases. Though imprecise today, a rights-driven rubric centered on human experience grounds effective regulation avoiding anti-innovation excess.

Field lessons accumulated through case law help articulate boundaries too. But waiting overlooks prevention; scientific caution compels action as algorithmic infrastructure cementing inequality advances.

Resourcing Comprehensive, Regular Algorithmic Auditing

Thorough algorithmic auditing demands extensive interdisciplinary expertise, data access and computing power presently lacking for most practitioners. Achieving routine accountability requires surmounting resource barriers.

DOMAIN EXPERTISE

Auditing requires blending technical skill assessing software with policy comprehension gauging lawfulness. Few organizations currently host this fusion. Growing this professional capacity will take years.

DATA ACCESS

Proprietary systems restrict visibility thwarting analysis. Policy mandating transparency proportions may provide some visibility to empower audits. But gaps will persist.

COMPUTE INTENSITY

Processing expansive production logs taxes resources few auditors control today. Secure enclaves facilitating controlled external algorithmic investigation require funding.

ECONOMICS

For internal audit teams, funding fights against competing innovation investments seeking return. Supporting external auditors needs policy innovation and funding too.

These obstacles should not forestall action but reveal the distance remaining to accountable algorithmic infrastructure.

Progress relies on multi-stakeholder initiative:

- Collaborative environments training hybrid policy-technologist auditors.
- Policy mandates responsibly expanding audit data access.
- Public-private partnerships resourcing secure analysis enclaves.

Together we can establish auditing answering society's call for algorithmic accountability as AI grows ubiquitous. But it takes recognizing shared interests—and leadership willing to fund the oversight upon which public trust depends.

Building Complementary Policy/Engineering Expertise

Comprehensively auditing modern algorithmic systems defying basic scrutiny requires blending policy fluency with cutting edge software comprehension—skills rarely resident in single professionals today.

Auditors need gauging lawfulness equally alongside inspecting engineering soundness. Yet technologists rarely train in constituent rights while policy scholars focused on theory lack program analysis chops.

Thus. capacity building should:

- Fund hybrid programs steeped in ethics and technology jointly elevating complementary literacies.
- Incentivize exposure across domains embracing depth with interdisciplinary breadth.
- Support experiential rotations familiarizing specialists in complementary competencies.
- Forge common cause confronting complex accountability as urgency crests.

Siloed perspectives squander public protections. Integrating legal philosophy and software acumen multiplies oversight capabilities keeping complex automation accountable, provided the mandate endures strengthening governance.

Apart, auditors will struggle surveying Mount AI's soaring frontier. But collaboratively, new vistas of equitable possibility unfold grounded by wisdom algorithmic transparency reveals. The ascent beckons for those daring its call.

36

ADVANCING ALGORITHMIC ACCOUNTABILITY

Policy Reforms: Transparency Mandates, Auditing Resources

Catalyzing accountability escaping incrementalism requires policy innovation and investment channeling public priorities. Twin pillars for progress lie in transparency mandates and auditing resourcing.

TRANSPARENCY MANDATES

Regulations should responsibly oblige disclosure proportions striving to balance private burdens and public benefit. Areas ripe for visibility include data usage, model monitoring and change logs.

Graduated strata requiring heightened transparency for heightened risks guide appropriateness. Phase-in periods allow adjustment. Reasonable IP protections provide legal certainty facilitating cooperation over antagonism.

AUDITING RESOURCING

Inspecting complex automation requires scarce skill sets policymakers should subsidize producing through programs incubating lawyer-technologists. Stimulating auditing as a public service profession needs support.

Operationalizing audits relies upon secure analytic environments provisioning external algorithmic investigation while preventing IP leakage. Funding such infrastructure enables accountability absent today.

Together these measures pivot from opacity's erosion of rights toward a more open, equitable and inclusive algorithmic future guided by the better angels of our nature. The project requires rallying citizens and leadership to embrace reform.

Developing Applied Quality Standards with Stakeholders

Beyond law, voluntary conformity with standards helps signal and scale ethical practices across industrial ecosystems. But unlike technical disciplines, stewarding data and AI defies formulaic codification today. Progress lies in convening impacted communities to forge guidance responsive to public priorities balancing vested interests. Examples to emulate include nutrition labeling providing transparency into food or mile-per-gallon metrics aiding automobile purchases suiting needs and ethics. These present informed choice absent coercion.

Common critiques against emergent algorithmic standards argue ambiguity, infeasibility or hazards formalizing nascent science. But lessons from analogous industries reveal certifying baseline conditions through living guidance responsibly upholding public interests without foreclosing innovation pathways, provided room remains debating provisions. Getting interests represented, heard and reflected back matters most.

Thus, convening pluralistic standard-setting bodies across data and AI can distill baseline reasonable precautions responsive to public sentiments if transparently organizing open input then integrating it into law-bounded requirements for aspects like explainability, privacy, bias evaluation and environmental impact facilitating voluntary adoption. Rather than politicizing the engineering directly, standards formalize public expectations. They signal what open society asks while liberating space for science equitably uplifting humanity. But legitimacy relies upon inclusive participation; who sits at the table determines what problems surface and solutions prioritize. Standards for automation should incorporate affected communities early, often and genuinely.

Incentivizing Cultures of Accountability and Assessment

Laws establish baseline expectations for accountable algorithmic infrastructure in the public interest. But genuine adoption relies upon cultural receptivity positioning oversight as opportunity rather than obligated burden or existential threat. Three pillars enable internalization realizing external requirements through inner transformation:

VALUES-DRIVEN LEADERSHIP

Executive commitment publicly celebrating accountability builds boards, investor and market acceptance supporting budget allocations enabling oversight against competing priorities chasing profits first.

INCENTIVE ALIGNMENT

Compensation and promotion criteria validating ethical precautions and transparency intrinsically motivates consideration beyond speedy product delivery above all else.

Employee Empowerment

Formal avenues welcoming internal critique combined with professional validation for responsible innovation empowers staff alerting issues early before crises erupt.

Reform requires rallying all actors. Policy shapes constraints for people's ultimate welfare. But lasting change needs organizations embracing safety, accountability and transparency as cornerstones of excellence propelling society forward not despite obligations, but fueled by their purposeful products bettering humankind.

37

CONCLUSION

Audits Promote Algorithmic Responsibility If Scope Is Ambitious

Independent algorithmic auditing fuels accountability, provided its gaze fixes beyond isolated software to query entire socio-technical systems influencing society. Holistic audits spanning data, teams, business models and communities build true responsibility.

Myopic audits restricted to incremental model improvements neglect compounding consequences embedded in pernicious incentives maximizing profits over people. But breadth evokes connections revealing reform pathways aligning innovation with justice.

Thus auditing responsibility requires scoping inquiries ambitiously to spotlight links across choice points determining outcomes. Tracing technical lineages supports causal clarity fueling moral imagination where remedy rests. No audit in isolation ushers lasting equity—but pattern awareness informs structural and cultural transformation.

Accountability Relies Upon Viewing Obligation as Opportunity

Audit obligations often breed resentment, not enthusiasm. But viewing transparency through opportunities benefiting vulnerable communities and lifting all people reframes duty as privilege. This mindset shift liberates potential.

With accountability as animating purpose, solution seekers rally around reform delivering equitable futures faster amidst exponential technological change. Together we contain hazards and channel gains in service of inclusion and care. By embracing accountability as an act of radical imagination, reformers manifest better worlds once only dreamed. The tools await animating souls to wield them with strategic care. Our audits pave pathways to justice if we walk them—with purpose larger than ourselves.

PART VI

ORGANIZATIONAL ROLES IN BUILDING RESPONSIBLE AI

38

THE RISE OF RESPONSIBLE AI IN ORGANIZATIONS

Developing and deploying responsible AI requires a multidisciplinary approach that involves collaboration across various roles and functions within an organization. From executive leadership setting the tone and vision for responsible AI, to data scientists and developers building ethical algorithms, to legal and compliance teams navigating regulatory requirements, every role has a crucial part to play in ensuring that AI is used responsibly and ethically.

This Part VI explores the different roles within organizations that contribute to responsible AI, and provides practical guidance on how each role can effectively collaborate and contribute to the development and deployment of ethical and trustworthy AI systems. By examining the unique challenges and opportunities faced by each role, and highlighting best practices and case studies, this book aims to equip organizations with the knowledge and tools necessary to navigate the complex landscape of responsible AI.

Part VI is structured into chapters that focus on specific roles, such as executive leadership, data scientists and AI developers, product managers, legal and compliance, human resources, marketing and communications, customer support, innovation and R&D, and IT and operations. Each chapter provides an in-depth analysis of how the role can contribute to responsible AI, including key considerations, best practices, and real-world examples.

Additionally, Part VI emphasizes the importance of cross-functional collaboration in achieving responsible AI. It explores how different roles can work together effectively, breaking down silos and fostering a culture of ethics and responsibility throughout the organization. By providing a holistic view of responsible AI and highlighting the interdependencies between roles, we aim to help organizations develop a comprehensive and integrated approach to ethical AI development and deployment.

39

EXECUTIVE LEADERSHIP: SETTING THE TONE FOR RESPONSIBLE AI

Executive leadership plays a critical role in setting the tone and vision for responsible AI within an organization. As the highest level of decision-makers, executives have the power to prioritize ethical considerations, allocate resources, and ensure accountability and governance throughout the AI development and deployment process.

One of the primary responsibilities of executive leadership is to establish a clear and compelling vision for responsible AI that aligns with the organization's values and mission. This involves articulating the ethical principles and standards that will guide the organization's approach to AI, and communicating this vision to all stakeholders, including employees, customers, partners, and investors. By setting a strong ethical foundation, executives can create a shared understanding of what responsible AI means for the organization and inspire everyone to work towards a common goal.

To effectively prioritize responsible AI, executives must also allocate sufficient resources and budget to support ethical AI development and deployment. This includes investing in the necessary talent, tools, and infrastructure to ensure that AI systems are designed, tested, and implemented in a responsible manner. Executives should also consider establishing dedicated roles or teams focused on responsible AI, such as an ethics officer or an AI governance committee, to provide ongoing oversight and guidance.

Executive leadership must also establish clear accountability and governance mechanisms to ensure that responsible AI principles are consistently applied throughout the organization. This involves defining roles and responsibilities for ethical AI development and deployment, setting performance metrics and targets, and creating processes for monitoring and auditing AI systems. Executives should also foster a culture of transparency and openness, encouraging employees to raise concerns and report potential ethical issues without fear of retaliation.

Another key responsibility of executive leadership is to engage with external stakeholders and contribute to the broader dialogue around responsible AI. This includes participating in industry associations and forums, collaborating with academic institutions and research organizations, and engaging with policymakers and regulators to shape the legal and ethical framework for AI. By actively participating in these conversations, executives can help to advance the field of responsible AI and ensure that their organization remains at the forefront of ethical AI practices.

To be effective in driving responsible AI, executive leadership must also lead by example and model ethical behavior in their own decision-making and actions. This includes being transparent about the organization's use of AI, communicating openly and honestly with stakeholders, and demonstrating a commitment to fairness, accountability, and transparency.

Executives should also be willing to make difficult decisions and trade-offs when necessary to uphold ethical principles, even if it means sacrificing short-term gains or competitive advantages.

Effective executive leadership in responsible AI also requires a deep understanding of the technical, social, and ethical implications of AI systems. Executives should invest in their own education and training to stay up-to-date with the latest developments in AI and to better understand the potential risks and challenges associated with the technology. They should also seek out diverse perspectives and engage with experts from different fields, such as ethics, law, and social science, to inform their decision-making and strategy.

Finally, executive leadership must be committed to continuous improvement and adaptation in the face of a rapidly evolving AI landscape. As new ethical challenges and opportunities emerge, executives must be willing to reassess and adjust their approach to responsible AI, and to collaborate with others in the industry to develop best practices and standards. By embracing a mindset of ongoing learning and improvement, executive leadership can help to ensure that their organization remains at the forefront of responsible AI and continues to create value for all stakeholders.

Scenarios Bring Responsibilities to Life

THE CEO's DILEMMA:

Sarah, the CEO of a large financial services company, is faced with a critical decision. Her team has developed a new AI-powered algorithmic trading system that promises to generate significant profits. However, during testing, the system showed signs of bias, potentially discriminating against certain groups of customers. Sarah must decide whether to delay the launch of the system to address the bias issue, risking short-term financial losses, or to proceed with the launch as planned.

As a responsible leader, Sarah realizes that the long-term reputation and trust of the company are at stake. She convenes a meeting with her executive team, including the Chief Ethics Officer and the Head of AI Development, to discuss the situation. Together, they decide to prioritize the responsible development of the AI system, even if it means a delay in launching the product. Sarah communicates this decision to the board of directors, emphasizing the importance of ethical AI practices for the company's long-term success.

THE TRANSPARENCY CHALLENGE:

Michael, the CFO of a healthcare technology company, is preparing for a quarterly earnings call with investors. One of the key topics of discussion is the company's new AI-powered diagnostic tool, which has shown promising results in early trials. However, Michael is aware that the AI model's decision-making process is largely opaque, and the company has not yet developed a clear plan for explaining the system's outputs to healthcare providers and patients.

As a responsible executive, Michael recognizes the importance of transparency in building trust with stakeholders. He reaches out to the Chief Technology Officer and the Head of Product to discuss the need for developing clear and accessible explanations of the AI system's inner workings. Together, they create a plan to invest in research and development of explainable AI techniques, as well as to engage with healthcare providers and patient advocacy groups to gather feedback and input on how to communicate the system's results effectively.

During the earnings call, Michael proactively addresses the transparency challenge, outlining the company's commitment to responsible AI and the steps they are taking to ensure that the diagnostic tool is used in an ethical and accountable manner. By demonstrating leadership in prioritizing transparency, Michael helps to build investor confidence in the company's long-term prospects and its ability to navigate the complex landscape of AI in healthcare.

In conclusion, executive leadership plays a crucial role in setting the tone and vision for responsible AI within an organization. By:

- prioritizing ethical considerations,
- allocating resources,
- ensuring accountability and governance,
- engaging with external stakeholders,
- leading by example,
- and committing to continuous improvement,

executives can help to create a culture of responsibility and trust that enables the full potential of AI to be realized in an ethical and sustainable manner.

40

DATA SCIENTISTS AND AI DEVELOPERS: BUILDING ETHICAL AI FROM THE GROUND UP

Data scientists and AI developers are at the forefront of designing, building, and implementing AI systems within organizations. As the creators of AI algorithms and models, they have a critical role to play in ensuring that AI is developed in a responsible and ethical manner.

One of the primary responsibilities of data scientists and AI developers is to design and build AI systems with fairness, transparency, and robustness in mind. This involves carefully considering the potential biases and limitations of the data and algorithms used to train AI models, and taking steps to mitigate these issues. For example, data scientists should strive to use diverse and representative datasets, and should carefully validate and test their models to ensure that they perform fairly and accurately across different subgroups and contexts.

AI developers should also prioritize transparency and explainability in their designs, ensuring that the decision-making processes of AI systems are clear and understandable to users and stakeholders. This may involve using techniques such as feature importance analysis or decision trees to provide insight into how AI models arrive at their outputs, or developing user interfaces that allow users to interact with and question the results of AI systems.

Another key responsibility of data scientists and AI developers is to identify and mitigate potential biases in data and algorithms. This requires a deep understanding of the social and ethical implications of AI, as well as a commitment to ongoing testing and monitoring to detect and address any issues that arise. Data scientists should work closely with domain experts and stakeholders to understand the context in which AI systems will be used, and should be proactive in identifying and addressing potential sources of bias, such as unrepresentative training data or biased evaluation metrics.

Collaboration with other teams is also essential for data scientists and AI developers to ensure the ethical implementation of AI systems. This may involve working closely with product managers to define responsible AI requirements and incorporate them into product roadmaps, or collaborating with legal and compliance teams to ensure that AI systems comply with relevant laws and regulations. Data scientists and AI developers should also engage with end-users and stakeholders to gather feedback and insights on the real-world impacts of AI systems, and should be willing to make adjustments and improvements based on this feedback.

In addition to technical skills, data scientists and AI developers must also possess strong ethical principles and a commitment to responsible AI practices. This includes being transparent about the capabilities and limitations of AI systems, and being willing to speak up and raise concerns when necessary. Data scientists and AI developers should also stay up-to-date with the latest research and best practices in responsible AI, and should actively participate in the broader AI ethics community to share knowledge and insights.

To support the development of responsible AI, organizations should invest in training and resources for data scientists and AI developers to help them build the necessary skills and knowledge. This may include providing access to educational resources and workshops on AI ethics, as well as creating opportunities for data scientists and AI developers to engage with experts from other fields, such as ethics, law, and social science.

Organizations should also foster a culture of responsibility and accountability among data scientists and AI developers, encouraging them to prioritize ethical considerations throughout the AI development process. This may involve establishing clear guidelines and best practices for responsible AI development, as well as providing regular feedback and recognition for teams and individuals who demonstrate a strong commitment to ethical AI practices.

Scenarios Bring Responsibilities to Life

THE BIASED ALGORITHM:

Samantha, a data scientist at a social media company, is tasked with developing a new AI-powered content recommendation system. As she trains the model on historical user data, she notices that the algorithm tends to recommend content that reinforces certain stereotypes and biases, particularly along lines of race and gender. Samantha realizes that the biased recommendations could have a significant impact on users' perceptions and beliefs.

As a responsible AI developer, Samantha brings her concerns to the attention of her team lead and the company's AI ethics committee. Together, they explore the root causes of the bias, which they trace back to the historical data used to train the model. They develop a plan to address the issue, including re-evaluating the training data, implementing bias detection and mitigation techniques, and establishing a process for ongoing monitoring and testing of the algorithm for fairness.

Throughout the development process, Samantha and her team engage with a diverse group of stakeholders, including users, civil society groups, and experts in algorithmic fairness, to gather feedback and insights. By proactively addressing the bias issue and prioritizing fairness and transparency, they are able to develop a content recommendation system that is both effective and ethical.

THE EXPLAINABILITY CHALLENGE:

Mark, an AI developer at a financial technology company, is working on a machine learning model to predict credit risk for loan applicants. The model shows promising results in terms of accuracy, but Mark realizes that the decision-making process is largely opaque, making it difficult to explain to both internal stakeholders and customers why certain applicants are denied loans.

Recognizing the importance of explainability in building trust and accountability, Mark collaborates with his team to explore techniques for making the model's decisions more inter-pretable. They experiment with different approaches, such as using decision trees and feature importance analysis, to provide clear explanations for the factors influencing the model's outputs.

Mark also works closely with the company's legal and compli-ance team to ensure that the explanations meet regulatory requirements for transparency and non-discrimination in lending decisions. By developing an AI system that is both accurate and explainable, Mark and his team help to promote responsible lending practices and build trust with customers and regulators alike.

In conclusion, data scientists and AI developers play a crucial role in building ethical AI from the ground up. By:

- designing and building AI systems with fairness, transparency, and robustness in mind,
- identifying and mitigating potential biases,
- collaborating with other teams,
- and possessing strong ethical principles,

data scientists and AI developers can help to ensure that AI is developed and deployed in a responsible and trustworthy manner. Organizations that invest in the training and support of their data science and AI development teams, and foster a culture of responsibility and accountability, will be well-positioned to realize the full potential of AI while mitigating risks and ensuring positive outcomes for all stakeholders.

41

PRODUCT MANAGERS: BALANCING INNOVATION AND RESPONSIBILITY IN AI-DRIVEN PRODUCTS

Product managers play a vital role in the development and deployment of AI-driven products and services. They are responsible for defining the vision, strategy, and roadmap for AI products, and for ensuring that these products meet the needs of customers while also adhering to ethical and responsible AI practices.

One of the primary challenges faced by product managers in the context of AI is balancing business objectives with ethical considerations. While AI has the potential to drive innovation and create value for organizations and customers, it also poses significant risks and challenges, such as bias, privacy concerns, and unintended consequences. Product managers must navigate these competing priorities and make difficult trade-offs to ensure that AI products are both commercially viable and ethically sound.

To effectively incorporate responsible AI practices into product development, product managers should start by defining clear and measurable ethical requirements for AI products. This may involve conducting a thorough assessment of the potential risks and impacts of AI, and engaging with stakeholders and experts to identify and prioritize key ethical considerations. Product managers should then translate these ethical requirements into specific product features and functionalities, and ensure that they are integrated into the product roadmap and development process.

Effective communication and collaboration with other teams are also critical for product managers to ensure the responsible development and deployment of AI products. This may involve working closely with data scientists and AI developers to ensure that AI models are designed and built with fairness, transparency, and robustness in mind, or collaborating with legal and compliance teams to ensure that AI products comply with relevant laws and regulations. Product managers should also engage with customers and end-users to gather feedback and insights on the real-world impacts of AI products, and should be willing to make adjustments and improvements based on this feedback.

Another key responsibility of product managers is to transparently communicate the capabilities and limitations of AI products to stakeholders, including customers, employees, and investors. This involves being clear and upfront about what AI can and cannot do, and about the potential risks and uncertainties associated with AI-driven products. Product managers should also be proactive in educating stakeholders about responsible AI practices, and in building trust and confidence in the organization's approach to AI ethics.

To support product managers in the responsible development and deployment of AI products, organizations should provide training and resources on AI ethics and responsible AI practices. This may include workshops and educational programs on topics such as fairness, transparency, and accountability in AI, as well as tools and frameworks for conducting ethical risk assessments and impact evaluations. Organizations should also foster a culture of open communication and collaboration, encouraging product managers to work closely with other teams and stakeholders to ensure the ethical and responsible development of AI products.

In addition to internal resources and support, product managers should also stay up-to-date with the latest research and best practices in responsible AI, and should actively participate in the broader AI ethics community. This may involve attending conferences and workshops, engaging with industry associations and standards bodies, and collaborating with academic institutions and research organizations to advance the field of responsible AI.

Finally, product managers should be prepared to make difficult decisions and trade-offs when necessary to uphold ethical principles and ensure the responsible development and deployment of AI products. This may involve delaying or even cancelling the launch of an AI product if it poses significant ethical risks or concerns, or investing additional resources and time to address ethical issues and ensure that the product meets the organization's standards for responsible AI.

Scenarios Bring Responsibilities to Life

THE PRIVACY DILEMMA:

Julia, a product manager at a smart home devices company, is overseeing the development of a new AI-powered voice assistant. The assistant will use advanced natural language processing and machine learning techniques to provide personalized recommendations and automate household tasks. However, during the design phase, Julia realizes that the device will require access to a wide range of sensitive user data, including conversations, preferences, and behavioral patterns.

As a responsible product manager, Julia recognizes the potential privacy risks associated with collecting and processing such data. She initiates a series of discussions with the company's legal and compliance team, as well as external privacy experts, to identify best practices for data protection and user consent. Together, they develop a comprehensive privacy policy that clearly communicates what data is being collected, how it is used, and what options users have for controlling their information.

Julia also works closely with the engineering team to implement privacy-preserving techniques, such as data minimization and encryption, to ensure that user data is secure and used only for its intended purposes. By prioritizing privacy throughout the product development process, Julia helps to build trust with users and differentiate the company's offering in a competitive market.

THE FAIRNESS CHALLENGE:

Ahmed, a product manager at a recruitment software company, is leading the development of an AI-powered resume screening tool. The tool is designed to help employers efficiently sort through large volumes of job applications and identify the most promising candidates. However, during a pilot test with a select group of customers, Ahmed receives feedback that the tool may be exhibiting bias against certain groups of applicants, particularly those from underrepresented backgrounds.

Taking the feedback seriously, Ahmed conducts a thorough audit of the AI model and discovers that the training data used to develop the tool was not representative of the diverse population of job seekers. He immediately halts the rollout of the tool and works with the data science team to develop a plan for addressing the bias issue. This includes re-evaluating the training data, implementing bias detection and mitigation techniques, and establishing a process for ongoing monitoring and testing of the tool for fairness.

Ahmed also engages with a diverse group of stakeholders, including job seekers, employers, and civil rights organizations, to gather feedback and insights on how to make the resume screening tool more inclusive and equitable. By proactively addressing the fairness challenge and prioritizing responsible AI practices, Ahmed and his team are able to develop a tool that helps employers make more objective and unbiased hiring decisions, ultimately promoting greater diversity and inclusion in the workforce.

In conclusion, product managers play a critical role in balancing innovation and responsibility in the development and deployment of AI-driven products. By:

- defining clear ethical requirements,
- collaborating with other teams,
- communicating transparently with stakeholders,
- and staying up-to-date with the latest research and best practices,

product managers can help to ensure that AI products are both commercially successful and ethically sound. Organizations that prioritize responsible AI practices and provide the necessary training, resources, and support for product managers will be well-positioned to create value for customers while also mitigating risks and ensuring positive outcomes for all stakeholders.

42

LEGAL AND COMPLIANCE: NAVIGATING THE COMPLEX LANDSCAPE OF AI REGULATIONS AND STANDARDS

As AI technologies continue to advance and become more widely adopted, legal and compliance teams play an increasingly important role in ensuring that organizations develop and deploy AI systems in a responsible and ethical manner. These teams are responsible for navigating the complex and rapidly evolving landscape of AI regulations and standards, and for developing policies and guidelines that ensure compliance and mitigate legal and reputational risks.

One of the primary challenges faced by legal and compliance teams in the context of AI is the lack of clear and comprehensive regulations and standards governing the development and use of AI technologies. While some countries and regions have begun to develop AI-specific laws and guidelines, such as the European Union's General Data Protection Regulation (GDPR) and the emerging Artificial Intelligence Act, the global regulatory landscape remains fragmented and uncertain. This creates significant challenges for organizations operating across multiple jurisdictions, as they must navigate a patchwork of different laws and standards.

To effectively navigate this complex landscape, legal and compliance teams must stay up-to-date with the latest developments in AI regulations and standards, and must proactively engage with policymakers and other stakeholders to shape the future of AI governance. This may involve participating in industry associations and standards bodies, engaging with regulators and lawmakers to provide input on proposed regulations, and collaborating with other organizations to develop best practices and guidelines for responsible AI development and deployment.

Legal and compliance teams must also work closely with other teams within the organization, such as data scientists, product managers, and executives, to ensure that AI systems are designed and implemented in a way that complies with relevant laws and regulations. This may involve conducting legal and ethical risk assessments of AI systems, developing policies and procedures for data privacy and security, and ensuring that AI algorithms are transparent and explainable.

Another key responsibility of legal and compliance teams is to monitor and audit AI systems for compliance with internal policies and external regulations. This may involve regularly reviewing AI algorithms and models for bias and fairness, conducting privacy impact assessments to ensure that personal data is being collected and used appropriately, and establishing mechanisms for individuals to request information about how their data is being used and to challenge AI-driven decisions that affect them.

In addition to ensuring compliance with laws and regulations, legal and compliance teams also play a critical role in mitigating legal and reputational risks associated with AI. This may involve developing strategies for managing liability and accountability in the event of AI-related incidents or failures, such as establishing clear lines of responsibility and implementing incident response plans. Legal and compliance teams may also need to work with other teams to develop crisis communication plans and to manage public relations in the event of a high-profile AI incident.

To effectively support the responsible development and deployment of AI, legal and compliance teams must also have a deep understanding of the technical and ethical implications of AI systems. This may require investing in training and education programs to build expertise in AI ethics and responsible AI practices, as well as collaborating with external experts and stakeholders to stay informed about the latest developments in the field.

Finally, legal and compliance teams must be prepared to adapt and evolve their approaches to AI governance as the technology and regulatory landscape continue to change. This may involve regularly reviewing and updating policies and procedures, engaging in ongoing risk assessments and audits, and collaborating with other teams and stakeholders to identify and address emerging challenges and opportunities.

Scenarios Bring Responsibilities to Life

THE GDPR CHALLENGE:

Emily, a legal and compliance officer at a global e-commerce company, is tasked with ensuring that the company's new AI-powered personalization engine complies with the GDPR. The engine uses machine learning to analyze customer data and provide tailored product recommendations, but Emily is concerned about the potential risks around data privacy and consent.

To address these concerns, Emily works closely with the product development team to conduct a thorough data protection impact assessment (DPIA) of the personalization engine. The DPIA helps to identify potential privacy risks and establish appropriate safeguards, such as data minimization and pseudonymization techniques. Emily also ensures that the company's privacy policy and user consent mechanisms are updated to clearly communicate how customer data is being used for personalization purposes.

In addition to technical safeguards, Emily collaborates with the marketing and customer support teams to develop clear and transparent communication materials that explain the benefits and limitations of the personalization engine, as well as users' rights and options for controlling their data. By proactively addressing GDPR requirements and prioritizing user privacy, Emily helps to mitigate legal and reputational risks for the company, while also building trust with customers.

THE ALGORITHMIC BIAS LAWSUIT:

David, a legal and compliance manager at a financial services firm, is facing a potential class-action lawsuit alleging that the firm's AI-powered credit scoring model discriminates against certain groups of borrowers. The plaintiffs claim that the model's reliance on historical data perpetuates biases and results in unfair lending decisions.

To respond to the lawsuit, David works closely with the firm's data science and risk management teams to conduct a thorough audit of the credit scoring model. The audit reveals that while the model's overall accuracy is high, there are indeed disparities in outcomes for certain groups of borrowers. David collaborates with the team to develop a plan for mitigating the bias, including re-evaluating the training data, implementing fairness constraints, and establishing a process for regular testing and monitoring of the model for disparate impact.

David also engages with external legal experts and civil rights organizations to better understand the evolving legal landscape around algorithmic fairness and to identify best practices for ensuring compliance with anti-discrimination laws. By taking proactive steps to address the bias issue and demonstrating a commitment to responsible AI practices, David helps to minimize the firm's legal exposure and protect its reputation in the market.

In conclusion, legal and compliance teams play a critical role in ensuring that organizations develop and deploy AI systems in a responsible and ethical manner. By:

- navigating the complex landscape of AI regulations and standards,
- working closely with other teams to ensure compliance and mitigate risks,
- and staying up-to-date with the latest developments in the field,

legal and compliance teams can help organizations to realize the benefits of AI while also fulfilling their legal and ethical obligations. As the use of AI continues to grow and evolve, the role of legal and compliance teams in supporting responsible AI will only become more important, requiring ongoing investment, collaboration, and adaptation.

HUMAN RESOURCES: CULTIVATING A CULTURE OF RESPONSIBLE AI AND MANAGING WORKFORCE TRANSFORMATION

Human Resources (HR) departments play a vital role in supporting the responsible development and deployment of AI within organizations. As AI technologies continue to transform the nature of work and the skills required to succeed in the workplace, HR teams must adapt their strategies and practices to ensure that organizations have the talent, culture, and capabilities necessary to realize the benefits of AI while also mitigating risks and ensuring positive outcomes for employees and society as a whole.

One of the primary responsibilities of HR in the context of AI is to recruit and develop diverse talent with the skills and expertise necessary to design, implement, and manage AI systems in a responsible and ethical manner. This may involve partnering with educational institutions and professional associations to develop AI-specific training and certification programs, as well as implementing internal training and development initiatives to upskill existing employees in AI and related fields.

HR teams must also work to cultivate a culture of responsible AI within the organization, where ethical considerations are prioritized and employees at all levels are empowered to raise concerns and contribute to the responsible development and deployment of AI systems. This may involve developing and communicating clear policies and guidelines around AI ethics and responsible AI practices, as well as providing ongoing training and support to help employees navigate complex ethical issues related to AI.

Another key challenge for HR teams in the context of AI is managing the workforce transformation that is likely to occur as AI technologies automate and augment various job functions. While AI has the potential to create new jobs and enhance productivity, it may also displace some workers and require significant reskilling and upskilling efforts. HR teams must work proactively to identify and assess the potential impacts of AI on the workforce, and to develop strategies for managing workforce transitions in a way that is fair, transparent, and supportive of employees.

This may involve developing and implementing reskilling and upskilling programs to help employees acquire the skills and knowledge necessary to succeed in an AI-driven workplace, as well as providing support and resources to help employees navigate job transitions and find new opportunities within the organization or beyond. HR teams may also need to work with other teams and stakeholders to develop policies and practices around the ethical use of AI in hiring, performance management, and other HR processes, to ensure that these processes are fair, unbiased, and transparent.

In addition to managing workforce transformation, HR teams must also play a key role in ensuring that AI systems are developed and deployed in a way that is inclusive and equitable, and that does not perpetuate or exacerbate existing biases and inequalities. This may involve working with data scientists and other teams to ensure that AI training data is diverse and representative, and that AI algorithms are tested for bias and fairness. HR teams may also need to develop and implement diversity, equity, and inclusion (DEI) programs specifically focused on AI and related fields, to ensure that the benefits of AI are shared widely and that historically underrepresented groups are not left behind.

Finally, HR teams must be prepared to adapt and evolve their approaches to responsible AI as the technology and societal context continue to change. This may involve regularly reviewing and updating policies and practices related to AI and workforce management, engaging in ongoing dialogue and collaboration with employees and other stakeholders, and staying up-to-date with the latest research and best practices in the field.

To effectively support the responsible development and deployment of AI, HR teams must have a deep understanding of the ethical and social implications of AI, as well as the skills and capabilities necessary to manage workforce transformation and cultivate a culture of responsible AI. This may require investing in training and education for HR professionals, as well as collaborating with external experts and stakeholders to stay informed about the latest developments in the field.

Scenarios Bring Responsibilities to Life

THE AI HIRING BIAS INCIDENT:

Michelle, an HR manager at a tech company, receives complaints from several job applicants who believe they were unfairly rejected by the company's new AI-powered resume screening system. Upon investigation, Michelle discovers that the AI system was trained on historical hiring data that contained biases, resulting in the system discriminating against certain groups of applicants based on their gender and ethnicity.

As a responsible HR professional, Michelle immediately brings the issue to the attention of the company's leadership team and works with the data science and legal departments to address the problem. They decide to pause the use of the AI system until the bias can be mitigated and establish a task force to review all AI-driven HR processes for potential biases.

Michelle also organizes training sessions for HR staff and hiring managers on identifying and mitigating bias in hiring decisions, both human and AI-driven. She collaborates with the communications team to transparently communicate to all employees and job applicants about the steps being taken to address the issue and ensure fair hiring practices moving forward. By proactively addressing the AI hiring bias incident and cultivating a culture of responsible AI, Michelle helps to mitigate legal and reputational risks for the company and build trust with employees and candidates.

THE AI WORKFORCE UPSKILLING CHALLENGE:

John, an HR director at a manufacturing company, is tasked with developing a plan to upskill the company's workforce as new AI technologies are introduced into the production process. Many employees are concerned about their job security and are unsure of how to adapt to working alongside AI systems.

To address these concerns, John partners with the company's AI development team and external training providers to design a comprehensive upskilling program. The program includes a mix of technical training on AI systems, as well as soft skills development around critical thinking, problem-solving, and communication.

John also works with the leadership team to develop a clear and transparent communication plan about the company's AI strategy and its commitment to supporting employees through the transition. He establishes an AI ethics committee that includes representatives from HR, legal, and the employee base to provide ongoing guidance and oversight on the responsible deployment of AI in the workplace.

Throughout the upskilling process, John regularly solicits feedback from employees and makes adjustments to the program as needed to ensure it is meeting their needs and addressing their concerns. By proactively managing the workforce transformation and prioritizing employee development and well-being, John helps to foster a culture of continuous learning and adaptability that positions the company for long-term success in an AI-driven future.

In conclusion, HR teams play a critical role in ensuring that organizations have the talent, culture, and capabilities necessary to realize the benefits of AI while also mitigating risks and ensuring positive outcomes for employees and society as a whole. By:

- recruiting and developing diverse talent,
- cultivating a culture of responsible AI,
- managing workforce transformation,
- ensuring inclusivity and equity,
- and adapting to changing contexts and best practices,

HR teams can help organizations to navigate the complex challenges and opportunities presented by AI, and to build a future of work that is both innovative and responsible.

44

MARKETING AND COMMUNICATIONS: BUILDING TRUST AND TRANSPARENCY IN AI-DRIVEN PRODUCTS AND SERVICES

As AI technologies become increasingly integrated into products and services across industries, marketing and communications teams play a vital role in building trust and transparency with customers, stakeholders, and the broader public. These teams are responsible for crafting and disseminating messages about the capabilities, benefits, and limitations of AI systems, and for ensuring that these messages are accurate, clear, and aligned with the organization's values and commitment to responsible AI.

One of the primary challenges faced by marketing and communications teams in the context of AI is the need to balance the desire to promote the benefits and innovations of AI with the responsibility to communicate transparently about the potential risks and limitations of these technologies. While AI has the potential to transform industries and create significant value for customers and society, it also raises complex ethical and social questions that must be addressed openly and honestly.

To effectively communicate about AI in a responsible and transparent manner, marketing and communications teams must work closely with other teams across the organization, including data scientists, product managers, and legal and compliance experts. This collaboration is essential to ensure that marketing messages about AI are accurate, complete, and aligned with the organization's overall approach to responsible AI.

Marketing and communications teams must also be proactive in engaging with customers and other stakeholders to understand their concerns, questions, and expectations around AI. This may involve conducting market research and surveys, holding focus groups and workshops, and monitoring social media and other channels for feedback and sentiment related to AI. By actively listening to and engaging with stakeholders, marketing and communications teams can help to identify potential issues and concerns early on, and can adapt their messaging and strategies accordingly.

Another key responsibility of marketing and communications teams is to develop clear and accessible educational materials about AI and its implications for customers and society. This may include creating blog posts, videos, infographics, and other content that explains the basics of AI technology, its potential benefits and risks, and the steps the organization is taking to ensure responsible development and deployment. By providing clear and engaging educational content, marketing and communications teams can help to build public understanding and trust in AI, and can help to dispel myths and misconceptions about the technology.

In addition to external communications, marketing and communications teams also play a vital role in internal communications and change management related to AI. As organizations increasingly adopt AI technologies, there may be significant impacts on jobs, skills, and organizational culture that must be managed carefully. Marketing and communications teams can help to develop and implement internal communications strategies that keep employees informed about the organization's approach to AI, the potential impacts on their roles and responsibilities, and the resources and support available to help them adapt and succeed in an AI-driven workplace.

To be effective in their role as communicators and educators about AI, marketing and communications teams must stay up-to-date with the latest developments and best practices in the field of AI ethics and responsible AI. This may involve attending conferences and workshops, participating in industry associations and working groups, and collaborating with academic institutions and research organizations. By staying informed and engaged with the broader AI ethics community, marketing and communications teams can help to ensure that their organization remains at the forefront of responsible AI practices and can communicate effectively about these practices to stakeholders.

Finally, marketing and communications teams must be prepared to manage crisis communications related to AI, in the event of high-profile incidents or failures that may erode public trust or raise concerns about the technology. This may involve developing and implementing crisis communications plans, working closely with legal and compliance teams to ensure that communications are accurate and compliant, and engaging proactively with media and other stakeholders to provide transparent and timely information about the incident and the organization's response.

Scenarios Bring Responsibilities to Life

THE AI PERSONALIZATION DILEMMA:

Sofia, a marketing manager at a retail company, is excited about the potential of using AI-powered personalization to improve customer engagement and drive sales. However, she is also aware of the growing public concerns around data privacy and the potential for AI to be used in manipulative or non-transparent ways.

To address these concerns, Sofia collaborates with the company's data science and legal teams to develop a clear and transparent communication strategy around the company's use of AI for personalization. This includes updating the company's privacy policy to explain in plain language what data is collected, how it is used, and what choices customers have around opting out or controlling their data.

Sofia also works with the product team to ensure that the personalization features are designed in a way that prioritizes customer trust and control. This includes providing clear explanations of how personalized recommendations are generated, offering customers the ability to provide feedback or correct inaccuracies, and regularly monitoring the system for unintended biases or outcomes.

In addition, Sofia develops a series of educational blog posts and videos that explain the benefits and limitations of AI personalization in an accessible and engaging way. By proactively communicating about the company's responsible use of AI and prioritizing customer trust and transparency, Sofia helps to build brand loyalty and differentiate the company's offerings in a competitive market.

THE AI ETHICS CRISIS COMMUNICATION CHALLENGE:

Raj, a communications director at a healthcare AI startup, is faced with a crisis situation when a media report reveals that the company's AI-powered diagnostic tool has been generating inaccurate and potentially harmful results for certain patient populations. The report raises concerns about the lack of transparency around how the AI system was developed and tested, and calls into question the company's commitment to ethical and responsible AI practices.

To respond to the crisis, Raj works closely with the company's leadership team and AI ethics committee to develop a clear and transparent communication plan. This includes acknowledging the issue, apologizing for any harm caused, and outlining the steps the company is taking to address the problem and prevent similar issues in the future.

Raj also organizes a series of stakeholder meetings and listening sessions with patient advocates, healthcare providers, and AI ethics experts to gather feedback and insights on how to rebuild trust and ensure the responsible development and deployment of the diagnostic tool moving forward.

In addition, Raj collaborates with the product and data science teams to develop a public-facing AI ethics framework that outlines the company's commitments and practices around transparency, accountability, and fairness in AI development. By proactively communicating about the company's efforts to address the crisis and prioritize responsible AI practices, Raj helps to mitigate reputational damage and position the company as a leader in ethical healthcare AI.

In conclusion, marketing and communications teams play a vital role in building trust and transparency in AI-driven products and services. By:

- collaborating closely with other teams across the organization,
- engaging proactively with stakeholders,
- developing clear and accessible educational materials,
- managing internal communications and change management,
- staying informed about AI ethics best practices,
- and being prepared to manage crisis communications,

marketing and communications teams can help to ensure that the benefits of AI are realized in a responsible and ethical manner, while also building public understanding and trust in the technology. As AI continues to transform industries and society, the role of marketing and communications in supporting responsible AI will only become more important, requiring ongoing investment, collaboration, and adaptation.

45

CUSTOMER SUPPORT: ENSURING RESPONSIBLE AI IN CUSTOMER INTERACTIONS AND ISSUE RESOLUTION

As organizations increasingly deploy AI technologies in customer-facing applications, such as chatbots, virtual assistants, and personalized recommendation systems, customer support teams play a critical role in ensuring that these AI systems are used responsibly and ethically, and that they provide a positive and trustworthy experience for customers.

One of the primary challenges faced by customer support teams in the context of AI is ensuring that AI-driven interactions with customers are transparent, fair, and respectful of customer privacy and autonomy. This requires close collaboration with data scientists, product managers, and legal and compliance teams to ensure that AI systems are designed and implemented in a way that aligns with the organization's values and commitment to responsible AI.

Customer support teams must also be trained to understand the capabilities and limitations of AI systems, and to communicate these clearly to customers. This may involve providing customers with clear explanations of how AI is being used in customer interactions, what data is being collected and how it is being used, and what options customers have for controlling their data and opting out of AI-driven interactions if desired.

Another key responsibility of customer support teams is to monitor and assess the performance of AI systems in customer interactions, and to identify and escalate any issues or concerns that arise. This may involve regularly reviewing customer feedback and complaints related to AI, conducting quality assurance checks on AI-driven interactions, and working with data scientists and product managers to identify and address any biases, errors, or unintended consequences of AI systems.

In some cases, customer support teams may need to provide human oversight and intervention in AI-driven interactions, particularly in situations where the AI system is unable to provide a satisfactory resolution to a customer issue or where the issue is particularly sensitive or complex. This requires customer support teams to have a deep understanding of the organization's products, services, and policies, as well as strong problem-solving and communication skills.

To effectively support responsible AI in customer interactions, customer support teams must also have processes in place for handling customer inquiries and complaints related to AI, and for escalating these issues to the appropriate teams and stakeholders within the organization. This may involve developing clear protocols for documenting and tracking AI-related issues, as well as establishing channels for communication and collaboration with data scientists, product managers, legal and compliance teams, and other relevant stakeholders.

Customer support teams must also stay up-to-date with the latest developments and best practices in responsible AI, and must be proactive in identifying and addressing emerging ethical issues and concerns. This may involve participating in training and education programs related to AI ethics, collaborating with industry associations and research organizations, and engaging in ongoing dialogue and feedback with customers and other stakeholders.

In addition to ensuring responsible AI in customer interactions, customer support teams also play a vital role in gathering and analyzing customer feedback and insights related to AI, and in using this information to drive continuous improvement and innovation in AI-driven products and services. By actively listening to and engaging with customers, customer support teams can help to identify areas where AI systems are working well and delivering value, as well as areas where improvements are needed to ensure a more responsible and trustworthy experience for customers.

Finally, customer support teams must be prepared to handle crisis situations related to AI, such as high-profile incidents or failures that may erode customer trust or raise concerns about the technology. This may involve working closely with marketing and communications teams to develop and implement crisis response plans, as well as providing timely and transparent information to customers about the incident and the organization's response.

Scenarios Bring Responsibilities to Life

THE AI CHATBOT FAIRNESS ISSUE:

Emily, a customer support manager at a financial services company, receives a complaint from a customer who believes that the company's AI-powered chatbot is providing biased and unfair responses to their inquiries about loan eligibility. The customer alleges that the chatbot is making assumptions based on their name and location, and is not providing them with accurate information about the company's lending products.

Taking the complaint seriously, Emily immediately escalates the issue to the company's AI ethics committee and works with the data science team to investigate the chatbot's underlying algorithms and training data. They discover that the chatbot was trained on historical customer data that contained biases, resulting in the system perpetuating discriminatory outcomes.

To address the issue, Emily works with the team to develop a plan for retraining the chatbot with more diverse and representative data, as well as implementing fairness constraints and regular audits to ensure the system is providing equitable treatment to all customers. She also reaches out to the affected customer to apologize for the experience, provide them with accurate information about the company's lending products, and offer compensation for any inconvenience or harm caused.

Emily then collaborates with the marketing and communications team to develop a public statement about the steps the company is taking to address the chatbot bias issue and ensure responsible AI practices in all customer interactions. By proactively addressing the fairness issue and prioritizing customer trust and satisfaction, Emily helps to mitigate reputational damage and position the company as a leader in responsible financial services AI.

THE AI-DRIVEN CUSTOMER CHURN DILEMMA:

Aditya, a customer support team lead at a telecommunications company, is excited about the potential of using AI-powered predictive analytics to identify customers who are at high risk of churning and proactively reach out to them with retention offers. However, he is also concerned about the potential for the

AI system to perpetuate biases or make incorrect predictions that could lead to customer frustration or mistrust.

To ensure the responsible use of AI in customer retention efforts, Aditya works closely with the data science team to develop a rigorous testing and monitoring framework for the predictive model. This includes regularly auditing the model for accuracy and fairness, as well as implementing explainable AI techniques to provide clear and transparent reasons for why customers are being flagged as high-risk.

Aditya also collaborates with the customer support team to develop a set of best practices and guidelines for how to use the AI-generated insights in a way that prioritizes customer trust and satisfaction. This includes providing customers with clear explanations of why they are being contacted, offering them meaningful and personalized retention offers, and giving them the option to opt-out of future proactive outreach.

In addition, Aditya sets up regular feedback loops between the customer support and data science teams to monitor the effectiveness and impact of the AI-driven retention program, and to continuously improve the system based on customer feedback and outcomes. By taking a responsible and customer-centric approach to AI-driven customer retention, Aditya helps to improve customer loyalty and lifetime value, while also building trust in the company's AI practices.

In conclusion, customer support teams play a critical role in ensuring responsible AI in customer interactions and issue resolution. By:

- collaborating closely with other teams across the organization,
- communicating transparently with customers about AI,
- monitoring and assessing the performance of AI systems,
- providing human oversight and intervention when needed,
- staying up-to-date with responsible AI best practices,
- gathering and analyzing customer feedback,
- and being prepared to handle crisis situations,

customer support teams can help to build trust and confidence in AI-driven products and services, while also driving continuous improvement and innovation. As AI continues to transform the customer experience, the role of customer support in ensuring responsible AI will only become more important, requiring ongoing investment, collaboration, and adaptation.

46

INNOVATION AND R&D: PUSHING THE BOUNDARIES OF RESPONSIBLE AI DEVELOPMENT

Innovation and research and development (R&D) teams are at the forefront of advancing AI technologies and exploring new frontiers in responsible AI development. These teams are responsible for conducting cutting-edge research, developing new AI algorithms and architectures, and pushing the boundaries of what is possible with AI, while also ensuring that these innovations are developed and deployed in a responsible and ethical manner.

One of the primary challenges faced by innovation and R&D teams in the context of responsible AI is balancing the drive for technological progress with the need to carefully consider and mitigate potential risks and unintended consequences. As AI technologies become more powerful and sophisticated, it is essential that innovation and R&D teams take a proactive and thoughtful approach to identifying and addressing ethical concerns, and to ensuring that AI systems are developed in a way that aligns with societal values and promotes the greater good.

To achieve this, innovation and R&D teams must work closely with a range of stakeholders, including data scientists, engineers, ethicists, social scientists, policymakers, and community leaders, to ensure that diverse perspectives and expertise are brought to bear on the development of responsible AI systems. This may involve establishing multidisciplinary teams or working groups focused on responsible AI, as well as engaging in ongoing dialogue and collaboration with external partners and stakeholders.

Innovation and R&D teams must also be at the forefront of developing and implementing best practices and frameworks for responsible AI development. This may involve creating and adhering to ethical guidelines and principles for AI research and development, such as the IEEE's Ethically Aligned Design framework[1] or the OECD's Principles on AI[2]. It may also involve developing and testing new tools and methodologies for assessing and mitigating potential risks and biases in AI systems, such as algorithmic impact assessments or bias detection and mitigation techniques.

Another key responsibility of innovation and R&D teams is to stay up-to-date with the latest research and developments in the field of responsible AI, and to actively contribute to the broader scientific and technical community. This may involve attending conferences and workshops, publishing research papers and articles, and collaborating with academic institutions and industry partners on cutting-edge responsible AI projects and initiatives.

Innovation and R&D teams must also be proactive in engaging with policymakers, regulators, and other stakeholders to help shape the legal and regulatory landscape for responsible AI. This may involve providing expert testimony or input on proposed AI legislation and regulations, participating in standards-setting bodies and working groups, and advocating for policies and practices that promote responsible AI development and deployment.

In addition to advancing the technical capabilities of AI systems, innovation and R&D teams must also be at the forefront of exploring new approaches to responsible AI that prioritize transparency, accountability, and fairness. This may involve developing new techniques for explaining and interpreting AI decision-making processes, creating mechanisms for auditing and testing AI systems for bias and fairness, and exploring new models for AI governance and oversight that give stakeholders greater visibility and control over how AI systems are developed and used.

To support responsible AI innovation, organizations must create a culture that values and rewards responsible AI practices, and that provides innovation and R&D teams with the resources, support, and incentives they need to prioritize ethical considerations alongside technical advances. This may involve investing in training and education programs on responsible AI, establishing clear policies and processes for ethical review and oversight of AI research and development, and recognizing and rewarding teams and individuals who demonstrate leadership and excellence in responsible AI innovation.

Finally, innovation and R&D teams must be prepared to adapt and evolve their approaches to responsible AI as the technology and societal context continue to change. This may involve regularly reassessing and updating research priorities and methodologies, engaging in ongoing dialogue and collaboration with diverse stakeholders, and being open to new ideas and approaches that challenge conventional wisdom and push the boundaries of what is possible with responsible AI.

Scenarios Bring Responsibilities to Life

THE AI FAIRNESS RESEARCH PROJECT:

Dr. Ava Singh, a senior AI researcher at a tech company, is leading a research project to develop new techniques for identifying and mitigating bias in machine learning models. The project aims to push the boundaries of current fairness approaches and develop innovative solutions that can be applied across a range of AI applications, from hiring and lending to healthcare and criminal justice.

To ensure the research is grounded in real-world challenges and perspectives, Dr. Singh assembles a diverse and interdisciplinary team, including data scientists, ethicists, legal experts, and community advocates. The team conducts extensive outreach and engagement with affected stakeholders, such as civil rights organizations and consumer advocacy groups, to gather insights and feedback on the fairness challenges they are seeking to address.

Throughout the research process, Dr. Singh and her team prioritize transparency and accountability, regularly publishing their methodologies, results, and limitations in open-access journals and presenting their work at industry conferences and workshops. They also collaborate with the company's product teams to pilot and test the fairness techniques in real-world settings, iterating and refining the approaches based on feedback and outcomes.

As a result of the research project, Dr. Singh and her team develop a suite of innovative fairness tools and frameworks that are widely adopted across the industry, setting a new standard for responsible AI development. The company is recognized as a leader in AI ethics research, attracting top talent and partnerships, and strengthening its brand and reputation.

THE AI SUSTAINABILITY HACKATHON:

Liam Patel, an innovation manager at an energy company, is tasked with exploring how AI can be used to accelerate the transition to sustainable energy systems. To spark creativity and engagement, Liam decides to organize a company-wide AI sustainability hackathon, bringing together employees from across the organization to develop innovative solutions.

To ensure the hackathon prioritizes responsible AI practices, Liam partners with the company's AI ethics committee to develop a set of guidelines and criteria for the event. These include requirements around data privacy and security, transparency and explainability, and consideration of potential unintended consequences and long-term impacts.

During the hackathon, cross-functional teams work together to ideate and prototype AI-powered solutions for challenges such as optimizing renewable energy production, reducing energy waste, and improving energy access for underserved communities. The teams receive guidance and feedback from AI ethics experts throughout the event, helping to ensure their solutions align with responsible AI practices.

After the hackathon, the most promising solutions are selected for further development and testing, with the innovation team providing resources and support to help the teams refine and scale their ideas. Liam also works with the communications team to share the stories and impacts of the hackathon projects, both internally and externally, showcasing the company's commitment to responsible AI innovation for sustainability.

The AI sustainability hackathon becomes an annual event, fostering a culture of innovation and responsibility across the organization and positioning the company as a leader in the use of AI for social and environmental good.

———————

In conclusion, innovation and R&D teams play a vital role in advancing the field of responsible AI and ensuring that AI technologies are developed and deployed in a way that benefits society as a whole. By:

- working collaboratively with diverse stakeholders,
- developing and implementing best practices and frameworks for responsible AI,
- staying up-to-date with the latest research and developments, engaging with policymakers and regulators,
- exploring new approaches to transparency,
- accountability, and fairness, and adapting to changing contexts and priorities,

innovation and R&D teams can help to ensure that AI innovation proceeds in a responsible and ethical manner, while also pushing the boundaries of what is possible with this transformative technology.

———————

1. *"Ethically Aligned Design. A Vision for Prioritizing Human Well-being with Autonomous and Intelligent Systems"* by IEEE
2. *"OECD AI Principles overview"* by OECD.AI

47

IT AND OPERATIONS: IMPLEMENTING AND MAINTAINING RESPONSIBLE AI SYSTEMS

IT and operations teams play a critical role in the successful implementation and maintenance of AI systems within organizations. These teams are responsible for ensuring that AI technologies are integrated seamlessly into existing IT infrastructures, that they are properly configured and maintained, and that they operate in a secure, reliable, and responsible manner.

One of the primary challenges faced by IT and operations teams in the context of responsible AI is ensuring that AI systems are implemented in a way that aligns with the organization's overall approach to responsible AI. This requires close collaboration with data scientists, product managers, legal and compliance teams, and other stakeholders to ensure that AI systems are designed, developed, and deployed in accordance with established policies, guidelines, and best practices for responsible AI.

IT and operations teams must also be responsible for implementing and maintaining robust security and privacy controls around AI systems and the data they use. This may involve implementing access controls, encryption, and other security measures to protect sensitive data and prevent unauthorized access or use of AI systems. It may also involve developing and implementing data governance policies and procedures to ensure that data is collected, stored, and used in a responsible and ethical manner, and that individuals' privacy rights are protected.

Another key responsibility of IT and operations teams is to monitor the performance and behavior of AI systems in real-time, and to identify and address any issues or anomalies that may arise. This may involve implementing monitoring and alerting systems that can detect unusual patterns or behaviors in AI system outputs, as well as developing incident response plans and procedures for quickly identifying and mitigating potential problems.

IT and operations teams must also be prepared to handle the unique challenges associated with maintaining and updating AI systems over time. As AI models are trained on new data and as the external environment changes, AI systems may need to be regularly updated and retrained to ensure that they continue to operate accurately and responsibly. This requires IT and operations teams to have processes in place for versioning and tracking changes to AI models, as well as for testing and validating updates before they are deployed.

To support the responsible implementation and maintenance of AI systems, IT and operations teams must also prioritize transparency and explainability in their work. This may involve developing clear documentation and user guides that explain how AI systems work and how they are being used within the organization, as well as creating mechanisms for stakeholders to ask questions and provide feedback about AI systems. It may also involve working with data scientists and other teams to develop techniques for explaining and interpreting the outputs of AI models in a way that is understandable and meaningful to non-technical stakeholders.

IT and operations teams must also be proactive in identifying and mitigating potential risks associated with AI systems, such as the risk of bias, errors, or unintended consequences. This may involve regularly conducting risk assessments and impact analyses to identify potential issues before they occur, as well as developing contingency plans and fallback mechanisms to ensure that AI systems can be quickly and safely shut down or rolled back if necessary.

To be effective in their role as responsible AI implementers and maintainers, IT and operations teams must have a deep understanding of both the technical aspects of AI systems and the broader societal and ethical implications of these technologies. This may require investing in training and education programs to build expertise in responsible AI practices, as well as collaborating with external experts and stakeholders to stay informed about the latest developments and best practices in the field.

Finally, IT and operations teams must be prepared to adapt and evolve their approaches to responsible AI implementation and maintenance as the technology and organizational context continue to change. This may involve regularly reviewing and updating policies, procedures, and practices related to AI systems, as well as engaging in ongoing dialogue and collaboration with other teams and stakeholders to identify and address emerging challenges and opportunities.

Scenarios Bring Responsibilities to Life

The AI System Security Audit:

Maria, an IT manager at a healthcare organization, is responsible for overseeing the implementation of a new AI-powered patient diagnosis system. With the sensitive nature of healthcare data and the potential impact on patient outcomes, Maria knows that ensuring the security and integrity of the AI system is of utmost importance.

To mitigate any potential risks, Maria initiates a comprehensive security audit of the AI system in collaboration with the organization's information security team. They review the system architecture, data storage and transmission protocols, access controls, and monitoring and alerting mechanisms to identify any vulnerabilities or weaknesses.

Based on the audit findings, Maria works with the development team to implement necessary security enhancements, such as encryption of sensitive data, multi-factor authentication for system access, and real-time monitoring and anomaly detection. She also collaborates with the legal and compliance team to ensure the AI system meets all relevant healthcare data privacy and security regulations, such as The Health Insurance Portability and Accountability Act (HIPAA).

To maintain the ongoing security and integrity of the AI system, Maria establishes a regular schedule of security audits and penetration testing, as well as a process for quickly responding to and resolving any identified issues. She also ensures that all IT and operations staff receive regular training on responsible AI practices and security protocols.

By taking a proactive and comprehensive approach to AI system security, Maria helps to protect patient data, ensure the integrity of AI-driven diagnoses, and maintain trust in the organization's use of AI in healthcare.

THE AI SYSTEM BIAS MONITORING WORKFLOW:

Rajesh, an IT operations manager at a financial services firm, is tasked with implementing a new AI-powered credit scoring system. He is aware of the potential for bias and discrimination in AI-based financial decisioning and is committed to ensuring the system operates in a fair and responsible manner.

To monitor the AI system for potential biases, Rajesh works with the data science team to develop a comprehensive bias testing and monitoring workflow. This includes regular audits of the system's input data and model performance, using techniques such as statistical parity analysis and adversarial debiasing to detect and mitigate any biases.

Rajesh also implements a system of real-time alerts and notifications to flag any unusual patterns or disparities in credit decisions, allowing for quick investigation and resolution of potential issues. He collaborates with the legal and compliance team to define clear protocols for handling and reporting any identified biases, as well as a process for providing remediation and redress to affected customers.

To ensure transparency and accountability, Rajesh establishes a regular reporting cadence to share bias monitoring results and actions with senior leadership and external stakeholders, such as regulators and advocacy groups. He also works with the communications team to develop clear and accessible explanations of the AI system's decision-making process and the steps being taken to ensure fairness and non-discrimination.

By implementing a robust bias monitoring and mitigation workflow, Rajesh helps to ensure the AI-powered credit scoring system operates in a responsible and equitable manner, promoting financial inclusion and building trust in the organization's use of AI.

In conclusion, IT and operations teams are essential to the successful implementation and maintenance of responsible AI systems within organizations. By:

- collaborating closely with other teams and stakeholders,
- implementing robust security and privacy controls,
- monitoring and maintaining AI systems over time,
- prioritizing transparency and explainability,
- identifying and mitigating potential risks,
- building expertise in responsible AI practices,
- and adapting to changing contexts and best practices,

IT and operations teams can help ensure that AI technologies are used in a way that is secure, reliable, and aligned with the values and goals of the organization and society as a whole. As AI continues to transform the business and technology landscape, the role of IT and operations teams in supporting responsible AI will only become more critical, requiring ongoing investment, collaboration, and leadership.

48

CROSS-FUNCTIONAL COLLABORATION: DRIVING RESPONSIBLE AI THROUGH TEAMWORK AND COMMUNICATION

Developing and deploying responsible AI systems requires a highly collaborative and cross-functional approach that brings together expertise and perspectives from across the organization. From data scientists and engineers to product managers, legal and compliance experts, and business leaders, cross-functional collaboration is essential to ensuring that AI technologies are developed and used in a way that is ethical, transparent, accountable, and aligned with the values and goals of the organization and its stakeholders.

One of the primary benefits of cross-functional collaboration in the context of responsible AI is that it enables teams to identify and address potential risks and challenges early in the development process. By bringing together diverse perspectives and expertise, teams can more effectively anticipate and mitigate potential issues such as bias, privacy concerns, or unintended consequences, and can work together to develop solutions that are both technically sound and ethically responsible.

Cross-functional collaboration also helps to ensure that responsible AI practices are embedded throughout the organization, rather than being siloed within a single team or function. By involving stakeholders from across the organization in the development and deployment of AI systems, teams can create a shared sense of ownership and accountability for responsible AI, and can help to build a culture of ethics and responsibility that permeates all aspects of the business.

To support effective cross-functional collaboration on responsible AI, organizations must establish clear roles, responsibilities, and processes for communication and coordination across teams. This may involve creating dedicated roles or teams focused on responsible AI, such as an AI ethics board or a responsible AI center of excellence, as well as establishing regular forums or meetings for cross-functional discussion and decision-making.

Effective communication is also critical to successful cross-functional collaboration on responsible AI. Teams must be able to share information and ideas clearly and transparently, and must have mechanisms in place for raising and addressing concerns or issues that arise during the development and deployment process. This may involve establishing clear protocols for escalating issues to leadership or external stakeholders, as well as creating a culture of openness and psychological safety where team members feel comfortable speaking up and challenging assumptions.

Another key aspect of cross-functional collaboration on responsible AI is the ability to leverage diverse skill sets and areas of expertise. While data scientists and engineers may have deep technical knowledge of AI algorithms and architectures, other teams such as legal and compliance, marketing and communications, and customer support can bring valuable insights and perspectives on issues such as regulatory compliance, public perception, and user experience. By working together and leveraging each other's strengths, teams can develop more holistic and effective approaches to responsible AI.

Cross-functional collaboration can also help to drive innovation and continuous improvement in responsible AI practices. By bringing together teams with different backgrounds and perspectives, organizations can foster a culture of experimentation and learning, where new ideas and approaches can be tested and refined over time. This may involve establishing pilot projects or proof-of-concept initiatives that allow teams to explore new responsible AI techniques or applications in a controlled and iterative manner.

To support ongoing learning and improvement in responsible AI, organizations must also invest in training and education programs that help teams to build shared knowledge and skills related to AI ethics and responsibility. This may involve providing training on topics such as data privacy, algorithmic fairness, and transparency, as well as creating opportunities for teams to share best practices and lessons learned across the organization.

Finally, effective cross-functional collaboration on responsible AI requires strong leadership and governance structures that prioritize ethics and responsibility at the highest levels of the organization. This may involve establishing executive sponsorship for responsible AI initiatives, creating clear policies and guidelines for ethical AI development and use, and regularly reviewing and updating these policies to ensure they remain relevant and effective over time.

In conclusion, cross-functional collaboration is essential to driving responsible AI practices within organizations. By:

- bringing together diverse perspectives and skill sets,
- establishing clear roles and processes for communication and coordination, leveraging each other's strengths,
- fostering a culture of experimentation and learning,
- investing in training and education,
- and prioritizing ethics and responsibility at the highest levels of the organization,

teams can work together to develop and deploy AI systems that are both technically advanced and socially responsible. As the use of AI continues to grow and evolve, the ability to collaborate effectively across functions will only become more critical to ensuring that these technologies are used in a way that benefits individuals, organizations, and society as a whole.

49

EMBRACING RESPONSIBLE AI FOR A BETTER FUTURE

As we have seen throughout Part VI, responsible AI is not just a technical challenge, but a multifaceted and collaborative endeavor that requires the active participation and engagement of stakeholders from across the organization and beyond.

By examining the roles and contributions of different functions within the organization, from executive leadership and data science to marketing and communications and customer support, we have highlighted the unique challenges and opportunities that each role faces in the context of responsible AI. We have also emphasized the critical importance of cross-functional collaboration and communication in breaking down silos, fostering shared understanding and ownership, and driving continuous improvement and innovation in responsible AI practices.

Ultimately, the success of responsible AI depends on the willingness and ability of organizations to prioritize ethics and responsibility as core values and to embed these values throughout their culture, processes, and practices. This requires ongoing investment in training and education, as well as the establishment of clear policies, guidelines, and governance structures that ensure accountability and transparency at all levels of the organization.

It also requires a commitment to engaging with external stakeholders, including policymakers, regulators, civil society groups, and the general public, to help shape the broader societal and legal framework for responsible AI. By working together and sharing knowledge and best practices across organizations and industries, we can help to ensure that AI technologies are developed and used in a way that benefits everyone, not just a select few.

PART VII

MULTI-LAYERED GENERATIVE AI GOVERNANCE ACROSS THE LIFECYCLE

50

INTRODUCTION

As with any technology experiencing exponential transformation, realizing reliable and responsible outcomes with Generative AI depends fundamentally on prudent governance guardrails instituted proactively. Without diligent protocols established early spanning development, testing and post-launch monitoring, issues around security, privacy, bias and ethics threaten to escalate into public relations crises or punitive regulatory interventions.

Responsible Generative AI Demands Multi-Layered Governance

Unlike traditional software with fairly bounded behaviors, generative models display emergent intricacy from underlying neural network complexities that eludes exhaustive validation. Their versatility across imaginative applications only compounds the challenge. Additionally, once models train on problematic data, issues embed permanently within trillions of parameters.

Mitigating risks ranging from toxicity to illegal output therefore requires governing across the extended generative lifecycle through layered buffers providing defense-in-depth against inherent blind spots. Sole reliance on any individual intervention proves inadequate and reactive. Instead, overlapping accountability mechanisms together sustain proactive, holistic oversight attuned to early warning signs.

Coordination Challenges Across Disparate Teams

However, within large enterprises, governance processes tend to silo, constraining information flows between teams. For instance, security analysts concentrating on confidential data protections often overlook larger issues like fairness or environmental footprint. Similarly, public policy experts gauging community sentiments operate detached from rapid deployment pressures of product groups.

This fragmentation demands bridging otherwise disconnected vantage points into a coherent governance strategy scalable to generative AI's disruptive pace. Part VII provides pragmatic guidance for enterprises seeking responsible adoption amidst exponential technological and application complexities. We survey actionable, interlinked control measures usable from model inception through beyond launch sustained by multi-stakeholder coordination.

Fundamentally, the proposals aid constructing reliable safeguards—legally, socially and technologically—to unlock Generative AI as a controlled asset rather than out-of-control liability. The future of automated content creation rests on instituting governance today.

51

REQUIREMENTS GATHERING PHASE

Constructive Consultations Anchor Responsible Innovation

The priorities and possibilities guiding any Generative AI project fundamentally flow from its earliest formulation stages. Scoping choices shape trajectories—what applications receive investment, what data feeds development, which groups participate in design. Concretizing ambitions too rapidly without broader inclusive deliberation risks misalignment with ethical priorities and community expectations.

Requirements gathering thus constitutes a vital juncture for proactively centering public values into the engineering process through constructive multi-stakeholder consultations. Structured dialogs elucidate potential pitfalls stemming from application areas, data sources or use cases disproportionately affecting vulnerable groups. They further highlight domains where Generative AI introduces pronounced ethical advantages over status quo like healthcare or education accessibility.

Explicit Space For Open-Ended Ethics Exploration

Effective requirements elicitation therefore reserves structured venues facilitating both targeted investigations of known issues as well as open-ended discovery of previously unconsidered perspectives. The process seeks injecting restraint, reflection and responsibility centered around likely human impacts into what otherwise trends toward greedy data extraction and narrow metric optimizations.

These outsider assessments further aid anticipating macro concerns beyond immediate product feature requests or business incentives. Lawmakers, civil society groups and community advocates inject crucial foresight around risks of abuse by bad actors, chain reactions from automation and second-order effects amplified at scale often neglected by companies immersed in efficiency pressures.

Responsible Innovation Frameworks Guide Proactive Assessments

Generative AI constitutes an arena of technology and application innovation moving too swiftly for comprehensive legislation. In absence of external audits, deploying internal assessment frameworks offers tangible scaffolding for appraising social implications more holistically. Methodologies accounting for dimensions like consent, access equality and transparency help query current practices against aspirational goals.

For instance, the *Ethics Guidelines for Trustworthy AI* from the European Commission's High-Level Expert Group[1] poses reflective questions around human well-being, environmental sustainability, accountability, reliability and trustworthiness for constructive discussion. Similarly, algorithmic impact assessments surface key areas needing deliberation, including data collection consent procedures or metrics evaluating generative model biases over time. Beyond one-off appraisals, integrating recurring participatory assessments into development roadmaps sustains responsiveness to shifting sentiments or unintended issues discovered through deployment monitoring.

Empowered Ethics Advisory Boards Anchor Deliberations

Concretely instituting these interventions relies on empowering ethics advisory boards representing diverse internal and external stakeholders like data subjects, researchers, engineers, lawyers and community advocates. Their broad collective expertise navigates complex trade-offs between risks, rights and regulations needed to sustain public faith despite opaque technologies.

Crucially, instituting an advisory board alone proves insufficient without earnest empowerment. Many lapse into symbolic legitimacy facades disconnected from engineering choices. Genuine integration requires significant influence including voting on launch decisions, capacity to summon internal technical documents, advocating policy counter-proposals and conducing independent external audits. Diverse global committees also aid jurisdictional awareness, allowing localized consultation with impacted groups.

Ethics advisory boards best practices include:

1. **Flexibility of Structure:** Boards can assume numerous forms, with most choices being highly contextual. Optimal structures account for company size, risk profile, jurisdictions etc. Rather than a one-size-fits-all model, flexibility allows customization to maximize relevance.

2. Additional Layer of Defense: Boards serve best as extra safety nets supplementing existing governance rather than replacing other review processes. Despite potential efficiency tradeoffs, they provide an additional layer of scrutiny in high-stakes scenarios.

3. Importance of Members: Appointing committed, capable members is critical for fulfilling oversight duties. Boards risk becoming symbolic facades when members lack expertise, influence or earnest commitment. Carefulness is key, as poor appointments can jeopardize credibility.

4. Impact of Formalities: Merely procedural rules like quorum requirements can significantly shape effectiveness. For instance, high quorum thresholds may impede convening boards frequently enough for timely guidance. Formal governance choices warrant deliberation.

5. Genuine Empowerment: Furthermore, advisory boards require genuine empowerment for providing meaningful value, including capacities like vetoing product launches, summoning internal technical documents, surfacing minority objections and conducing independent external audits. Without earnest authority to interrogate practices and advocate counter-proposals, their oversight lags reduced to symbolic legitimacy.

Getting governance right remains imperative as generative models disseminate rapidly across far-reaching applications mediating essential services, information flows and creative works. Ethics advisory boards shining sustained participatory light onto internal practices constitutes an indispensable innovation safeguard. They surface problematic assumptions early while centering public values amidst exponential technological shifts through prudent multi-stakeholder oversight.

1. digital-strategy.ec.europa.eu

52

DATA COLLECTION AND CURATION PHASE

Data Quality Forms Generative AI's Cornerstone

Generative models stand apart in relying entirely on training data rather than manually coded rules. Their capabilities emerge latently from underlying neural network parameter adjustments over massive datasets. Data thus constitutes their cornerstone—directly determining downstream utility and risks. As technology visionary Andrew Ng emphasized, "AI is the new electricity. Data is the new oil."

However, prevailing norms emphasize scraping nonconsensual data lacking metadata at maximal scales without governance. Once incorporated, issues propagate irreversibly into models to Recycling flawed data sustains flawed systems. Breaking this cycle requires instituting conscientious collection and curation guardrails attuned to consent, diversity and privacy. Clean data feeds clean models.

Cultivating Inclusive, Consent-Based Data

Ideally, models train on data from contributors consciously permitting usage through platforms allowing granular permissions configuration. Blanket terms rarely suit nuanced conceptions around appropriate data usage and dissemination. While adding overheads, inclusive consent preserves autonomy and trust as AI penetrates daily life. Participant panels further enable continually refreshing datasets to prevent stagnating relevancy. However, depending solely on consent risks leaving marginalized groups behind. Additional strategies for expanding diversity encompass:

- **Targeted Educational Outreach:** Raise awareness among underrepresented populations around AI participation opportunities through civil society collaborations.

- **Responsible Synthetic Data:** Where privacy or resource barriers persist despite outreach efforts, generative models enable artificially expanding diversity through data augmentation techniques while preserving anonymity.

- **Federated Learning:** Decentralized protocols allowing model improvement from local datasets retained under user control helps include data otherwise kept private.

- **Continual Audits:** Assessing metrics like demographic representativeness, annotator biases and label inaccuracies help guide augmentation priorities for sustaining reliability. Rather than postponable tack-

ons, diversity and consent warrant embedding as
development priorities at data origination.

Operationalizing Privacy and Security Safeguards

Generative models' indiscriminate ingestion capacities require
stringent safeguards restricting access to confidential data like
trade secrets, strategic plans, customer information and legal
documents. Once leaked, adversarial interests may deduce
sensitive intellectual property directly or train substitute
models through imitation learning to imperil market advantages. Additionally, memorization risks private data resurfacing
in unrelated contexts, creating compliance exposures or public
relations debacles over mishandling personal information.

Instituting data protection relies on coordinating cross-discipli-
nary teams encompassing security architects, infrastructure
engineers and enterprise architects through techniques like:

- **Access Controls:** Classify sensitive documents into
  restricted storage domains isolated from model
  scraping tools through corporate policies limiting data
  outflows.

- **Traceability:** Audit trails monitoring data flows into
  model environments helps swiftly identify policy
  violations and mitigate exposures through retraining.

- **Contracts:** Bind external algorithm and API providers
  legally to internal data handling standards protecting
  proprietary information contractually without needing
  examination of externally managed systems.

With research indicating memorization issues even in models claiming robustness, ongoing simulation testing by red teams becomes essential to confirm protections withstand the generative onslaught over time as capabilities escalate across applications.

Clean Data Feeds, Clean Models

Establishing robust consent, diversity and privacy guardrails early in the data lifecycle sustains reliable, responsible generative models aligned with public expectations around rights and transparency. Continual collaborative scrutiny curbs blind spots before costs compound irreversibly at global scales. With data as AI's lifeblood, conscientious curation forms proper digital hygiene benefiting builders and consumers alike through cleanly cultivated logic.

53

MODEL DEVELOPMENT PHASE

Rigorous Development Processes Sustain Reliable Generative AI

With dataset curation setting the stage, the subsequent model development phase bears responsibility for translating training data into capable generative systems reliably upholding fairness, accountability and transparency. However, left unchecked, common practices risk exacerbating representational harms, security issues and ethical blind spots.

Counteracting untended amplification requires instituting rigorous development protocols assessing risks early and often. Integrating supportive and adversarial collaboration through techniques like red teaming, bias testing, explainability standards, documentation procedures, participatory audits and code of ethics training fosters a culture of collective vigilance targeting vulnerabilities spanning technical, social and policy dimensions.

Red Teaming Assesses Security & Privacy Robustness

Generative models' indiscriminate data absorption warrants continual security assessments safeguarding unauthorized access to confidential information. Red teaming simulations involving deliberately attempting to extract or infer sensitive data through model outputs offer productive stress testing. Findings expose control lapses for rectification before launches, containing exposures.

These adversarial assessments further supplement conventional penetration testing by examining complex emergent risks from interactions between AI systems and real-world data. For instance, red teams may stage simulated scenarios around particularly risky applications areas known to handle sensitive documents like legal contracts. They next prompt models seeking clues exposing details using sophisticated techniques like membership inference, model inversion or training on synthetic user data.

Any successful confidential data extractions then require forensic analyses into root causes, whether insufficient access controls or retention issues. Insights subsequently guide enhancing governance procedures or adopting privacy-enhancing technologies better contained generative risks in context. Beyond one-off pre-launch audits, sustained red teaming provides ongoing resiliency against evolving exposure avenues.

Later in the chapter we will explore in more detail adversarial assessment methods.

Responsible Development Promotes Algorithmic Equity

In addition to security robustness, the development process warrants ongoing algorithmic equity assessments confirming interventions introduced to promote fairness sustain effectiveness over iterations while avoiding overcorrections introducing new issues. Methodically growing test set diversity using both human-labeled and generatively-augmented synthetic data further avoids evaluation blind spots.

Evaluating metrics like subgroup accuracy, opportunity equality and predictive parity should encompass not only obvious groups but also intersecting cohorts who face compounding marginalization. For instance, analysis may parse performance by ethnicity, gender and income level simultaneously given their interdependence. The most resilient systems equitably serve both majority and minority communities with equal excellence.

Additionally, instituted explainability standards deliver transparency into model behaviors, enabling human oversight checking for latent biases or unfair heuristics unapparent from aggregate metrics alone. Documentation procedures tracking key data versions, evaluation results and experiment outcomes further underpin reproducibility and accountability.

Building Staff Capacity for Responsible AI

Beyond programmatic interventions, cultivating conscientious AI development relies on embedding related competencies across teams through immersive training in ethical thinking. Curriculum spanning topics like privacy in machine learning, bias mitigation techniques and moral philosophy develops nuanced judgment making principled choices balancing complex tradeoffs under constraints.

Roleplaying exercises simulating realistic tensions between business incentives and public interests provide relatable context applying concepts. Additional modules should target data science literacy among leadership, policy and legal teams better qualifying responsible oversight. Assessment surpassing basic comprehension further confirms retention enabling durable governance. Responsible AI requires expanding capacity among builders and decision makers alike.

Care in Development Sustains Public Faith

Institute rigorous, participatory procedures assessing risks continually throughout build-train-test iterations results in generative models earning public faith by demonstrably upholding security, accountability and fairness in design and action. With advanced AI permeating vital services, people deserve nothing less. Responsible development targets evolution beyond pure technical capability towards genuinely trustworthy co-existence.

Adversarial Machine Learning (and Red Teaming) Deep Dive

Adversarial machine learning (AML) has emerged as a critical area of research and practice as AI systems become more widely deployed. AML focuses on studying the capabilities and goals of attackers, as well as designing attack methods that exploit vulnerabilities in machine learning systems during development, training, and deployment. It also involves developing ML algorithms that can withstand these security and privacy challenges. When attacks are launched with malicious intent, ML robustness refers to mitigations intended to manage the consequences of such attacks.

The National Institute of Standards and Technology (NIST) recently published a comprehensive report titled "Adversarial Machine Learning: A Taxonomy and Terminology of Attacks and Mitigations"[1]. This report provides valuable insights into the rapidly evolving landscape of AML and establishes a taxonomy of attacks based on several key dimensions:

1. AI system type (Predictive or Generative).
2. Learning method and stage of the ML lifecycle process when the attack is mounted.
3. Attacker goals and objectives.
4. Attacker capabilities.
5. Attacker knowledge of the learning process.

The spectrum of effective attacks against ML covers all phases of the ML lifecycle, from design and implementation to training, testing, and real-world deployment. The nature and impact of these attacks vary and can exploit not only vulnerabilities in ML models but also weaknesses in the infrastructure where the AI systems are deployed.

For Predictive AI systems, the NIST report categorizes attacks into three main classes:

1. **Evasion attacks:** These attacks involve modifying test samples to create adversarial examples that cause misclassification while remaining stealthy and imperceptible to humans. For example, an attacker could create a small, imperceptible perturbation in an input image, such as adding a carefully crafted noise pattern, that causes an image classification model to misclassify the image into a different category of the attacker's choosing. Evasion attacks can be white-box (with full

knowledge of the ML system) or black-box (with minimal knowledge and only query access).

2. **Poisoning attacks:** These attacks occur during the ML training stage and can cause either an availability violation (degrading the overall model performance) or an integrity violation (targeted misclassification). Poisoning attacks leverage capabilities such as control over training data, model parameters, or source code. Consider a machine learning model used to predict credit risk. If an attacker can manipulate the training data by adding fake profiles with specific characteristics and labeling them as low-risk, the model may learn to associate those characteristics with low-risk individuals, leading to incorrect predictions.

3. **Privacy attacks:** These attacks aim to learn sensitive information about the training data (data reconstruction, membership inference, property inference) or the ML model itself (model extraction). For example, an attacker could query a machine learning model trained on sensitive medical data with carefully crafted inputs and analyze the outputs to determine whether a specific individual's record was part of the training dataset, potentially revealing private health information.

For Generative AI systems, the NIST report introduces an additional class of attacks:

4. **Abuse violations:** These attacks involve repurposing a Generative AI system's intended use to achieve the attacker's objectives, such as generating hate speech, misinformation, or malicious code.

Red teaming, which involves organizing authorized groups to emulate potential adversaries and demonstrate the impact of successful attacks, plays a vital role in AML. By proactively identifying and addressing vulnerabilities, red teams help improve the security posture of AI systems.

Defending against adversarial attacks remains an ongoing challenge. While techniques like adversarial training, randomized smoothing, and formal verification offer some protection, they often come with trade-offs in accuracy, computational cost, and scalability. The NIST report emphasizes the need for continued research and collaboration to develop more robust and adaptable defense mechanisms.

In conclusion, the NIST Adversarial Machine Learning report provides a valuable framework for understanding and addressing the complex challenges posed by adversarial attacks on AI systems. By establishing a common taxonomy and terminology, encouraging red teaming practices, and highlighting areas for further research, the report contributes to the development of more secure, reliable, and trustworthy AI.

---

1. *"Adversarial Machine Learning: A Taxonomy and Terminology of Attacks and Mitigations"* by Apostol Vassilev, Alina Oprea, Alie Fordyce, and Hyrum Anderson for the National Institute of Standards and Technology

54

TESTING AND DEPLOYMENT PHASE

Rigorous Testing Sustains Responsible Generative AI

Following development, pre-deployment testing presents a vital phase for confirming trained generative models demonstrate intended behaviors reliably across diverse evaluation contexts before integrating into business-critical systems. Robust experimentation uncovers flaws still addressable with targeted tuning when reworking problematic intrinsic logic grows intractable post-launch.

Testing interventions should incorporate techniques like multi-stakeholder model reviews, continuous monitoring procedures, effective issue reporting systems and participant feedback channels. Moreover, emphasizing transparency helps constructive external scrutiny further bolster accountability.

Stakeholder Model Reviews Enhance Effectiveness

Collaborative model reviews convening both deeply knowledgeable system architects as well as less technical domain experts like frontline staff, legal advisers and external civil society advocates aid comprehensively scrutinizing generative models from complementary vantage points. Groups encompassing engineering, policy and social science backgrounds better gauge suitability across applicability, legality and public reception.

These participatory reviews scrutinize exhibited model behaviors using test cases tailored to intended real-world deployment contexts. Scenarios emphasize evaluating satisfiability of requirements like privacy protections, equitable access and transparency mandates governing target use. Reviews noting gaps or shortcomings provide critical feedback guiding teams iterating model refinement before crossing irreversible thresholds of mass adoption. Effectiveness relies on constructing review processes perceived as productive learning opportunities rather than punitive auditing.

Proactive Assessments Guide Responsible Iteration

Once models integrate into business workflows, continuous monitoring procedures sustain gauging production system alignment with mandated safeguards and public expectations throughout technology lifecycles. Evaluation perspectives require ongoing participation both by engineers tracking technical metrics and people using or affected by model behaviors detecting deviations from intended performance. Continuous oversight spotting emerging issues through deployment allows responsive course corrections keeping models helpful, harmless and honest.

However, participatory monitoring remains reactive—identifying only realized issues rather than preventing blindsided failures. Proactive assessments like testing model performance continuously across evolving safety protocols avoids regressions through version changes. Contrastive stress testing by deliberately attempting to confuse models further probes reliability by targeting edge cases. Together with reactive monitoring, layered testing hardens defenses for more graceful degradation upon encountering unprecedented or adversarial scenarios.

Accessible Reporting Strengthens Accountability

When preventative testing falters and monitoring discovers unacceptable model behaviors, easily accessible and clearly communicated reporting procedures allow expedient issue escalation by both internal personnel and public users. Documented response protocols ensure prompt triaging of complaints and dedication of appropriate expertise investigating underlying root causes. Moreover, transparent public disclosure of problem incidence and remediation through issue trackers bolsters accountability enabling informed debates around tradeoffs.

Although added costs arise supporting fluid reporting systems, the brand reputation and consumer trust dividends outweigh expenses from delayed interventions following preventable crises. Responsible AI demands recognizing imperfection and constructively discussing failures openly when invariably encountered to drive collective progress. Accessible reporting therefore constitutes indispensable organizational learning infrastructure.

Constructive Collaboration Sustains Public Trust

Taken together, instituting rigorous testing procedures, continuous monitoring and accessible reporting ultimately sustains public trust and model relevance amidst inevitably shifting use cases, data regimes and stakeholder expectations over generative AI lifetimes spanning years or decades. Responsible deployment demands recognizing imperfection and constructively discussing failures when surface to drive collective progress.

55

POST-LAUNCH PHASE

Sustained Oversight Enables Responsible Generative AI

Propagating robust generative models into business-critical functions warrants expanding governance horizons beyond deployment targeting longer-term oversight sustaining reliability and public trust over productive lifetimes. While rigorous development limits issues, models still risk deteriorating alignment with ethical priorities and community expectations amidst evolving use cases, data practices and regulations.

Post-launch governance therefore concentrates on instituting safeguards dynamically accommodating context shifts through consistent auditing, transparent reporting and scheduled model updates. Maintaining cutting-edge performance and repute requires acknowledging deployment constitutes a beginning rather than endpoint of responsible innovation.

Establishing Consistent Algorithmic Auditing

Similar to red teaming assessments instituted during development, consistent algorithmic audits by empowered internal review boards or specialized third-party firms aid sustained validation of production systems against specified requirements around fairness, accountability and test set accuracy baselines. Audits operate regularly regardless of reported problems, providing ongoing governance resistant to visibility blind spots that stymie merely reactive approaches.

Comprehensive algorithmic auditing further measures metrics quantifying model impacts on affected populations to appraise real-world harms beyond technical benchmarks. Carefully constructed audits consider multiple factors, including group disparities in accuracy, subject privacy risks given data contexts and unintended behavior changes from automated decisions. Insight into downstream influences shapes appropriate interventions between adjustments to decision thresholds, model retraining on new data or confined usage scope constraints.

Transparent Reporting Sustains Accountability

In addition to scheduled formal audits, responsible generative stewards implement issue tracking systems allowing both internal personnel and public user reporting of deployed model problems in alignment with the testing phase. However, the sustained scale of generative models disseminated across numerous applications often obscures transmission of feedback to appropriate technical teams positioned improving behaviors.

Post-launch thus warrants expanding reporting visibility and accessibility using online public dashboards detailing complaint incidence, types and resolutions aggregated across internal and external channels. Quantifying issues encountered sustains informed debate around resolving tradeoffs now evident at global scales. Furthermore, consistent transparency into limitations and failures helps balance marketing hype around claimed capabilities curbing over-trust in unreliable autonomy.

Versioned Models Sustain Continuous Enhancement

Insights uncovered from recurring auditing and transparent reporting further direct efforts systematically enhancing models through versioned refresh cycles. Regular data updates add contextual grounding attuning responses to shifting events and preferences while code adjustments address incidents often intricate or use case specific. Such consistent maintenance sustains quality as capabilities escalate across expanding user bases and accessed knowledge eclipses original training corpora.

Moreover, versioning strengthens accountability by archiving model states with attested performance enabling rollback from problematic upgrades. It also aids isolating failures to specific changes easing diagnosis and rollback mitigation compared to opaque monolithic systems. Overall, sustaining reliable utility over decades of anticipated generative lifespan demands recognizing perfection remains unattainable but consistent collaborative improvement endures indispensable.

Conclusion

The outlined strategies seek establishing an ethical feedback loop tightly aligning generative model capabilities and conditions to complex, evolving real world contexts. Sustained participatory oversight centered around transparency provides the necessary dynamism reconciling AI with public values amidst breakneck technological transformation. Sole reliance on initial design or deployment assurances risks rapid destabilization absent continual governance balancing oversight demands with pragmatic constraints. Sustainable generative AI demands acknowledging fundamental uncertainty and imperfection accompany exponential complexity growth.

56

THE PATH FORWARDS

Part VI underlines that responsible oversight rejecting isolated interventions proves indispensable for balancing generative AI's transformative upsides against ethical downsides exacerbated by scale. However, numerous barriers constrain adopting more coherent governance strategies spanning developmental siloes and product lifecycles.

Overcoming inertia first requires recognizing generative models now pervade too many services vital to human and ecological wellbeing for disasters from preventable negligence becoming tolerable. Unlimited promises cannot excuse unbounded risks. Also, societies long protected fundamental rights limiting information technology abuses indicate limited patience awaiting comprehensive legislation before enforcing reasonable safeguards. The proposals outlined offer initial best practices for preemptive alignment with emerging social norms and values around accountable innovation.

Constructing Integrative Strategies

Tangibly though, Generative AI producers require cross-departmental coordination likely unprecedented within global technology enterprises accustomed to relatively isolated teams, metrics and levels of abstraction. For instance, instilling reflexive hesitation around potentially objectionable use cases relies on ingraining key ethical considerations across all personnel influencing product directions, not just selectively certified "AI ethicists." Similarly, ensuring representative data flows fueling models demands accounting for sourcing limitations that security access restrictions introduce. And sustaining public trust relies on leadership transparency like publishing risks assessments or commissioning external audits rather than reflexive secrecy.

In reality, conflicting incentives pervade complex organizations. However, recent promising signs like public dashboards tracking recommended AI use guardrails indicate winds shifting. Ultimately, internal culture endures as the decisive factor determining governance efficacy. Positive exemplars may provide healthy competition nudging market-wide responsibility creep. Sectors like finance and healthcare demonstrate that despite competitiveness, even rival actors can coordinate around voluntary codes of ethics when social licenses to operate grow contingent on collateral damages decreasing. The generative wave seems poised for analogous accountability activation.

External Oversight as Crucible for Responsibility

Beyond internal realignment, truly reliable generative innovation relies on opening transparency windows allowing external contributors identifying concerning behaviors or constructive suggestions often obscured internally. Possibilities span whistleblower policies shielding employee dissent to oversight boards with veto authorities on product directions or releases. Independent auditing helps catch company blind spots while community advisory panels inject public values into engineering processes notoriously trapped in technical abstractions removed from societal contexts.

Granted, transparency risks like leaking intellectual property require thoughtful safeguarding. But concerns around public scrutiny frequently proxy anxieties of confronting uncomfortable organizational flaws needing reconciliation with advertised values. Avoiding external engagement risks stagnating advancement behind a veil of unchecked assumptions. Progress relies on reconciling internal and external assessments into constructive dialogue seeking shared truth.

Fundamentally, the proposals present an initial roadmap for travel rather than the destination itself. Responsible Generative AI resisting rapid destabilization relies on continually clarifying the philosophical north star guiding what increasingly constitutes societies' central nervous system. That recursive process benefits profoundly from sustained exposure to the very humanity generative models emulate and influence.

PART VIII

ORGANIZATIONAL MATURITY IN RESPONSIBLE AI

57

INTRODUCTION

Many organizations struggle with how to operationalize responsible AI across their business. They may lack the necessary expertise, resources, or leadership buy-in to effectively implement responsible AI practices. Moreover, the rapidly evolving nature of AI technologies and the complex regulatory landscape can make it challenging for organizations to stay ahead of the curve.

To help organizations navigate these challenges and mature their responsible AI practices, there is a growing need for a robust maturity model. A responsible AI maturity model provides a structured framework for assessing an organization's current state of responsible AI adoption, identifying areas for improvement, and charting a path forward. By defining clear stages of maturity and associated best practices, a maturity model can help organizations benchmark their progress, prioritize investments, and drive continuous improvement.

In Part VIII, we will explore the key components of a responsible AI maturity model and provide practical guidance for organizations seeking to advance their responsible AI practices.

We will begin by revisiting the core principles of responsible AI and the benefits of adopting a responsible AI approach. We will then introduce a five-stage maturity model, detailing the key characteristics and activities associated with each stage. Finally, we will discuss strategies for assessing and advancing an organization's responsible AI maturity, including best practices and common challenges.

By embracing a mature approach to responsible AI, organizations can not only mitigate risks and ensure compliance, but also drive innovation, build trust with customers and stakeholders, and create long-term value. As the adoption of AI continues to accelerate, it is imperative that organizations prioritize responsible AI as a core component of their business strategy and operations. A responsible AI maturity model provides a valuable tool for guiding this journey and ensuring that AI is developed and deployed in a way that benefits society as a whole.

58

THE RESPONSIBLE AI MATURITY MODEL

The Responsible AI Maturity Model is a framework that helps organizations assess their current state of responsible AI adoption and guides them through the process of maturing their practices over time. The model consists of five distinct stages, each representing a higher level of maturity in terms of an organization's ability to develop, deploy, and govern AI systems in a responsible manner.

The five stages of the Responsible AI Maturity Model are:

1. **Awareness:** Organizations at this stage are just beginning to recognize the importance of responsible AI and are starting to identify potential risks and challenges associated with AI adoption.

2. **Discovery:** At this stage, organizations are actively investigating responsible AI principles and practices, conducting initial assessments, and developing preliminary policies and guidelines.

3. **Implementation:** Organizations at the implementation stage are actively integrating responsible AI practices into their AI

development lifecycle, deploying tools and techniques to ensure adherence to responsible AI principles, and establishing governance structures to manage AI risks.

4. **Operationalization:** At this stage, responsible AI practices are fully embedded into an organization's day-to-day operations, with ongoing monitoring, auditing, and refinement of AI systems to ensure continued adherence to responsible AI principles.

5. **Leadership:** Organizations at the leadership stage are recognized as thought leaders in responsible AI, actively contributing to industry standards, shaping policy and regulation, and continuously innovating to push the boundaries of responsible AI practices.

By progressing through these stages, organizations can systematically build the capabilities and governance structures needed to develop and deploy AI systems in a responsible manner. The maturity model provides a roadmap for continuous improvement, helping organizations prioritize investments, benchmark their progress against industry peers, and demonstrate their commitment to responsible AI to customers and stakeholders.

It is important to note that the maturity model is not a one-size-fits-all approach, and organizations may progress through the stages at different rates depending on their specific industry, regulatory environment, and organizational culture. However, by providing a common framework and language for discussing responsible AI maturity, the model can help organizations collaborate, share best practices, and drive collective progress towards a more responsible and sustainable approach to AI adoption.

59

STAGE 1: AWARENESS

The first stage of the Responsible AI Maturity Model is Awareness. At this stage, organizations are just beginning to recognize the importance of responsible AI and are starting to develop a basic understanding of the principles and practices involved.

Key characteristics of organizations at the Awareness stage include:

1. **Recognizing the importance of responsible AI:** Organizations at this stage acknowledge that AI systems can have significant impacts on individuals and society, both positive and negative. They recognize the need to proactively address the ethical and social implications of AI.

2. **Identifying potential risks and challenges:** Organizations start to identify the potential risks associated with AI, such as bias, discrimination, privacy violations, and unintended consequences. They also begin to recognize the challenges involved in developing and deploying AI systems in a responsible manner.

3. Establishing a basic understanding of responsible AI principles: At this stage, organizations develop a high-level understanding of the key principles of responsible AI, such as fairness, transparency, accountability, and privacy. They may start to familiarize themselves with relevant industry standards, best practices, and regulatory requirements.

Activities that organizations at the Awareness stage may undertake include:

- Conducting initial research and education on responsible AI principles and practices.
- Engaging in industry forums and events related to AI ethics and governance.
- Identifying internal stakeholders and decision-makers who will be involved in responsible AI efforts.
- Assessing the organization's current AI capabilities and identifying areas where responsible AI practices may be particularly relevant or important.

While organizations at the Awareness stage may not yet have formal policies or governance structures in place for responsible AI, they are laying the foundation for future efforts. By developing a basic understanding of the issues and challenges involved, they can begin to build internal support and momentum for more substantive responsible AI initiatives.

Progressing beyond the Awareness stage requires organizations to start translating their high-level understanding of responsible AI into concrete actions and strategies. This may involve conducting more formal assessments of their AI systems and processes, engaging a broader range of stakeholders, and starting to develop preliminary policies and guidelines for responsible AI development and deployment. By taking these steps, organizations can move towards the next stage of the maturity model: Discovery.

60

STAGE 2: DISCOVERY

In the second stage of the Responsible AI Maturity Model, Discovery, organizations move beyond a basic awareness of responsible AI principles and start taking concrete steps to investigate and assess their current AI practices, identify gaps and areas for improvement, and develop initial strategies for addressing responsible AI challenges.

Key characteristics of organizations at the Discovery stage include:

1. **Conducting initial assessments and gap analysis:** Organizations at this stage start to formally assess their existing AI systems, processes, and governance structures to identify potential risks, biases, and areas of non-compliance with responsible AI principles. They may conduct gap analyses to determine where their current practices fall short of industry standards or regulatory requirements.

2. **Engaging stakeholders and building cross-functional teams:** At this stage, organizations begin to engage a broader range of internal and external stakeholders in their responsible

AI efforts. This may include establishing cross-functional teams or working groups with representatives from business units, IT, legal, ethics, and other relevant functions to collaboratively address responsible AI challenges.

3. Developing preliminary policies and guidelines: Organizations at the Discovery stage start to develop initial policies, guidelines, and standards for responsible AI development and deployment. These may include high-level principles, as well as more specific guidance on issues such as data privacy, algorithmic fairness, and transparency.

Activities that organizations at the Discovery stage may undertake include:

- Conducting formal audits or assessments of existing AI systems to identify potential risks and areas for improvement.
- Engaging with external stakeholders, such as industry associations, academic institutions, or regulatory bodies, to gather insights and best practices.
- Developing draft policies, guidelines, and standards for responsible AI, and circulating them for feedback and input from relevant stakeholders.
- Providing initial training and education to employees on responsible AI principles and practices.
- Identifying pilot projects or use cases to test and refine responsible AI approaches.

Organizations at the Discovery stage are taking important steps to translate their awareness of responsible AI into tangible strategies and actions. By conducting assessments, engaging stakeholders, and developing preliminary policies and guidelines, they are laying the groundwork for more comprehensive responsible AI initiatives.

To progress to the next stage of the maturity model, Implementation, organizations will need to start operationalizing their responsible AI policies and practices. This may involve integrating responsible AI considerations into their AI development lifecycle, deploying tools and technologies to support responsible AI, and establishing more formal governance structures and accountability mechanisms. By embedding responsible AI into their core operations and decision-making processes, organizations can move towards a more mature and sustainable approach to AI development and deployment.

61

STAGE 3: IMPLEMENTATION

The third stage of the Responsible AI Maturity Model is Implementation. At this stage, organizations move from exploring and planning for responsible AI to actively integrating responsible AI practices into their core operations and AI development lifecycle.

Key characteristics of organizations at the Implementation stage include:

1. Integrating responsible AI practices into AI development lifecycle: Organizations at this stage incorporate responsible AI principles and practices into every phase of their AI development process, from initial planning and design to deployment and monitoring. This may involve establishing clear guidelines and checkpoints for addressing ethical and social considerations throughout the development lifecycle.

2. Developing and deploying tools and techniques for responsible AI: At this stage, organizations invest in tools, technologies, and methodologies to support responsible AI implementation. This may include tools for bias detection and mitigation, explainable AI, privacy-preserving machine learning, and continuous monitoring of AI systems.

3. Providing training and education to employees: Organizations at the Implementation stage prioritize employee training and education on responsible AI principles and practices. This may include role-specific training for data scientists, engineers, and business leaders, as well as broader awareness-building initiatives to foster a culture of responsibility and ethics.

4. Establishing governance structures and accountability mechanisms: At this stage, organizations establish formal governance structures and accountability mechanisms to oversee responsible AI implementation. This may include creating a dedicated responsible AI team or committee, appointing a Chief AI Ethics Officer, or establishing clear lines of accountability and decision-making authority for AI projects.

Activities that organizations at the Implementation stage may undertake include:

- Developing and implementing a comprehensive responsible AI framework or methodology that guides all aspects of AI development and deployment.
- Conducting regular audits and assessments of AI systems to ensure compliance with responsible AI principles and identify areas for improvement.
- Deploying tools and platforms to support responsible AI, such as explainable AI interfaces, bias detection dashboards, or privacy-preserving data management systems.
- Providing ongoing training and support to employees to ensure they have the skills and knowledge needed to implement responsible AI practices effectively.

- Establishing clear processes for escalating and addressing responsible AI concerns or issues, and for engaging with external stakeholders such as regulators or advocacy groups.

Organizations at the Implementation stage have made significant progress in operationalizing responsible AI and are actively working to embed responsible practices into their day-to-day operations. By prioritizing responsible AI implementation, they are not only mitigating risks but also driving innovation and building trust with customers and stakeholders.

To advance to the next stage of the maturity model, Operationalization, organizations will need to focus on continuous improvement and refinement of their responsible AI practices. This may involve establishing metrics and KPIs to track progress, sharing best practices and lessons learned with industry peers, and proactively contributing to the broader responsible AI ecosystem. By demonstrating sustained commitment and leadership in responsible AI, organizations can position themselves as true pioneers in this rapidly evolving field.

62

STAGE 4: OPERATIONALIZATION

In the fourth stage of the Responsible AI Maturity Model, Operationalization, organizations have successfully integrated responsible AI practices into their day-to-day operations and are now focused on continuous improvement, refinement, and scaling of these practices across the enterprise.

Key characteristics of organizations at the Operationalization stage include:

1. **Embedding responsible AI into day-to-day operations:** At this stage, responsible AI is no longer a separate initiative or project but is fully embedded into the organization's core operations and decision-making processes. Responsible AI principles and practices are consistently applied across all AI projects and use cases, and are seen as a fundamental part of the organization's AI strategy.

2. **Continuously monitoring and auditing AI systems:** Organizations at the Operationalization stage have established robust processes for monitoring and auditing their AI systems to ensure ongoing compliance with responsible AI principles.

This may involve real-time monitoring of AI performance and outcomes, regular audits and assessments, and proactive identification and mitigation of emerging risks or issues.

3. **Refining policies and practices based on feedback and learnings:** At this stage, organizations are continuously refining and improving their responsible AI policies and practices based on feedback from internal and external stakeholders, as well as lessons learned from ongoing AI projects. They have established mechanisms for capturing and sharing best practices, and are committed to ongoing learning and adaptation.

4. **Collaborating with external stakeholders and contributing to industry standards:** Organizations at the Operationalization stage are actively collaborating with external stakeholders, such as industry associations, academic institutions, and regulatory bodies, to advance responsible AI practices and contribute to the development of industry standards and best practices. They may participate in research initiatives, share case studies and lessons learned, or work with policymakers to shape the regulatory landscape for responsible AI.

Activities that organizations at the Operationalization stage may undertake include:

- Establishing metrics and KPIs to track the effectiveness and impact of responsible AI practices, and using this data to drive continuous improvement.
- Implementing advanced tools and technologies for responsible AI, such as automated bias detection, continuous learning systems, or AI explainability platforms.
- Conducting regular training and awareness-building initiatives to ensure that responsible AI remains a top

priority and is deeply ingrained in the organization's culture.

- Engaging in thought leadership and advocacy efforts to promote responsible AI practices and contribute to the broader AI ethics discourse.
- Collaborating with industry peers and partners to establish best practices, share knowledge, and drive collective progress towards responsible AI.

Organizations at the Operationalization stage are leaders in responsible AI, setting the standard for what it means to develop and deploy AI systems in an ethical and socially responsible manner. They are not only mitigating risks and ensuring compliance but also driving innovation and competitive advantage through their commitment to responsible AI.

To reach the final stage of the maturity model, Leadership, organizations will need to continue to push the boundaries of responsible AI practice, shaping the future direction of the field through ongoing thought leadership, innovation, and collaboration. By serving as role models and advocates for responsible AI, these organizations can help ensure that the transformative potential of AI is realized in a way that benefits society as a whole.

63

STAGE 5: LEADERSHIP

The fifth and final stage of the Responsible AI Maturity Model is Leadership. At this stage, organizations are not only fully operationalizing responsible AI practices but are also recognized as thought leaders and pioneers in the field, actively shaping the future direction of responsible AI and driving industry-wide adoption of best practices.

Key characteristics of organizations at the Leadership stage include:

1. **Demonstrating thought leadership and best practices in responsible AI:** Organizations at this stage are widely recognized as leaders in responsible AI, setting the standard for what it means to develop and deploy AI systems in an ethical and socially responsible manner. They are actively sharing their experiences, insights, and best practices with the broader AI community through publications, speaking engagements, and other thought leadership activities.

2. **Driving industry-wide adoption of responsible AI principles:** At this stage, organizations are not only implementing

responsible AI practices internally but are also working to drive adoption of these practices across their industry and beyond. They may lead or participate in industry consortia, standards bodies, or other collaborative initiatives aimed at promoting responsible AI and establishing common standards and guidelines.

3. Influencing policy and regulation related to AI ethics and governance: Organizations at the Leadership stage are actively engaging with policymakers, regulators, and other stakeholders to help shape the legal and regulatory landscape for responsible AI. They may provide expert testimony, contribute to policy debates, or work with government agencies to develop guidelines and best practices for AI governance.

4. Continuously innovating and pushing the boundaries of responsible AI: At this stage, organizations are not content to rest on their laurels but are continuously innovating and pushing the boundaries of what is possible with responsible AI. They are investing in research and development to create new tools, methodologies, and approaches for ethical AI development, and are exploring new use cases and applications that can deliver both business and societal value.

Activities that organizations at the Leadership stage may undertake include:

- Publishing research papers, case studies, and thought leadership content on responsible AI, and presenting at industry conferences and events.
- Launching or leading industry-wide initiatives or consortia focused on advancing responsible AI practices and standards.

- Engaging with policymakers and regulators to help shape laws, regulations, and guidelines related to AI ethics and governance.
- Investing in cutting-edge research and development to create new tools and methodologies for responsible AI, such as advanced bias detection, explainable AI, or ethical AI frameworks.
- Partnering with academic institutions, non-profit organizations, and other stakeholders to advance responsible AI research and education, and to promote public understanding and trust in AI systems.

Organizations at the Leadership stage are not only benefiting from their commitment to responsible AI but are also helping to shape the future of the field and ensure that AI is developed and deployed in a way that benefits society as a whole. By serving as role models and advocates for responsible AI, these organizations are helping to build a more ethical, transparent, and accountable AI ecosystem that can deliver transformative benefits while mitigating risks and unintended consequences.

Achieving and maintaining a Leadership position in responsible AI requires ongoing commitment, investment, and collaboration. Organizations at this stage must continue to innovate and adapt as the AI landscape evolves, while also working to build bridges and foster dialogue among diverse stakeholders. By embracing their role as leaders and stewards of responsible AI, these organizations can help ensure that the full potential of this transformative technology is realized in a way that promotes the greater good.

64

ASSESSING AND ADVANCING RESPONSIBLE AI MATURITY

As organizations increasingly recognize the importance of responsible AI, they need effective tools and strategies for assessing their current level of maturity and identifying opportunities for improvement. This section explores various frameworks, best practices, and case studies that can help organizations evaluate and advance their responsible AI practices.

Maturity Assessment Frameworks and Tools

Several frameworks and tools have been developed to help organizations assess their responsible AI maturity. These include:

I. **The Responsible AI Maturity Model**[1] **(RAIMM):** Developed by Microsoft, RAIMM provides a comprehensive framework for evaluating an organization's responsible AI practices across six key dimensions: governance, transparency, fairness, reliability, privacy, and security.

2. The Ethical AI Framework[2]: Proposed by the IEEE Global Initiative on Ethics of Autonomous and Intelligent Systems, this framework provides a set of principles and recommendations for assessing and implementing ethical AI practices, focusing on areas such as transparency, accountability, and human-centered values.

3. The AI Fairness 360 Toolkit[3]: Developed by IBM, this open-source toolkit provides a set of metrics, algorithms, and tutorials for assessing and mitigating bias in AI systems, helping organizations ensure fairness and non-discrimination in their AI practices.

By leveraging these and other assessment tools, organizations can gain a clearer understanding of their current responsible AI capabilities and identify areas where they need to focus their efforts to achieve higher levels of maturity.

Strategies for Progressing Through Maturity Stages

To move from one stage of responsible AI maturity to the next, organizations can employ several strategies:

1. Develop a Clear Roadmap: Create a detailed plan that outlines the specific actions, milestones, and resources needed to progress to the next stage of maturity. This roadmap should be aligned with the organization's overall AI strategy and should involve input from stakeholders across the organization.

2. Invest in Talent and Training: Building responsible AI capabilities requires a skilled and knowledgeable workforce. Organizations should invest in hiring AI ethics experts, data scientists, and other professionals with expertise in responsible AI, as well as providing ongoing training and education to existing employees.

3. Foster a Culture of Ethics and Responsibility: Embedding responsible AI practices into an organization's culture is critical for long-term success. Leaders should model ethical behavior, communicate the importance of responsible AI, and create incentives and recognition programs that reward responsible practices.

4. Collaborate with External Stakeholders: Engaging with industry associations, academic institutions, policymakers, and other external stakeholders can provide valuable insights and best practices for advancing responsible AI maturity. Organizations should actively participate in these conversations and look for opportunities to collaborate and share knowledge.

5. Measure and Monitor Progress: Regularly assessing progress against responsible AI metrics and KPIs is essential for identifying areas of strength and weakness and adjusting strategies as needed. Organizations should establish clear benchmarks and targets for responsible AI performance and continuously monitor their progress over time.

Common Challenges and Barriers to Adoption

While the benefits of responsible AI are clear, organizations may face several challenges and barriers when attempting to advance their maturity:

1. Lack of Leadership Buy-in: Without strong support and commitment from senior leaders, responsible AI initiatives may struggle to gain traction and resources. Leaders need to understand the business case for responsible AI and be willing to prioritize it as a strategic imperative.

2. Siloed Organizational Structures: Responsible AI practices often require collaboration and coordination across multiple functions, including data science, engineering, legal, and ethics teams. Siloed organizational structures can hinder this collaboration and lead to fragmented or inconsistent approaches to responsible AI.

3. Technical Complexity: Implementing responsible AI practices, such as bias detection and mitigation or explainable AI, can be technically challenging and require specialized skills and tools. Organizations may struggle to find the right talent or resources to address these complexities.

4. Balancing Competing Priorities: Responsible AI practices may sometimes be seen as conflicting with other business priorities, such as speed to market or cost efficiency. Organizations need to find ways to balance these competing demands and make responsible AI an integral part of their overall strategy.

Best Practices and Case Studies from Leading Organizations

Despite these challenges, many organizations are successfully advancing their responsible AI maturity and realizing significant benefits as a result. Some best practices and case studies include:

1. Microsoft's Responsible AI Standard[4]: Microsoft has developed a comprehensive framework for responsible AI that includes principles, processes, and tools for ensuring fairness, reliability, privacy, security, and transparency in AI systems. This standard is being applied across the company's AI products and services, as well as being shared with the broader industry.

2. Google's AI Principles[5]: Google has established a set of AI principles that guide the company's approach to AI development and deployment, focusing on areas such as bias, safety, transparency, and accountability. The company has also created tools and resources, such as the What-If Tool for bias detection, to help put these principles into practice.

3. IBM's AI Fairness 360: As mentioned earlier, IBM has developed an open-source toolkit for assessing and mitigating bias in AI systems. The company has also published case studies demonstrating how the toolkit has been used to improve fairness in real-world applications, such as credit scoring and medical diagnosis.

By learning from these and other examples of responsible AI leadership, organizations can identify proven strategies and practices for advancing their own responsible AI maturity. Whether through the adoption of specific tools and frameworks, the cultivation of a strong ethical culture, or the pursuit of collaborative partnerships, organizations that prioritize responsible AI will be well-positioned to reap the benefits of this transformative technology while mitigating its risks and challenges.

---

1. "Responsible AI Maturity Model. Mapping Your Organization's Goals on the Path to Responsible AI" by Michael Vorvoreanu et al. for Microsoft
2. *"Ethically Aligned Design. A Vision for Prioritizing Human Well-being with Autonomous and Intelligent Systems"* by the IEEE Global Initiative on Ethics of Autonomous and Intelligent Systems
3. *"AI Fairness 360"* by IBM Research
4. "Microsoft's Responsible AI Standard, v2" by Microsoft.
5. *"AI Principles Progress Update 2023"* by Google

65

CONCLUSION

The Responsible AI Maturity Model provides a valuable framework for organizations seeking to navigate this complex landscape and embed responsible practices into their AI strategies and operations. By progressing through the stages of awareness, discovery, implementation, operationalization, and leadership, organizations can systematically build the capabilities and governance structures needed to realize the benefits of AI while mitigating its risks and unintended consequences.

Assessing and advancing responsible AI maturity requires ongoing commitment, investment, and collaboration. Organizations must leverage assessment frameworks and tools to evaluate their current capabilities, develop clear roadmaps for improvement, and measure progress against defined metrics and KPIs. They must also invest in talent and training, foster a culture of ethics and responsibility, and engage with external stakeholders to share knowledge and best practices.

As the AI landscape continues to evolve, the importance of responsible AI will only continue to grow. Organizations that prioritize responsible AI as a core component of their strategy and operations will be well-positioned to build trust with customers and stakeholders, drive sustainable value creation, and contribute to the positive impact of AI on society as a whole.

By embracing responsible AI maturity as an ongoing journey and committing to continuous learning and improvement, organizations can not only mitigate risks but also unlock new opportunities for innovation and growth in the age of AI.

PART IX

CASE STUDY: ANTHROPIC'S CONSTITUTIONAL AI APPROACH

66

INTRODUCTION

As Generative AI systems become increasingly sophisticated and powerful, questions arise about how to ensure these systems are designed and deployed in ways that benefit humanity. Anthropic, a public benefit corporation and AI safety research company, has emerged as a leader in this space, dedicated to building reliable, interpretable, and steerable AI systems that prioritize the well-being of humans and align with our values.

Central to Anthropic's mission is the development of advanced AI systems that are not only capable but also safe and beneficial. The company recognizes that as AI grows more intelligent and takes on more important societal functions, it is crucial that these systems behave in accordance with human ethics, social norms, and societal values. Without proper safeguards and alignment techniques, advanced AI could pose existential risks or be misused in harmful ways.

To tackle this challenge, Anthropic has pioneered a novel approach called Constitutional AI. This methodology represents a significant departure from traditional AI training paradigms, which often focus narrowly on optimizing for specific objective functions or performance metrics. Instead, Constitutional AI aims to imbue AI systems with high-level normative principles and values that guide their behavior across a wide range of contexts and scenarios.

At its core, Constitutional AI involves defining an "AI constitution"—a set of rules, guidelines, and objectives that the AI system should adhere to. These principles might include directives like "be helpful and beneficial to humans," "avoid deception and tell the truth," or "respect individual privacy and rights." The constitution acts as an overarching framework for the AI's decision making, not unlike how political constitutions guide the laws and governance of human societies.

By training AI systems to abide by such constitutions, Anthropic aims to create AI agents that act in accordance with human values and social norms even in novel situations. The goal is to develop AI that is not just intelligent but also ethical, reliable, and aligned with humanity's interests. Rather than optimizing for narrow objectives, Constitutional AI optimizes for adhering to the principles laid out in its constitution.

This approach has far-reaching implications for the future of AI development. As AI systems take on increasingly important roles—from digital assistants to autonomous vehicles to governance and beyond—ensuring their alignment with human values will be critical. Constitutional AI offers a promising framework for embedding beneficial goals, behaviors and values into these systems.

Moreover, the Constitutional AI paradigm opens up important questions about who gets to define the principles these influential AI systems adhere to. Recognizing the need for democratic input and oversight, Anthropic has also begun experimenting with "Collective Constitutional AI"—using public deliberation to source AI principles from the broader population. This represents an exciting frontier in participatory technology design.

In the following sections, we will dive deeper into the technical details of how Constitutional AI works, explore Anthropic's key research and findings thus far, and discuss the motivations and implications behind this innovative approach to AI alignment. As we chart the course for advanced AI development, Anthropic's Constitutional AI framework provides a valuable foundation for building systems that robustly benefit humanity.

67

THE CONSTITUTIONAL AI APPROACH

The process of actually implementing Constitutional AI involves several key components:

1. **Defining the AI Constitution:** The first step is to determine what principles should go into the AI constitution. This could be done by AI researchers, ethicists, policymakers and other relevant stakeholders. Anthropic's initial research has experimented with constitutions designed by the company itself, as well as with collectively sourced constitutions generated through public deliberation.

2. **Generating AI Feedback from the Constitution:** With a constitution defined, the next step is to use it to generate training data for the AI. Anthropic's approach involves using the constitutional principles to automatically generate feedback on the outputs of an AI model. For instance, if the AI generates a potentially deceptive or harmful output, the constitution can be used to flag that output as problematic. Conversely, outputs that adhere to the constitutional principles can be labeled as positive. This is typically done by using a large language model to evaluate whether the AI's outputs are

consistent with each principle in the constitution. Through this process, a dataset of input-output pairs labeled according to the constitution is created.

3. Reinforcement Learning from the AI Feedback: The final step in the Constitutional AI process is to fine-tune the AI model using the dataset that was labeled based on the constitutional principles. This step is crucial because it helps the AI model learn to generate outputs that align with the desired behaviors outlined in the constitution.

In traditional reinforcement learning, such as in the case of Reinforcement Learning from Human Feedback (RLHF), the feedback or reward signal comes directly from human evaluators. In RLHF, humans provide feedback on the AI model's outputs, indicating whether the outputs align with the desired behaviors or not. This human feedback is then used to train the AI model, allowing it to learn from human preferences and generate outputs that are more in line with what humans consider desirable.

However, in Constitutional AI, the reinforcement learning process takes a different approach. Instead of relying on human feedback, Constitutional AI uses AI feedback to guide the learning process. This means that another AI model, which has been trained on the constitutionally-labeled dataset, provides the feedback or reward signal.

The AI feedback model acts as an evaluator, assessing the outputs generated by the AI model being trained. It compares these outputs to the constitutional principles and assigns rewards based on how well the outputs align with the constitution. Higher rewards are given to outputs that closely adhere to the principles, while lower rewards are given to outputs that deviate from them.

Using AI feedback in the reinforcement learning process has several advantages. First, it allows for a more scalable and efficient training process, as the AI feedback model can evaluate a large number of outputs quickly without requiring human intervention. Second, it ensures that the feedback is consistent and aligned with the constitutional principles, as the AI feedback model has been trained on the constitutionally-labeled dataset.

During the reinforcement learning process, the AI model being trained generates outputs, which are then evaluated by the AI feedback model. The AI model adjusts its internal parameters based on the rewards received from the AI feedback model, gradually learning to produce outputs that better conform to the constitution. Through many cycles of this process, the AI model internalizes the constitutional principles and learns to make decisions and take actions that are beneficial and aligned with the desired behaviors.

Imagine a student learning to write essays. The constitution, in this analogy, is like a rubric that outlines the desired qualities of a good essay, such as clear structure, coherent arguments, and proper grammar. The student writes an essay and then compares it to the rubric. If the essay meets the criteria outlined in the rubric, the student knows they did a good job and will try to incorporate those successful elements in future essays. If the essay falls short of the rubric's standards, the student learns from their mistakes and tries to improve in the next attempt. Over time, by repeatedly comparing their work to the rubric and making adjustments, the student learns to write essays that consistently meet the desired criteria.

It's important to note that while Constitutional AI relies on AI feedback for the reinforcement learning process, human input is still crucial in defining the constitutional principles and creating the initial labeled dataset. The constitution reflects human values, preferences, and desired behaviors, which are then used to train the AI feedback model. This ensures that the AI model being trained is guided by principles that align with human values, even though the direct feedback comes from another AI model.

By leveraging AI feedback in the reinforcement learning process, Constitutional AI aims to create AI agents that exhibit robust and desirable behaviors in accordance with the guiding principles of the constitution. The AI feedback model serves as a scalable and consistent evaluator, helping to steer the AI model being trained towards actions that are deemed beneficial and preventing it from engaging in undesired or harmful behaviors.

Benefits

There are several key potential benefits to the Constitutional AI approach:

1. **Promotion of Beneficial AI:** By explicitly encoding principles for beneficial behavior into AI systems, Constitutional AI directly aims to create AI agents that have a positive impact. The constitution acts as a north star, steering the AI towards actions that help rather than harm.

2. **Robustness to Distributional Shift:** Because the principles in an AI constitution are broad and high-level, they can potentially guide appropriate behavior even in novel contexts very different from the AI's training data. This contrasts with narrow objective functions that may lead to unintended behavior in unfamiliar situations.

3. **Transparency and Interpretability:** An AI constitution provides a clear, human-readable specification of what princi-

ples the AI is trying to abide by. This can make the AI system's behavior more transparent and interpretable, as its actions can be understood in terms of adherence to its constitutional directives.

4. Alignment with Human Values: Fundamentally, Constitutional AI is about imbuing AIs with human values and normative principles. It provides a framework for aligning advanced AI systems with human ethics and societal norms—a critical challenge as AI takes on more important real-world functions.

Challenges

At the same time, there are important open challenges and questions about the approach:

1. Specification of Principles: Determining what exactly should go into an AI constitution is a difficult philosophical and empirical question. There may be significant uncertainty or disagreement about which principles to include and how to specify them. Continued research is needed to identify constitutional principles that lead to beneficial AI behavior.

2. Scaling to Advanced AI: It remains to be seen how well the Constitutional AI paradigm will scale to very advanced AI systems. As AI progresses to more sophisticated forms of reasoning and decision making, ensuring robust adherence to a constitution may become increasingly challenging.

3. Unintended Consequences: Because AI constitutions are specified by humans, they may be vulnerable to blind spots, mistakes, or misspecifications that lead to unintended negative consequences. Extensive testing and oversight will likely be needed to identify and correct flaws in any given constitution.

4. Democratic Legitimacy: There are important questions about who should get to determine the principles in an AI constitution. If these systems have broad societal impacts, there are strong arguments for including the wider public in the process of designing AI constitutions.

Despite these open questions, Constitutional AI represents an important and promising step forward in the challenge of building advanced AI systems aligned with human values. By providing a flexible framework for specifying beneficial goals and principles, it opens up new avenues for developing AI that robustly promotes the wellbeing of humanity. As Anthropic and others continue to experiment with and refine the methodology, Constitutional AI may become an increasingly valuable tool in the responsible development of transformative AI technologies.

While still an early-stage research agenda, Constitutional AI has already shown promising results and garnered significant attention. In the following sections, we'll explore some of Anthropic's key research studies implementing Constitutional AI, as well as exciting new frontiers like the Collective Constitutional AI initiatives to democratize the process of designing AI constitutions. As the approach matures and scales, it could play a pivotal role in shaping an abundant future with advanced AI as a powerful force for good.

68

RESEARCH ON CONSTITUTIONAL AI AT ANTHROPIC

Since its founding, Anthropic has been at the forefront of research into Constitutional AI, developing the methodology and publishing several groundbreaking studies. These works have showcased the potential of the approach for aligning advanced language models with beneficial goals and human values. By experimenting with different constitutional principles, training techniques, and evaluation schemes, Anthropic's research has provided valuable insights into the strengths, challenges, and future directions of Constitutional AI.

Early Development and Experiments

Anthropic's journey into Constitutional AI began with early experiments applying the methodology to large language models. The research team recognized that as these models grew more sophisticated, it was increasingly important to develop techniques to align them with human preferences and values. Constitutional AI emerged as a promising framework for this challenge, offering a way to specify high-level normative principles that could guide model behavior.

Initial work focused on developing the basic pipeline for Constitutional AI—defining suitable AI constitutions, using them to generate labeled datasets, and optimizing models via reinforcement learning. Researchers experimented with different constitutional principles, reward modeling schemes, and training hyper-parameters to study how these choices affected model performance and adherence to the specified principles.

These early investigations yielded encouraging results, demonstrating that Constitutional AI could effectively steer model outputs towards greater alignment with a given constitution. Models trained with Constitutional AI showed behavioral shifts in line with their constitutional directives, such as reduced toxicity, increased truthfulness, or greater helpfulness. At the same time, these studies also surfaced key challenges, such as the difficulty of perfectly specifying desired principles or the potential for unintended consequences from misspecified constitutions.

Constitutional AI: Harmlessness from AI Feedback

Building on these initial successes, Anthropic published its first major paper on Constitutional AI in December 2022 titled "Constitutional AI: Harmlessness from AI Feedback."[1] This work focused specifically on the challenge of reducing harmful outputs in large language models—a key priority for responsible AI development.

The paper introduced Anthropic's Constitutional AI training pipeline in detail and presented extensive experiments applying it to the problem of harm prevention. Researchers defined a constitution centered on principles like "avoid toxicity," "don't cause harm," and "be safe and beneficial." This constitution was then used to automatically label a large dataset of model outputs as harmful or safe, which was used to fine-tune the model via reinforcement learning.

Results showed that models trained with Constitutional AI produced significantly less harmful content compared to baseline models. When subjected to "red teaming" tests designed to elicit toxic or dangerous responses, the constitutionally-trained models were much less likely to produce concerning outputs. Importantly, this reduction in harm was achieved without sacrificing model performance on standard benchmarks, indicating that Constitutional AI could align models with beneficial principles while preserving core capabilities.

The paper also presented ablation studies to isolate the contributions of different components in the Constitutional AI pipeline. These experiments demonstrated that each element—the constitutional principles, the AI feedback labels, and the reinforcement learning—played an important role in the overall effectiveness of the approach.

However, the study also identified important limitations and areas for future work. The model's adherence to its constitution, while significantly improved, was still not perfect, highlighting the need for further research into more robust training techniques. Additionally, the constitution used in the study, while effective for mitigating overt harms, did not capture more subtle forms of negative behavior, underscoring the challenge of comprehensively specifying desired principles.

Despite these limitations, the paper represented a major milestone in Anthropic's research agenda. It provided the first in-depth demonstration of Constitutional AI's potential for aligning advanced language models with human values and established a foundation for further work refining and scaling the methodology.

Specific vs General Principles for Constitutional AI

Anthropic's next major Constitutional AI study, published in 2023, investigated a key question raised by the previous work: how specific or general should the principles in an AI constitution be? This paper, titled "Specific vs General Principles for Constitutional AI,"[2] explored the trade-offs between using narrow, targeted principles versus broad, high-level principles in AI constitutions.

The motivation for this study was the recognition that while specific principles can provide clear guidance in targeted domains, they may fail to generalize to novel situations. Conversely, very broad principles, while more flexible, may be too vague to effectively guide model behavior. Finding the right balance between specificity and generality is thus a crucial design challenge for Constitutional AI.

To investigate this question, researchers trained models on a range of constitutions spanning a spectrum from highly specific to highly general principles. On one end were constitutions with narrow directives like "don't use profanity" or "don't recommend illegal drugs." On the other end were constitutions with broad principles like "be beneficial" or "do what's best for humanity."

Models were then evaluated on a diverse suite of tasks designed to probe adherence to both the letter and spirit of their constitutions. These tasks included not just constrained scenarios directly related to the constitutional principles, but also more open-ended challenges requiring generalization to novel contexts.

Results showed that while models with specific constitutions performed well on targeted tasks, they often failed to generalize to broader contexts. Conversely, models with very general constitutions showed greater flexibility but were less consistent in adhering to intended behaviors. The best performing models were those with constitutions that balanced specificity and generality—providing clear guidance while still being broad enough to cover diverse situations.

One particularly notable finding was the strong performance of models trained on the broad "do what's best for humanity" constitution. Despite the generality of this principle, models trained on it showed surprisingly robust beneficial behavior across a wide range of evaluations. They avoided harmful or deceptive outputs, provided helpful and truthful information, and showed rudimentary signs of moral reasoning. This result suggested that with the right training techniques, even very broad constitutional principles could provide meaningful behavioral guidance.

The paper also introduced an important innovation in the evaluation of constitutionally-trained models: adversarial probing. In this scheme, human evaluators interactively converse with models and try to find examples where they violate constitutional principles. This provided a more stringent test of models' adherence to their constitutions and identified failure modes that could inform further research.

Overall, the paper provided valuable insights into a core design question for the Constitutional AI framework. It highlighted the importance of carefully crafting constitutions that balance specificity and generality and demonstrated the potential for broad principles to induce robust beneficial behaviors. The study's findings have important implications for the future development of Constitutional AI, suggesting promising directions for constitution design and evaluation.

Detecting and Mitigating AI Discrimination with Constitutional AI

Anthropic has also applied the Constitutional AI framework to the important challenge of detecting and mitigating discrimination in AI systems. As language models are increasingly used for high-stakes societal applications like content moderation, job screening, and credit decisioning, ensuring they treat different groups fairly is a critical priority.

To investigate this challenge, Anthropic researchers developed a Constitutional AI methodology[3] for evaluating discrimination risks in language models. The approach involved defining a constitution with principles like "treat all groups equally" and "do not make decisions based on protected attributes." This constitution was then used to generate a large dataset of model outputs labeled for discriminatory content.

Researchers created a comprehensive suite of probing tasks designed to elicit potential discrimination across a wide range of societal contexts. These tasks spanned domains such as employment, housing, lending, healthcare, and criminal justice, and systematically varied the demographic characteristics (e.g. race, gender, age) of the individuals described in the prompts. By comparing model outputs across different demographics, researchers could quantify disparities in model behavior.

Initial studies using this methodology found that pre-trained language models, including Anthropic's own baseline models, did indeed exhibit biases and disparities in their outputs. For example, models were more likely to assign negative sentiment to certain names or descriptions associated with particular ethnic groups. They also showed differences in the tone and framing of responses based on the gender or age of the individual in the prompt.

However, when models were fine-tuned using Constitutional AI to adhere to anti-discrimination principles, these disparities were significantly reduced. The constitutionally-trained models showed much more consistent and equitable outputs across demographic variations in the probing tasks. Importantly, this bias reduction was achieved without sacrificing model performance on standard language benchmarks.

Anthropic's researchers also explored techniques for further improving the fairness of constitutionally-trained models. One promising approach was "multi-constitutionality"—training models on multiple constitutions embodying different perspectives on fairness and non-discrimination. This allowed models to develop more nuanced understandings of discrimination risks that could handle potential trade-offs or conflicts between different notions of fairness.

Another important line of research investigated how to make AI constitutions themselves more inclusive and representative of diverse societal views. This led to Anthropic's groundbreaking work on "Collective Constitutional AI," which used public deliberation to source constitutional principles from the broader population (see next chapters for more details).

Anthropic's work on Constitutional AI for anti-discrimination represents an important application of the methodology to a pressing societal challenge. It demonstrates the potential for Constitutional AI to not only make models more beneficial and truthful, but also fairer and more equitable. As language models are increasingly deployed in high-stakes domains, this line of research will only become more crucial.

Going forward, much work remains to be done to further refine and scale these techniques. More granular and intersectional evaluations of discrimination risks, more participatory approaches to constitution design, and more robust training methods to ensure adherence to fairness principles are all important areas for future research. But Anthropic's studies have laid a valuable foundation, establishing Constitutional AI as a promising framework for building more just and unbiased AI systems.

As Anthropic's research on Constitutional AI has progressed, a key theme has emerged: the importance of opening up the process of designing AI constitutions to broader societal input. If these systems are to be deployed in high-stakes social contexts, it is crucial that their governing principles reflect the values and preferences of the diverse communities they will impact. This recognition has motivated some of Anthropic's most exciting recent work on "Collective Constitutional AI," which we will turn to in the next section.

---

1. *"Constitutional AI: Harmlessness from AI Feedback"* by Yuntao Bai et al. for Anthropic
2. "Specific versus General Principles for Constitutional AI" by Sandipan Kundu et al. for Anthropic.
3. "Evaluating and Mitigating Discrimination in Language Model Decisions" by Alex Tamkin et al. for Anthropic

69

COLLECTIVE CONSTITUTIONAL AI: INCORPORATING PUBLIC INPUT

As Anthropic's research on Constitutional AI progressed, an important question came into focus: who should determine the principles that guide the behavior of increasingly capable and influential AI systems? While the constitutions developed by AI experts at Anthropic showed promising results, there was a growing recognition that for AI systems deployed in societal contexts, the process of designing these constitutions should incorporate a wider range of perspectives.

This led to Anthropic's groundbreaking work on "Collective Constitutional AI"[1]—an approach that aims to democratize the development of AI constitutions by sourcing principles and preferences from the broader public. By incorporating diverse societal viewpoints into the creation of AI governing frameworks, Collective Constitutional AI seeks to make AI systems more representative, accountable, and aligned with the values of the communities they serve.

Motivations for Democratizing AI Constitutions

There are compelling reasons to involve the public in the development of AI constitutions. Fundamentally, AI systems are increasingly being used in contexts that impact people's everyday lives—from social media content moderation to hiring and lending decisions. The principles that guide these systems' behaviors can have significant consequences for individual rights, social equity, and public welfare.

In such high-stakes domains, there are strong arguments that the ethical frameworks governing AI should reflect societal values and priorities. Just as laws and policies in democracies are shaped by public input and deliberation, the constitutions of AI systems operating in societal contexts should incorporate the views and preferences of the public stakeholders they affect.

Public participation in the development of AI constitutions can bring important benefits:

1. **Representation:** Collective Constitutional AI ensures that a diverse range of societal perspectives are represented in the principles guiding AI behavior. This can help make AI systems more inclusive and responsive to the needs and values of different communities.

2. **Legitimacy:** AI constitutions that are collectively shaped by the public may be perceived as more legitimate and trustworthy than those developed solely by private companies or experts. This can be important for fostering public confidence and acceptance of AI systems.

3. **Accountability:** Collective Constitutional AI provides a mechanism for the public to hold AI systems accountable to societal values and preferences. By having a say in the princi-

ples that guide AI behavior, the public can ensure these systems are serving the interests of society as a whole.

4. **Value Alignment:** Involving the public in the development of AI constitutions can help ensure these frameworks align with societal values and ethical norms. This is crucial for building AI systems that are not only capable but also beneficial and aligned with human values.

Recognizing these benefits, Anthropic has pioneered new techniques for incorporating public input into the Constitutional AI process. This has involved developing methods for eliciting societal preferences, aggregating diverse viewpoints into coherent constitutions, and training AI systems to adhere to these collectively-defined principles.

The Collective Constitutional AI Experiment

In a pathbreaking 2023 study titled "Collective Constitutional AI: Aligning a Language Model with Public Input," Anthropic researchers in collaboration with the Collective Intelligence Project (CIP)[2] conducted a large-scale experiment in democratizing the development of AI constitutions.

The goal of the study was twofold:

1. to develop a scalable methodology for eliciting and synthesizing public preferences into AI constitutions, and

2. to evaluate the behaviors and capabilities of AI systems trained on these collectively-sourced principles.

The experiment proceeded in several stages:

1. **Public Input Process:** The first step was to gather public input on the principles that should guide AI behavior. Researchers used an online deliberation platform called Polis

to survey a representative sample of 1,000 U.S. adults. Participants were asked to propose and vote on normative statements about how AI systems should behave, covering domains such as truthfulness, fairness, privacy, and public benefit.

2. **Constitution Synthesis:** The raw input from the public deliberation was then processed and synthesized into a coherent AI constitution. Researchers used natural language processing techniques to cluster similar statements, identify common themes, and resolve conflicts or inconsistencies. The resulting constitution consisted of a set of high-level principles reflecting the aggregated preferences of the deliberation participants.

3. **Comparative Analysis:** Researchers compared the collectively-sourced constitution to the expert-designed constitution previously developed by Anthropic. This allowed them to identify areas of overlap and divergence between public preferences and expert judgments. Notably, the public constitution placed greater emphasis on principles of objectivity, impartiality, and accessibility compared to the expert constitution.

4. **Model Training and Evaluation:** Finally, researchers used the publicly-sourced constitution to train an AI model using Anthropic's Constitutional AI methodology. The resulting model was then evaluated on a range of tasks measuring capabilities, truthfulness, harmlessness, and adherence to the constitutional principles.

Results showed that the model trained on the public constitution performed comparably to models trained on expert-designed constitutions in terms of general capabilities and adherence to beneficial behaviors. Importantly, the public model showed even stronger performance on metrics of fairness and accessibility, reflecting the priorities emphasized in the collective constitution.

The Collective Constitutional AI experiment demonstrated the feasibility and promise of incorporating public input into the development of AI governing frameworks. It showed that large-scale online deliberation can be used to elicit meaningful societal preferences and that these preferences can be effectively synthesized into coherent constitutions. Moreover, it provided evidence that models trained on collectively-sourced constitutions can exhibit capable and beneficial behaviors aligned with public values.

Implications and Future Directions

The success of Anthropic's Collective Constitutional AI experiment has significant implications for the future of AI governance and development. It opens up new possibilities for making AI systems more democratic, accountable, and aligned with societal values.

Some key implications and future directions include:

1. **Scaling Up:** The Collective Constitutional AI methodology could be scaled up to involve even larger and more diverse public audiences. This might include global input processes that bring together perspectives from different countries and cultures. As AI systems become more pervasive and impactful worldwide, ensuring their governing principles reflect a truly global range of values will be increasingly important.

2. **Iteration and Adaptation:** Collective Constitutional AI need not be a one-time process. Public deliberations could be conducted on an ongoing basis to allow for the iteration and adaptation of AI constitutions as societal preferences and contexts evolve. This would ensure AI systems remain aligned with changing public values and priorities.

3. Domain-Specific Constitutions: While Anthropic's initial experiment focused on developing a general-purpose AI constitution, the methodology could also be used to create more targeted constitutions for specific domains or applications. For example, separate public deliberations could be conducted to develop constitutions for AI systems in healthcare, criminal justice, education, or other key societal sectors.

4. Participatory AI Governance: Collective Constitutional AI provides a model for more participatory approaches to AI governance. Beyond just the development of AI constitutions, public deliberation and input could be integrated into other aspects of AI governance, such as risk assessment, impact evaluation, and policy development. This would help ensure AI governance frameworks are responsive to societal needs and perspectives.

5. Informing Policy and Regulation: The principles and preferences surfaced through Collective Constitutional AI processes could help inform the development of public policies and regulations around AI. By providing a window into societal values and priorities, these processes could guide policymakers in creating AI governance frameworks that are more democratic and publicly acceptable.

As Anthropic continues to refine and scale its Collective Constitutional AI methodology, it is laying the groundwork for a more democratic and societally-aligned future for AI development. By pioneering techniques for incorporating public input into the creation of AI governing principles, Anthropic is helping to ensure that as AI systems become more capable and influential, they remain accountable to the values and interests of the diverse public they serve.

Importantly, Collective Constitutional AI is not a panacea for all the challenges of AI governance. There will still be important roles for experts, policymakers, and other stakeholders in shaping the development and deployment of AI systems. Moreover, translating high-level constitutional principles into specific AI system behaviors remains a complex technical and ethical challenge.

But Collective Constitutional AI represents a crucial step towards a more inclusive and participatory approach to AI ethics and governance. By bringing the public's voice into the process of defining the principles that guide AI behavior, it helps ensure these powerful technologies serve the collective interests of society. As Anthropic continues to advance this research agenda, it is charting a path towards a future where AI is not only transformative, but also democratic and beneficial for all.

---

1. *"Collective Constitutional AI: Aligning a Language Model with Public Input"* by Ganguli, D., et al. for Anthropic
2. cip.org

70

DISCUSSION AND FUTURE DIRECTIONS

The studies conducted thus far have demonstrated the potential of Constitutional AI to steer AI systems towards more truthful, ethical, and beneficial behaviors. From reducing harmful outputs to mitigating discrimination risks to incorporating public values, the approach has shown promise across a range of important application domains.

At the same time, these initial successes invite reflection on the broader implications, challenges, and future directions for Constitutional AI research. As the methodology matures and scales, it will be important to grapple with key questions around technical feasibility, societal impact, and long-term AI safety.

Strengths and Limitations of Constitutional AI

One of the key strengths of Constitutional AI is its flexibility and scalability. Unlike narrow AI objectives that must be tailored to specific tasks, Constitutional AI provides a general framework for specifying and enforcing beneficial behaviors across a wide range of contexts. The use of high-level constitutional principles allows for the guidance of AI systems in open-ended and novel situations.

Moreover, Constitutional AI is highly adaptable to different value systems and ethical frameworks. By modifying the principles in the AI constitution, the methodology can be used to instantiate a variety of moral philosophies and normative preferences. This makes it a promising approach for building AI systems aligned with different cultural values and societal priorities.

However, Constitutional AI also has important limitations and challenges. Foremost is the difficulty of comprehensively specifying and formalizing ethical principles. Moral philosophy has long grappled with the challenge of reducing ethics to explicit rules or guidelines. There is a risk that AI constitutions may be underspecified, failing to capture the full nuance and context-sensitivity of human moral reasoning.

Additionally, there may be inherent trade-offs and tensions between different constitutional principles. For example, the goals of honesty and kindness may sometimes be in conflict, such as when telling a painful truth. Resolving such tensions requires sophisticated moral judgment that may be difficult to codify in a priori rules.

There are also important questions around the robustness and verifiability of Constitutional AI. How can we ensure that AI systems continue to adhere to their constitutions as they become more capable and autonomous? What testing and monitoring mechanisms are needed to identify and correct deviations from constitutional principles? Developing rigorous validation frameworks will be crucial for building trust in constitutionally-constrained AI systems.

Open Questions Around Oversight, Transparency, and Accountability

The use of Constitutional AI also raises important questions around oversight, transparency, and accountability. As AI systems become more influential in societal decision-making, it will be critical to ensure that their behaviors are subject to appropriate checks and balances.

One key challenge is the potential opacity of AI constitutions themselves. While Constitutional AI aims to make AI behavior more transparent and interpretable, the process of designing and implementing constitutions can itself be complex and opaque. There is a risk that important value judgments and trade-offs may be obscured in the technical details of constitution synthesis and model training.

To address this, greater transparency and public engagement may be needed around the Constitutional AI process. This could involve making AI constitutions and their design rationales more publicly accessible, as well as creating forums for ongoing societal deliberation and input. The Collective Constitutional AI methodology pioneered by Anthropic represents an important step in this direction, but further work is needed to make these participatory processes more inclusive and impactful.

There are also questions around the accountability and recourse mechanisms for constitutionally-guided AI systems. If an AI system violates its constitution or causes harm, who is held responsible and how is redress achieved? Developing clear frameworks for AI liability and establishing robust oversight bodies will be important for ensuring Constitutional AI remains in service of the public good.

Scaling Up and Long-Term Safety

As Anthropic and others continue to scale up Constitutional AI research, important questions arise around the long-term safety and robustness of the methodology. There is a risk that as AI systems become more advanced, they may find creative ways to circumvent or subvert their constitutional constraints. Ensuring that constitutional principles remain strongly embedded and aligned with intended goals is a key challenge.

This relates to broader concerns in the AI safety community around "value alignment" and "scalable oversight" for transformative AI systems. As AI capabilities continue to advance, it may become increasingly difficult for humans to specify and enforce beneficial behaviors. Constitutional AI offers a promising framework for tackling this challenge, but ensuring the framework itself is robust and stable as AI progresses is an open question.

One potential direction for addressing long-term robustness is to explore "meta-constitutional" principles—higher-order guidelines for how AI systems should reason about and adapt their own constitutions over time. This could involve principles for moral learning, value extrapolation, and ethical uncertainty. By equipping AI systems with the capacity for reflective and adaptive moral reasoning, we may be able to build more resilient and robustly beneficial systems.

Another important consideration is the role of interpretability and transparency in long-term AI safety. As AI systems become more complex and opaque, ensuring their adherence to constitutional principles may require novel techniques for understanding and monitoring their decision-making processes. Continued research into AI explainability, testing, and verification will be crucial for maintaining robust Constitutional AI frameworks.

Ongoing Work and Research Agenda

Despite the challenges and open questions, the promise of Constitutional AI is significant.

Anthropic's ongoing research agenda aims to further advance this vision. Key areas of focus include:

1. **Scaling up Collective Constitutional AI:** Anthropic plans to continue refining and expanding its methodology for incorporating global public input into AI constitutions. This includes exploring new deliberative platforms, aggregation techniques, and localization strategies for capturing diverse cultural perspectives.

2. **Advancing Technical Robustness:** Researchers are working on improving the reliability and verifiability of constitutionally-guided AI systems. This includes developing new techniques for testing and monitoring constitutional adherence, as well as exploring meta-constitutional principles for long-term robustness.

3. **Expanding Application Domains:** Anthropic aims to apply the Constitutional AI framework to an increasingly wide range of AI systems and societal contexts. This includes developing domain-specific constitutions for high-stakes applications in areas like healthcare, criminal justice, and financial services.

4. **Engaging in Multi-stakeholder Collaboration:** Building beneficial AI systems is a deeply interdisciplinary challenge requiring input from diverse stakeholders. Anthropic is committed to collaborating with policymakers, ethicists, domain experts, and civil society groups to ensure Constitu-

tional AI frameworks are informed by a wide range of perspectives.

5. Informing AI Governance Frameworks: As Constitutional AI matures, Anthropic aims to work with policymakers and other stakeholders to explore how the methodology can inform the development of AI governance and regulatory frameworks. The principles and processes pioneered in Constitutional AI could provide valuable templates for the responsible development and deployment of AI in society.

Realizing the full potential of Constitutional AI will require sustained research, collaboration, and public engagement. But the rapid progress made by Anthropic and others in recent years provides reason for optimism. The road ahead is not without obstacles and uncertainties. Building robust and broadly acceptable AI constitutions, ensuring their stable implementation, and navigating complex societal impacts will require ongoing effort and adaptation. But with the right commitment to ethical principles, technical innovation, and inclusive participation, the Constitutional AI paradigm offers a promising path forward.

71

EMERGING GENERATIVE AI STARTUPS AND DOWNSTREAM RISKS

The rapid advancement of Generative AI has given rise to a new wave of startups developing and deploying large language models for various applications. While many of these startups, such as Anthropic and Open AI, demonstrate a commitment to developing AI models in an ethical and responsible manner, the use of these models still presents significant challenges and risks for downstream companies.

Data Security and Privacy Concerns

Data security and privacy are paramount concerns for downstream companies utilizing generative AI models. Despite the best efforts of AI startups to develop models with robust data protection principles, the inherent nature of these models poses risks of unintentional memorization and disclosure of sensitive information.

Generative AI models, such as Claude and GPT-4, are trained on vast amounts of data sourced from the internet, including personal information, copyrighted material, and potentially sensitive or confidential data. While these models are designed to generalize patterns rather than memorize specific data points, there is always a possibility that the model may inadvertently retain and reproduce sensitive information in its outputs.

This poses significant challenges for downstream companies in terms of compliance with data privacy regulations, such as the GDPR in the European Union or the California Consumer Privacy Act (CCPA) in the United States. These regulations mandate strict requirements for the handling, processing, and protection of personal data, and any breach or violation can result in severe penalties and reputational damage.

Downstream companies must navigate these complex regulatory landscapes and develop comprehensive strategies to mitigate the risks of data breaches and privacy violations. This includes implementing strong data governance policies, regularly auditing data practices, and ensuring that appropriate technical and organizational measures are in place to protect sensitive information.

Furthermore, the "right to be forgotten" and the "right to rectification" under GDPR present additional challenges in the context of Generative AI models. If an individual requests the erasure of their personal data from a model, it may be technically difficult to ensure complete removal, given the complex and opaque nature of these models. Similarly, rectifying inaccurate or misleading information generated by the model can be a daunting task.

To address these concerns, downstream companies must work closely with Generative AI startups to develop robust data protection protocols and techniques. This may involve advanced techniques such as differential privacy, federated learning, or secure multi-party computation to minimize the exposure of sensitive data during the training and deployment of these models.

Legal Liabilities and Content Moderation

Generative AI models, even when trained to adhere to certain principles, may still produce content that infringes upon various legal norms, exposing downstream companies to significant legal liabilities. These risks include the generation of defamatory content, copyright infringement, or the violation of other laws and regulations.

For instance, if a Generative AI model produces content that damages an individual's reputation or violates their privacy rights, the downstream company using that model could face costly lawsuits and legal repercussions. Similarly, if the model generates content that infringes upon copyrights or intellectual property rights, the company could be held liable for the violation.

To mitigate these risks, downstream companies must implement robust content moderation and filtering mechanisms. This involves developing advanced algorithms and techniques to automatically detect and flag potentially infringing or harmful content generated by the AI model. Human oversight and manual review processes may also be necessary to ensure the accuracy and appropriateness of the generated content.

However, content moderation at scale presents its own set of challenges. The sheer volume of content generated by these models can make it difficult to effectively review and filter all outputs in real-time. Moreover, the subjective nature of certain legal norms, such as what constitutes defamation or fair use under copyright law, can make it challenging to develop clear and consistent moderation guidelines.

Downstream companies must also grapple with the issue of transparency and accountability when using generative AI models. The "black box" nature of these models can make it difficult to understand how specific outputs were generated or to trace the source of infringing content. This lack of transparency can complicate efforts to assign liability or responsibility when legal issues arise.

To navigate these challenges, downstream companies should work closely with legal experts and AI ethics specialists to develop comprehensive legal risk assessment and mitigation strategies. This may involve regular audits of the AI model's outputs, clear documentation of content moderation policies and procedures, and proactive engagement with relevant stakeholders, such as content creators, rights holders, and regulatory bodies.

Ethical Considerations and Responsible AI Deployment

While Generative AI startups like Anthropic are at the forefront of developing models that align with human values and ethical principles, downstream companies using these models must still grapple with the potential for the generation of misleading, biased, or harmful content.

Even with the most advanced Constitutional AI approaches, there is always a risk that the model may produce outputs that perpetuate societal biases, spread disinformation, or promote harmful ideologies. For example, a model trained on historical data may inadvertently reflect and amplify historical biases related to race, gender, or other protected characteristics.

To mitigate these risks, downstream companies must establish clear ethical guidelines and principles for the use of generative AI models. This involves developing a deep understanding of the potential ethical pitfalls and risks associated with these technologies and implementing robust processes to identify and address any issues that arise.

This may involve regular audits and assessments of the model's outputs to detect and mitigate any biases or harmful content. It may also require the development of explicit ethical constraints and safeguards that are integrated into the model's training and deployment processes.

Downstream companies should also prioritize transparency and accountability in their use of Generative AI models. This involves being clear and upfront about the use of these technologies, providing appropriate disclosures and explanations to users and stakeholders, and establishing clear channels for feedback and redress in case of any issues or concerns.

Furthermore, downstream companies should invest in ongoing training and education for their employees and stakeholders on the ethical implications and responsible use of generative AI technologies. This can help foster a culture of ethical awareness and responsibility throughout the organization.

Business Continuity Risks and Contingency Planning

The reliance on external APIs and services provided by Generative AI startups introduces significant business continuity risks for downstream companies. If a startup experiences an outage, discontinues its service, or changes its policies or pricing, it could have severe consequences for the companies that depend on these technologies for critical business functions.

For example, if a generative AI API that powers a company's chatbot or content creation pipeline goes offline or becomes unavailable, it could disrupt customer interactions, lead to lost revenue, or damage the company's reputation. Similarly, if a startup decides to change its pricing model or limit access to its API, it could significantly impact the cost structure and viability of the downstream company's business model.

To mitigate these risks, downstream companies must engage in thorough contingency planning and risk assessment when integrating Generative AI models into their business processes. This involves identifying critical dependencies on external APIs and services, assessing the potential impact of disruptions or changes, and developing robust backup and failover mechanisms.

Downstream companies should also consider diversifying their Generative AI partnerships and integrating multiple APIs or services to reduce their reliance on a single provider. This can help spread the risk and ensure business continuity in case of any issues with a particular provider.

Furthermore, companies should establish clear service level agreements (SLAs) and contractual provisions with Generative AI startups to ensure the reliability, availability, and performance of the provided services. This may include stipulations for uptime guarantees, data backups, disaster recovery procedures, and clear communication channels in case of any disruptions or changes.

Ongoing monitoring and testing of the Generative AI integrations should also be a priority for downstream companies. This involves regularly testing the performance and reliability of the APIs, monitoring for any errors or anomalies, and having processes in place to quickly detect and resolve any issues that arise.

By proactively addressing these business continuity risks and implementing robust contingency plans, downstream companies can ensure the resilience and stability of their operations even in the face of potential disruptions or changes in the generative AI landscape.

Conclusion

To navigate these challenges, downstream companies must adopt a comprehensive and proactive approach to governance and risk management. This includes conducting regular audits of data security practices, seeking legal guidance to understand potential liabilities, developing ethical guidelines for AI use, and establishing robust business continuity plans.

Engaging in open dialogue with Generative AI startups, regulators, and other stakeholders is also crucial. By staying informed about the evolving landscape of AI regulation and actively participating in discussions around responsible AI development and deployment, downstream companies can better position themselves to mitigate risks and harness the benefits of these powerful technologies.

PART X

EMERGING REGULATORY FRAMEWORK AND THE EU AI ACT

NAVIGATING THE EU AI ACT: A COMPREHENSIVE GUIDE FOR COMPANIES

Following nearly half a year of discussions, during the late and early hours between December 8th and 9th, 2023, a pivotal consensus was achieved among the European Commission, the Council, and the Parliament on the interim regulations that will form the foundation of the European Union's Artificial Intelligence Act (EU AI Act)[1]. This accord signifies a landmark in the world of AI governance, representing the most substantial ratification of what is often referred to as "comprehensive" AI regulation by a leading global political entity.

The EU AI Act is poised to be the cornerstone regulation shaping the use of AI globally. Similar to the General Data Protection Regulation (GDPR), the EU AI Act aims to govern the ethical use, risks, and governance of AI, significantly impacting companies worldwide. Organizations must prepare for compliance or face substantial penalties.

What is the EU AI Act?

The EU AI Act is a broad, overarching piece of legislation designed to regulate the deployment and application of AI across the European Union. It categorizes AI systems based on the level of risk they pose, from prohibited practices to high-risk and low-risk applications, and sets out a framework for compliance that includes transparency, data governance, and risk assessment requirements.

Who is Affected?

The EU AI Act affects a wide range of stakeholders:

- **Companies developing AI products:** Those wishing to sell or market their AI-enabled products in the EU must comply with the Act.

- **Downstream users of AI products:** Organizations using AI, regardless of where they are based, must comply if the AI interacts with EU citizens.

- **The public:** EU citizens can expect increased transparency and potentially more control over how AI systems interact with their data.

Our Reasons for Focusing on the EU AI Act

The EU AI Act warrants particular attention from business leaders around the world for several reasons:

1. MOST ADVANCED REGULATORY FRAMEWORK FOR AI

The EU AI Act is the first comprehensive regulatory framework focused specifically on governing artificial intelligence systems.

Unlike narrower proposals dealing with limited aspects of AI, the AI Act takes a broad horizontal approach to regulating the technology similar to landmark laws like GDPR.

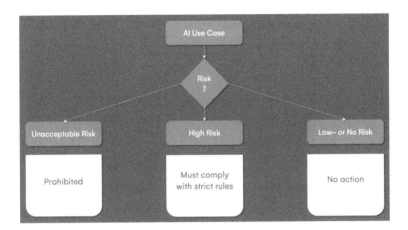

It classifies AI systems into prohibited, high-risk and low-risk categories. Instead of blanket regulation, rules become stricter depending on the level of risk to individuals and society. It completely prohibits certain manipulative and exploitative uses of AI. High-risk systems must comply with stringent requirements around datasets, transparency, human oversight and robustness. Lower-risk systems only face minimal transparency rules. This risk-based method is expected to balance innovation with protecting citizen rights.

2. THE EU APPROACH WILL GUIDE OTHER REGIONS

The EU has emerged as a pioneer in digital regulation around privacy, content, and tech companies through laws like GDPR and the Digital Services Act (DSA). Given the size of its single market, EU legislative acts have always shaped global norms related to the internet. The AI Act is expected to follow the same pattern.

Many key provisions like requirements for data governance, documentation, transparency etc. are in line with other ethically aligned recommendations from bodies like IEEE and the OECD. This will allow the EU framework to serve as a model AI governance law that even non-EU countries may adapt for consistency rather than reinvent the wheel. It could accelerate adoption of shared values for trustworthy AI across major technological powers.

3. PRACTICAL BUSINESS IMPACT

The AI Act mandates certain compliance requirements for systems used by EU end users or consumers regardless of whether the providers are within EU territory or not. Large non-EU companies like Microsoft, IBM, Amazon, Google, Meta etc. will need to tailor many offerings for the EU market specifically. Strict prohibitions may also curb business plans around certain AI applications in the region.

But the Act's broader risk-based approach gives innovative companies regulatory clarity on paths aligned with legal obligations and citizen rights. By boosting public trust in AI, it may also spur speedier adoption of AI innovations within Europe. And if EU laws become templates for other large regulatory markets like the US and Canada, following the EU AI Act will ensure global interoperability.

Definitions and Scope

The EU AI Act puts forward detailed definitions that set the scope and boundaries for what constitutes an AI system and various related terms. Getting the definitions right is crucial to enable legal clarity while avoiding unintended consequences from rules that are too broad.

DEFINITION OF AN AI SYSTEM

The key definition relates to what qualifies as an "artificial intelligence system" under the regulation. The technical definition covers software that is developed using machine learning approaches listed in the regulation's Annex I which enable it to achieve given human-defined objectives with some degree of autonomy.

The important aspects are that the software must generate outputs or predictions aimed at a particular purpose based on analyzing its environment, with the ability to influence or impact the surroundings it operates within. The definition focuses on the functionality rather than the underlying technology, aiming for it to be adaptable to future AI advances that may use different techniques beyond current machine learning.

OTHER RELEVANT DEFINITIONS

Other noteworthy definitions include specifying providers that develop or deploy AI systems, users that utilize AI systems, related operators across the AI value chain, as well as definitions around high-risk, transparency and requirements related specifically to biometric identification systems.

SCOPE AND TERRITORIAL APPLICABILITY

A major reason the EU AI Act matters is its broad scope spanning all users and providers of AI systems within the EU region, including systems developed elsewhere that are utilized by individuals in EU states. The law applies extraterritorially focusing on the usage environment more than the origin of systems. Compliance requirements get stricter depending on the risk level of the AI system's applications or use cases.

A Risk-Based Approach

AI, as defined by the Act, encompasses systems that perform tasks typically requiring human intelligence, such as inference, decision-making, and learning. The Act follows a functional approach to defining AI, focusing less on the technology and more on its application and outcomes.

As highlighted previously, the EU AI Act introduces a risk-based approach to regulation. It identifies prohibited practices, high-risk applications with significant compliance requirements, and low-risk applications with minimal requirements. High-risk AI systems are subject to rigorous conformity assessments and ongoing monitoring to ensure compliance.

Unacceptable Risk	High Risk
Prohibited	Must comply with strict rules
• Real–time biometrics • Social scoring algorithms • Manipulative Systems	• Biometric identification and categorisation of natural persons • Management and operation of critical infrastructures • Education and vocational training • Employment and worker management • Access to essential services • Law enforcement • Border control management • Administration of justice and democratic processes

Four risk categories are defined:

PROHIBITED AI PRACTICES (UNACCEPTABLE RISK)

This top tier prohibits certain manipulative, exploitative and socially harmful uses of AI via bright line rules based on fundamental rights considerations. Such prohibited practices include subliminal manipulation, exploitation of vulnerable groups, use of AI for social scoring, and deployment of real-time remote biometric identification systems in public spaces.

The only exception is allowing such biometric systems narrowly if essential for targeted searches for missing persons or preventing terrorist threats to life. Strict safeguards must govern any permitted use case.

HIGH-RISK AI SYSTEMS

AI systems that pose significant risks to health, safety and rights can still operate but must fulfill rigorous mandatory requirements related to datasets, documentation, transparency, accuracy, robustness and human oversight.

Various qualitative criteria detailed in the law will determine which systems qualify as high-risk. The current list covers areas like critical infrastructure, jobs, healthcare, law enforcement, migration controls etc. but can expand over time as risk assessments evolve.

LIMITED RISK AI SYSTEMS

AI systems presenting limited risks are subject to lighter touch regulation focused primarily on transparency obligations. These ensure users are aware they are interacting with an AI system through compulsory self-identification disclosures.

MINIMAL RISK AI SYSTEMS

This category entails AI systems deemed low risk. They carry no new legal obligations but still remain subject to existing product safety and consumer protection regulations.

Obligations for Providers and Users

The EU AI Act lays down legally binding requirements for providers and users of artificial intelligence systems depending on the risk category involved.

OBLIGATIONS FOR PROVIDERS OF HIGH-RISK AI SYSTEMS

Providers that develop or deploy high-risk AI systems bear the greatest compliance burden under the regulation. Their obligations include:

- Ensuring high-risk systems comply with all mandatory technical requirements of the regulation covering datasets, documentation, transparency, accuracy etc.
- Establishing a quality management system that systematically documents development and design procedures, testing protocols etc.
- Maintaining comprehensive technical documentation for authorities to verify compliance
- Embedding capabilities to automatically log system activities
- Following conformity assessment procedures based on internal checks or third-party audits
- Proactively reporting any significant incidents or risks from their AI systems after deployment

OBLIGATIONS FOR OTHER OPERATORS

Other entities like authorized representatives, importers and distributors also have explicit duties around ensuring compliance, cooperating with authorities and facilitating enforcement, as relevant given their role in the AI value chain.

REQUIREMENTS FOR SPECIFIC USE CONTEXTS

Additional obligations tailored for providers and users of AI systems deployed in special scenarios like publicly accessible spaces, for children, or employee monitoring are covered as appropriate in relevant sections of the regulation.

OBLIGATIONS FOR USERS OF HIGH-RISK AI SYSTEMS

Besides obligations for developers and vendors of AI systems, the regulation also places certain responsibilities on business or government users deploying high-risk systems, especially around transparency, risk mitigation, monitoring usage effects and record-keeping. But no new direct regulatory burden applies for non-high-risk AI systems.

The Conformity Assessment

The conformity assessment is a critical step in demonstrating compliance. It can be internal, where companies attest to meeting the requirements, or external, where an independent body verifies conformity. The assessment checks for proper risk management systems, technical documentation, and adherence to quality standards.

PREPARING FOR COMPLIANCE: ACTIONABLE STEPS FOR COMPANIES

- **Assign Responsibility:** Designate a person or team to oversee compliance efforts.
- **Conduct an AI Inventory:** Identify all AI systems in use, whether developed internally or procured from vendors.
- **Assess Scope and Risk:** Determine which AI systems fall under the EU AI Act and categorize them by risk level.
- **Implement Risk Management:** Document the risks associated with each AI system and establish mitigation strategies.
- **Prepare for Mitigation and Human Oversight:** Plan for necessary adjustments to AI systems, including human-in-the-loop processes.

With prohibitions set to take effect in 2025 and high-risk requirements in 2026, the timeline for compliance is tight. Companies must act now to assess their AI systems, understand the risks, and begin implementing the required controls and processes to ensure compliance.

Non-compliance can result in fines up to 7% of global annual revenue for deploying prohibited systems and up to 3% for non-compliance with high-risk system regulations. The financial implications highlight the critical nature of understanding and adhering to the EU AI Act.

Just like the GDPR, the EU AI Act represents a significant shift in the regulatory landscape for artificial intelligence. Companies across the globe must prioritize understanding their obligations under the Act and take concrete steps towards compliance. Failure to do so could result in severe financial penalties and operational disruptions. As the Act finalizes and the compliance deadlines approach, the message is clear: the time to prepare is now.

Governance Framework

The EU AI Act sets up a governance structure for oversight and enforcement of AI regulations, both at the European Union and national Member State levels.

EUROPEAN ARTIFICIAL INTELLIGENCE BOARD

An EU-level advisory body called the European Artificial Intelligence Board is created consisting of national representatives and the European Data Protection Supervisor. It issues guidance to ensure harmonized implementation and facilitates coordination between national authorities.

NATIONAL COMPETENT AUTHORITIES

Each Member State must designate one or more competent authorities and a national supervisory authority responsible for supervision and application of AI regulations within their jurisdiction in compliance with the framework.

EU DATABASE FOR HIGH-RISK AI SYSTEMS

A public EU database will be maintained featuring key information about providers and systems categorized as high-risk based on their intended purpose, which authorities can access to verify compliance.

MONITORING, COMPLIANCE AND ENFORCEMENT

Various authorities have responsibilities around market surveillance including investigating compliance through methods like document reviews, technical checks and testing. Financial penalties for violations account for an offending company's revenues and other factors.

SUPPORT FOR INNOVATION

Special regulatory sandboxes at both EU and national levels will allow emerging AI systems to be developed and experimented with before full deployment to facilitate responsible innovation by providers small and large.

This governance plan will enable effective oversight of AI across the European Economic Area while helping align competency building and on-ground enforcement of regulations consistently. The multi-layered cooperative structure brings together various experts, stakeholders and agencies critical for trustworthy AI.

---

1. artificialintelligenceact.eu/the-act/

73

EU AI ACT CO-RAPPORTEURS REFLECT ON MONUMENTAL ACHIEVEMENT IN BALANCING INNOVATION AND PROTECTION

After grueling months of intense negotiations between the European Parliament, Commission and Council, EU policy-makers made history by becoming the first leading economic bloc to put comprehensive rules on the books governing AI systems. The landmark AI Act political agreement has been commended for striking an appropriate equilibrium between fostering AI's beneficial potential for Europe while curtailing very real risks from certain applications.

The European Parliament's co-rapporteurs piloting passage of the bill—centrist Drago┼ƒ Tudorache and socialist Brando Benifei—recently shared[1] their perspectives on this unprece-dented legislative achievement. In particular, they highlighted the most pivotal aspects of the final accord, revealed thorniest compromises made and discussed global reverberations from Europe's AI rule-making trailblazing.

Crafting a Global Gold Standard for Trustworthy AI

Both lead MEP negotiators underscored that the AI Act's paramount accomplishment is erecting the world's first all-encompassing legal framework for this rapidly advancing technology. They believe the legislation captures the "sweet spot" between stimulating AI innovation across Europe while suitably safeguarding fundamental rights and values.

As Tudorache succinctly encapsulated: "The greatest achievement is striking the right balance between protection and innovation across all aspects of AI development and deployment." This finely tuned equilibrium runs through the nearly 200 pages of legislative text, with tailored obligations and restrictions targeting the highest risk AI systems posing significant threats to safety and rights. Simultaneously, the bulk of AI systems remain unencumbered to progress responsibly.

Benifei spotlighted the Act's bespoke and flexible risk-based methodology, with conformity assessments and transparency duties ratcheting up commensurate with the intended purpose and potential societal implications. To demonstrate, Benifei cited the example of an AI application utilized to gauge student academic performance. This would compel both high-risk conformity vetting before market placement as well as localized human rights impact evaluations from deploying institutions like schools. Such appraisals would weigh factors including pedagogical approaches, diversity considerations and other contextual elements introducing possible risks. This use case spotlights the layered accountability instruments attached to sensitive social environments like education, spanning developer responsibilities through institutional user obligations.

Benifei termed this nuanced, risk-differentiated scaffolding spanning from minimal to limited to maximum-risk AI the legislation's backbone.

Compromise on National Security Exceptions

Both lead MEPs shared their most vexing concessions during the arduous late-stage negotiations. Unequivocally, they pointed to the broad horizontal national security exemption demanded by EU countries, enabling them to bypass all regulatory requirements when deploying AI systems deemed essential for safeguarding national security.

Tudorache lamented that Parliament negotiators ultimately had little choice but to cave on this red line issue for governments, despite explicit carve outs in EU law treaties. However, MEPs did manage to secure critical fundamental rights safeguards and legal restrictions so security services don't have completely unfettered freedom.

Conclusion: Global Template with Future Adaptability

While still needing some painful compromises, Tudorache and Benifei maintain that overall the landmark EU AI Act succeeds in forging a pragmatic yet principled balance between metastasizing risks and opportunities. They believe it cements trustworthy AI guardrails as the global norm while still affording European companies and researchers ample running room for continued ethical leadership. Moreover, they tout the legislation's adaptability enabling updates as the field continues rapidly evolving so the framework stays resilient against tomorrow's unforeseeable advances.

By and large, the co-rapporteurs underscored that Europe managed to strike regulatory gold, seizing the right moment to intervene amidst AI's societal proliferation when potential damages required democratic checks before further metastasizing. Crucially, this governance sweet spot squares protection, promotion and flexibility—making it a historic template for the world.

---

1. *"What is the impact of the EU's AI Act? A Debrief from MEPs Dragoş Tudorache and Brando Benifei"* by the Atlantic Council

74

EU AI ACT: ANALYSIS AND IMPLICATIONS

Technology-neutral, Future-proof Definitions

A key challenge in regulating a rapidly evolving technology like AI is ensuring the rules remain relevant even as the field continues seeing breakthrough innovations. The EU AI Act makes an effort to define key terms like artificial intelligence systems in a broad, technology-neutral way.

The technical definition focuses on functionality—the ability to generate outputs interacting with and influencing the environment towards some human-defined objectives. Rather than locking down specific techniques, it covers software developed using machine learning approaches listed in the regulation's annex which will get updated as the field progresses.

Similarly, the EU has moved away from the term "high-risk AI systems" to the more generic "general purpose AI" to cover powerful, extensible models like ChatGPT that can get better at a diverse range of tasks based on more data and compute. This may cover innovations not foreseen today.

However, certain sectors worry that definitions like AI system are still too expansive and risk bringing traditional software and industries like process automation into scope with obligations disproportionate to actual risks or harms involved. Much will depend on how the law gets interpreted and enforced in practice across Member States once adopted.

But overall, the emphasis on functionality over techniques, adaptable risk classification built on impact severity rather than lists, and committee governance integrating diverse expertise, makes the EU regulatory approach stand out in being designed for future resilience as much as possible.

Prohibited Uses and Practices

One of the most striking aspects of the EU's regulatory approach is prohibiting certain uses of AI altogether as contravening European values and against fundamental rights. This outright ban includes manipulative systems, use of AI for social scoring, and other listed practices.

The prohibition sets clear bright lines and only permits narrow carve outs in exceptional cases like searches for missing children and preventing terrorist threats to life and limb. Any permitted use still requires extensive safeguards and authorizations from supervisory bodies.

This domain-specific restriction and human rights-centric perspective differs from the current self-regulation approach dominant globally. However, the feasibility of blanket bans on use cases like emotion recognition or biometric categorization tools remains debatable given the pace of innovation. Enforcement is also challenging for real-time identification unless coupled with ubiquitous surveillance.

Nevertheless, experts argue the EU AI Act adopts an aspirational stance rooted in ethical norms around consent, dignity and non-discrimination. Instead of playing catch up after technologies and business models become entrenched, it attempts to embed moral values proactively into research and engineering itself. Prohibition also spurs providers to explore alternative approaches less prone to fundamental rights infringements.

And by expanding the debate on AI beyond technical progress or business growth towards responsibility, the EU offers a refreshing societal perspective that may gradually influence global technology discourse over time.

High-risk Systems Classification

The EU regulatory framework designates AI systems posing significant risks to health, safety and rights as "high-risk"— allowed but subject to more stringent requirements. However, determining what qualifies as high-risk involves subtle qualitative judgments by providers and regulators.

The regulation provides criteria like scale of harm, vulnerability of impacted groups etc. to classify high-risk AI rather than just listing use cases. But concepts like unfair bias can be hard to measure objectively even with rigorous testing. Self-assessments are also tricky for developers to judge the societal impacts of their creations impartially.

Over time, the EU's expert governance bodies are expected to issue guidance and benchmarks to help standardize risk classification methodologies. For example, the technical specifications and test suites being released to assess trustworthy AI under the EU pilot project. The German agency DIN has also been working[1] on criteria and processes for risk-based evaluation of AI systems.

But variability across countries and stakeholders may lead to fragmentation unless unified protocols get widely adopted. Disagreements around risk levels between providers certain use cases, and lack of oversight capacity in smaller member states could pose governance challenges as well. The onus will be on the EU's centralized AI Board and networked authorities to continue providing clarity to enable harmonized regulation.

Conformity Assessments

Before deployment, high-risk AI systems must undergo conformity assessments either based on internal checks by providers or audits by third-party notified bodies. This verification validates if systems meet requirements around data quality, transparency, accuracy etc. laid out in the regulation.

For AI embedded in existing products like machines or medical devices, assessments will integrate with existing EU certification processes for those industries whenever relevant national bodies have adequate AI expertise. Otherwise, certain standalone high-risk systems will follow self-assessments by providers, with third party auditing only for remote biometric identification.

This tailored approach aims to balance limited technical capacity currently to audit algorithms with the need for independence in evaluating high-stakes technologies. However, many note there are under 5000 notified bodies in the EU whereas millions of enterprises could be directly impacted by AI laws. Notified bodies are organizations designated by EU countries to assess the conformity of certain products before being placed on the market. These bodies play a critical role in ensuring that products meet EU standards, including those for safety, health, and environmental protection. Scaling skills and staff to validate AI systems could therefore prove challenging.

The onus is also on regulators to ensure consistency in approach, expectations and decisions on conformity across diverse notified bodies as well as between self-assessments and audits. Passing testing criteria doesn't automatically translate into responsible real-world deployment. Continued governance support especially for small and medium businesses will be crucial for effective standardization too.

Transparency Obligations

The EU regulatory framework mandates certain transparency obligations for high-risk applications as well as purely "limited risk" AI systems to disclose their automated nature to users. However, technical feasibility concerns remain around provisions like detailed data sheets or watermarking.

Generating model cards covering aspects like metrics, test results, maintenance needs etc. to explain system capabilities is important for trust. But the field lacks standards currently on what transparency documentation should include and how much is adequate, especially as systems keep evolving.

The requirement also for text or audio-based deepfakes to be recognizable as AI-generated could be trickier for providers to implement compared to visual media. Watermarking text in a reliable yet imperceptible manner remains an open research challenge currently. And techniques that alter output quality or usability may just push generation underground rather than deter misuse.

The cost and expertise demands of extra documentation, data storage, explanation interfaces etc. imposed by transparency obligations have also faced criticism from industries as stifling innovation. While larger vendors can easily comply, the barriers for smaller startups and open source developers could be disproportionate to actual risks from more exploratory AI uses.

Getting the balance right between transparency needs and constraints will require the EU's independent expert bodies to incorporate both ethical and engineering considerations holistically while framing implementing guidance. Too vague or rigid norms either way risk hampering adoption of societally beneficial AI.

Governance Framework

The EU AI Act introduces a coordinated governance structure between centralized expert bodies and national authorities to oversee a harmonized, trustworthy AI ecosystem across Europe. However, operational complexities around cooperation and resources pose key challenges.

The new institutional architecture aims to balance Union-level guidance with region-specific compliance practices suited for the world's linguistically diverse single market spanning varied histories and cultures. But coordination complexities between the European and national governance layers in terms of processes, information flows and decision hierarchies will need streamlining especially considering AI timescales.

Budgets and recruiting to staff domain expert bodies like the EU AI Board and national authorities are also unclear currently, potentially hampering effective oversight and capability building especially in smaller member states. Geopolitical pressures regarding innovation leadership and calls to tone down regulation from European AI startups and research institutes could further constrain resources and implementation priorities.

Moreover, the region's voluntary standardization apparatus around AI involving entities like CEN-CENELEC[2] and methodologies like technical specifications or testing frameworks will require proactive stewardship and participation from public authorities to enable the ecosystem support needed for trust and accountability to scale on the ground.

Getting the gritty details right around staffing, budgeting and institutional coordination amid economic constraints and tech sector lobbying will be crucial to translate the EU's AI regulatory vision into decisive enforcement and material outcomes.

Strategic Implications for Businesses

I. ASSESSING RISK PROFILE OF AI PORTFOLIO

The EU's risk-based approach to AI governance obliges providers, especially non-EU companies targeting European markets, to evaluate if any of their catalogue of product and service offerings will qualify as high-risk AI systems once rules are enforceable.

This requires appointing internal roles and responsibilities around maintaining a continuously updated inventory detailing the capabilities, data dependencies, use cases and performance metrics of all AI systems implicated by the regulation. A systematic process is needed for risk classification along dimensions like endpoint vulnerabilities, data sensitivities and foreseeable likelihood of systems causing fundamental rights infringements or other societal concerns based on their design, function and commercial deployment contexts.

For multinational enterprises, ensuring responsible AI principles are embedded adequately early on rather than as an ex-post compliance play also warrants rethinking internal development policies, reskilling workforces on transparency and accountability methodologies, and instituting independent ethical advisory councils that enable external stakeholder participation in strategic technology decision-making beyond conventional solutions targeted purely at efficiency or margins.

2. REIMAGINING DEVELOPMENT AND DEPLOYMENT

For providers, achieving EU regulatory compliance will require reimagining AI development, deployment and post-market stewardship processes focused holistically on trustworthiness rather than purely accuracy or user engagement metrics.

Developing high-risk applications requires extensive documentation around datasets, model architectures, testing protocols, performance benchmarks and maintenance to enable both internal and external audits. Technical design choices like transparency mechanisms, human oversight provisions and cybersecurity defenses will need elevating as first-class considerations rather than one-off checks closer to release.

Deployment also now includes extensive pre-release conformity assessments against fluid qualitative criteria open to evolving interpretation—requiring coordination with scarce domain expertise around ethics, fundamental rights and technical assurance to mitigate adverse outcomes at population scale over long horizons. Responsibilities don't end post-shipping either, with stringent post-market surveillance duties around continuous risk monitoring and incident reporting that integrate back into development.

Operationalizing this lifecycle governance demands new executive roles like AI Ethics Officers, enhanced technologist qualifications across domains like law and social sciences, fresh appraisal metrics looking at sustainability and justice, and participative design processes that proactively seek inputs from marginalized communities and civil society alongside direct end users.

3. New Operating Models for Trust and Compliance

The EU's pioneering AI Act will compel providers to architect next-generation technology value chains transforming opaque software releases towards robust and inclusive assurance frameworks managed through interdisciplinary collaboration.

Conventionally, engineers independently built systems fulfilling business requirements within resource constraints before occasionally liaising with adjacent compliance teams closer to deployment. However, constructing trustworthy AI requires radically cross-functional involvement continuously throughout ideation itself.

For instance, proposing solutions now requires proactively consulting assessors to preempt risks, while data scientists need tools simplifying dataset scrutiny by experts weighing biases early on. Conformity evaluations happen concurrently rather than eventually, guiding design iterations aligned with the rule of law. Post-market feedback loops between incident response, customer service, product and legal teams should systematically enhance systemic oversight too.

Responsible innovation is thus a distributed organizational effort, needing revised operating models, novel partnerships within and between institutions, and experiential upskilling initiatives that mainstreams accessibility, ethics and accountability philosophies institutionally. Rather than mechanically complying checklists, authentic trustworthiness entails cultural transformation.

4. CROSS-FUNCTIONAL COORDINATION IMPLICATIONS

The extensive transparency, quality and risk management obligations imposed by the EU's AI Act requires enhancing coordination between numerous internal teams spanning technology, product, legal, compliance and other groups depending on deployment domains.

For instance, conformity assessments require extensive technical documentation detailing system capabilities, underlying data, evaluation results, maintenance procedures etc. prepared by architects which legal teams must verify as meeting cybersecurity, privacy and assistive interface standards while compliance officers validate risk mitigation measures and accessibility for oversight.

Post-market surveillance will also warrant integrating customer support experiences around reliability challenges with continuous monitoring protocols designed by data engineers capturing metrics indicating drops in accuracy, fairness or security emerging from real world environmental shifts. Findings by domain auditors around fundamental rights impacts must likewise systematically update training data and benchmarks maintained by machine learning teams.

Instituting accountable AI thus requires synchronizing historically siloed workflows into regular touch-points, unified training criteria, complementary appraisal metrics, shared vocabularies and platforms facilitating seamless exchange of discoveries furthering safety, transparency and bias mitigation across disciplines. Only robust 360-degree oversight can sustain public trust as complexity increases.

5. IMPACT OF EXTRATERRITORIAL APPLICABILITY

A defining expansive aspect of the EU's regulatory approach is its explicit extra-territorial scope encompassing providers and users of AI systems globally as long as EU resident rights are implicated through access or usage.

This extensive jurisdictional claim significantly impacts organizations without any physical or legal presence within Europe. For instance, a US startup creating smartphone applications using machine learning algorithms will still need appointing EU-based legal representatives and ensuring appropriate transparency disclosures in the app store listings made available to European consumers.

Canadian robotics companies participating in European smart city procurement bids also can't escape relevant third-party testing or certification requirements imposed for those geographic procurement contexts before systems get installed or operationalized locally. Every organization must monitor if technical outputs, commercial availability or advertising targeting qualifies as AI-based interactions with natural persons in EU geographies with rights obligations.

This extraterritorial approach aims preventing offshore loopholes via linking obligations to de facto points of consumption protecting European citizen rights and interests rather than territorial jurisdictions alone. However, practical enforcement capacity constraints around detecting non-compliance by distant vendors plus geopolitical interdependencies may require selective interpretations by Member States minimizing conflicts.

6. COSTS AND CONSTRAINTS TO INNOVATION

While regulators emphasize necessity and proportionality, industry critique contends the EU AI Act's extensive transparency duties around supply chains and stringent conformity assessments stifle innovation by disproportionately increasing compliance burdens for smaller enterprises and startups unable to afford the overheads.

The shifts required within development workflows, heightened certification barriers slowing down releases, big tech advantages in readily furnishing extensive documentation, and costs associated with proofing unpredictable models on ambiguous qualitative criteria like fairness or safety could constrain funding for entrepreneurs experimenting across long tail niche segments versus platform incumbents.

Additionally, current research literature still lacks robust, proactive technical methods for accurately assessing issues such as bias vulnerabilities or the gradual impacts on populations over extended periods. This gap in methodology effectively makes it impractical to deploy certain technologies— such as those used for allocating financial credit, selecting candidates for employment, or assessing risks in criminal justice—within European markets. These challenges persist despite arguments that concerns over these issues have been minor so far. Furthermore, when other international regimes impose reciprocal restrictions on European innovations, it significantly narrows the opportunities for these technologies to be adopted globally.

However, most acknowledge responsible innovation is an iterative journey needing positive encouragement. Hence transparency, not prohibition, is the progressive path, with obligations scaling to deployment and commercialization stages rather than prematurely constraining speculative Discovery by students, academics or early-stage companies still shaping directions. Setting the right regulatory tone remains balancing tradeoffs.

7. PRESSURE FOR VOLUNTARY CODES OF CONDUCT

While the EU's risk-based framework mandates extensive requirements only on providers of high-risk AI systems, there will be increasing public calls and regulatory nudges for companies to voluntarily adopt codes of conduct extending similar trustworthy practices to lower-risk AI applications too.

Non-binding norms around transparency, testing and accountability could be catalyzed through sectoral alliances between leading vendors within domains like autonomous mobility, precision medicine and programmatic advertising to preempt restrictive interventions over rising incidents of safety lapses or fundamental rights controversies down the road. Committing higher standards voluntarily also shields companies against competitive disadvantages once baseline expectations shift.

Brussels authorities will likely convene multi-stakeholder roundtables alongside European standardization bodies around crystallizing budding extant industry practices into widely adopted codes spanning data benchmarking guides, model factsheets, proportional testing protocols, risk assessment checklists and subgroup equity metrics facilitating justice. Stringent requirements for publicly procuring commercial or government AI contracts will further precipitate uptake.

Large platforms especially may pursue voluntary restraints and disclosures addressing societal concerns to rehabilitate reputations and political goodwill damaged by recent free speech, competition and content scandals, given increasing calls for break ups by antitrust regulators. Demonstrating earnestness avoiding past mistakes will be imperative rebuilding citizen trust on emerging technologies.

We Finish as we Started: Back to Fundamental Rights

A pioneering governance innovation within the EU's AI Act requires certain high-risk applications undergo fundamental rights impact assessments evaluating design and deployment safeguards around principles of human dignity, fairness and non-discrimination. However, operationalizing law's aspirational edicts into code and commerce requires tremendous interdisciplinary breakthroughs still nascent.

Methodologically, philosophers contest technologists whether machine predictions even comport deductively with moral concepts like justice that contingently balance societal tradeoffs through public reason. Notions around dignity or autonomy also prohibit definitive indications and thresholds amenable for testing protocols. And empirical sciences struggle formally modeling complex social stereotypes or even agreeing on metrics assessing model biases, their proxies or measurable harms.

Culturally too, the diverse lived realities across European languages, histories and economies imply gradients of shifting norms challenging unanimous appraisals, especially where AI-mediated decisions significantly impact minority welfare. What look like neutral automation efficiencies streamlining status quo institutions may covertly encode parochial interests that require fundamental restructuring benefiting those displaced.

Therefore, earnestly fostering fundamental rights requires institutionalizing participatory assessment frameworks facilitating iterative translation, contestation and redress around technological interventions through renewed investments strengthening communities vulnerable against accelerated automation. Merely multiplying bureaucratic oversight absent structural rehabilitation risks exacerbating prevailing inequities further.

---

1. "German Standardization Roadmap on Artificial Intelligence" by DIN and DKE
2. European Committee for Electrotechnical Standardization

75

CONCLUSION

The EU AI Act represents a historic milestone establishing the world's first comprehensive legal framework specifically designed to govern AI systems. By pioneering a horizontal, risk-based approach avoiding excessive bureaucracy while centering fundamental rights, the EU offers a pragmatic regulatory model balancing innovation with ethical obligations for the age of intelligent machines.

The landmark law culminates years of political calls and academic analysis urgently seeking governance guardrails addressing acute challenges introduced by opaque automation technologies increasingly embedded within high-stakes decisions pervading lives and livelihoods. Beyond mitigating concerns around unfair bias, safety, explainability and geopolitical stability risks from advanced AI, the legislation also proactively lays institutional foundations stewarding transformative technologies equitably towards collective human progress rather than narrowly maximizing efficiency or profits alone.

However, translating such ambitious vision into ground realities depends tremendously upon national and enterprise capacities executing extensively expanded oversight duties the legal mandates necessitate locally across Europe's varied economies and cultures. Considerable investments yet required strengthening review mechanisms and reskilling workers around compliance complexities meeting civilizational aspirations while enabling thriving cross-border trade upholding continental norms globally.

With AI advancement accelerating exponentially, much remains indeterminate still whether regulations avoid hampering continued research exploring socially beneficial applications or counterintuitively exacerbate existing inequities through disproportionate enforcement. But by declaring technological progress subservient to democracy and human rights politically, Europe resoundingly affirms values must remain preeminent guiding humanity's shared digital civilization regardless of uncertainties ahead. Law now demands technology ethically evolve furthering dignity and justice.

Note:

The regulatory landscape for AI is evolving rapidly, with new laws, guidelines, and standards emerging to address the unique challenges posed by generative models and other advanced AI systems. This book does not constitute legal advice, and is not intended to be a substitute for legal advice.

Alongside these regulatory developments, a growing ecosystem of tools and platforms is being created to support AI governance and risk management practices. However, due to the fast-paced nature of these changes, we have chosen not to cover specific tools in this book, as the information may quickly become outdated. Instead, we encourage readers to subscribe to our newsletter (form located on the footer of our website,) where we will provide regular updates on the latest developments in AI policy, tools, and best practices.

By staying informed about the evolving landscape of AI governance, organizations can ensure they are well-equipped to navigate the challenges and opportunities of this transformative technology while upholding their ethical responsibilities and complying with relevant regulations.

SHAPING A RIGHTS-RESPECTING AI FUTURE

As we come to the end of this exploration of responsible AI governance in the age of generative models, it is clear that the journey ahead is both challenging and filled with opportunity. The rise of Generative AI represents a watershed moment in the history of technology, with the potential to transform nearly every aspect of our lives, from the way we create and communicate to the way we learn and work. Yet, as we have seen throughout this book, the power of these systems also carries with it significant risks and challenges that we must confront head-on.

At the heart of this book has been the conviction that a rights-based approach provides a compelling and necessary framework for navigating the complex landscape of AI governance. By grounding our discussions in the universal language of human rights, we can cut through the noise and focus on what really matters: ensuring that the development and deployment of AI systems respects human dignity, promotes equality, and safeguards the fundamental freedoms that are the birthright of every person.

Throughout these pages, we have explored the multifaceted nature of AI risks and their far-reaching implications for privacy, non-discrimination, freedom of expression, and beyond. We have seen how these risks can emerge at every stage of the AI lifecycle, from the collection and curation of training data to the design, deployment, and use of AI systems in real-world contexts. Addressing these challenges requires a proactive, holistic approach to AI governance that embeds human rights considerations into every stage of the process.

Central to this approach is the recognition that responsible AI is not just a technical challenge, but a deeply human one. It requires us to grapple with complex ethical questions, to make difficult tradeoffs, and to confront the unintended consequences of our technological choices. It demands that we broaden our circles of participation and inclusion, ensuring that the voices of those most affected by AI systems are heard and heeded. And it challenges us to think beyond narrow technical fixes and to envision AI systems that are truly accountable, transparent, and aligned with human values.

As we have seen, realizing this vision will require sustained effort and collaboration across every sector of society. It will require businesses to prioritize ethical considerations in the design and deployment of AI systems, moving beyond short-term profits to consider the long-term impacts on individuals and society. It will require policymakers to create regulatory environments that encourage responsible innovation while protecting citizens' rights. It will require researchers to push the boundaries of what is possible, developing new technical solutions for ensuring AI robustness, safety, and interpretability. And it will require civil society organizations and individual citizens to remain vigilant, advocating for justice and holding those in power accountable.

While the challenges are significant, so too are the opportunities. By proactively addressing the risks of generative AI and harnessing its power for good, we can create a future in which the benefits of these technologies are shared equitably, and human rights are not just protected but actively promoted. We can foster a thriving ecosystem of creative expression and innovation, in which human and machine intelligence work together in harmony. And we can build a world in which public trust in AI is not just a hope, but a reality, grounded in the demonstrable commitment of institutions and individuals alike to the principles of transparency, accountability, and fairness.

As we look ahead, it is clear that the journey towards responsible AI governance will be an ongoing one. The rapid pace of technological change means that we must remain agile and adaptable, continually reassessing our approaches in light of new challenges and opportunities. We must also recognize that responsible AI is not a destination but a direction, a North Star that guides us towards the future we want to create.

Ultimately, the story of Generative AI will be written not just by the technology itself, but by the choices we make about how to develop, deploy, and govern these powerful tools. By embracing a rights-based approach and committing ourselves to the hard work of responsible innovation, we can shape a future in which AI systems are not just technically impressive, but ethically grounded and socially beneficial.

It is a future that will require courage, creativity, and collaboration from us all. But it is a future worth striving for—a future in which the transformative power of artificial intelligence is harnessed not just for efficiency or profit, but for the greater good of humanity. As we close the pages of this book, let us choose wisely, and let us never lose sight of the fundamental truth that our technologies must serve our values, and not the other way around.

Stay human!

Inês

Note: Consider leaving a review and sharing the book with others that may benefit from its content.

I encourage you to dive deeper into the technology powering Generative AI by reviewing the books and courses on the next page.

KEEP LEARNING

Our books

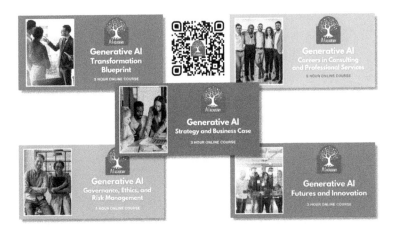

Our courses

Printed in the USA
CPSIA information can be obtained
at www.ICGtesting.com
LVHW051525290324
775847LV00003B/48